# **Pina Bausch** DANCE THEATRE

Norbert Servos

# PINA BAUSCH
# DANCE THEATRE

Photographs by Gert Weigelt

Translated by Stephen Morris

**K·Kieser**

The translator would like to thank the *Ministerpräsident* of the state of North Rhine Westphalia for assistance with translating this book in the form of a grant for a residency at the *Europäisches Übersetzer-Kollegium*, Straelen.

Front cover: Nazareth Panadero in *Vollmond*. Back cover: *1980*

© K. Kieser Verlag · Dr. Klaus Kieser, Munich 2008
Published originally in German under the title *Pina Bausch. Tanztheater* (2008)
All photographs by Gert Weigelt (www.gert-weigelt.de)
Cover design by Katja Fliedner after a sketch by Thomas Betz and Sara Hoffmann
Typeset by Uwe Steffen, Munich
Printed in Germany by ulenspiegel druck gmbh, Andechs
ISBN 978-3-935456-22-7

# Contents

# Foreword

It is almost thirty years since the first book on Pina Bausch and the Tanztheater Wuppertal appeared, published in Germany by the Ballett-Büh-
nen-Verlag which I co-founded. Still deeply controversial within the
country at the time, the company was on the verge of international recognition and success. Since then not only have its detractors largely fallen
silent, but the term "dance theatre", or *Tanztheater*, has entered the vocabulary. The Wuppertal model launched a world theatre rich in colours and
forms, moods and moving images; one in which fundamental hopes and
fears, needs and desires can be tackled. It is understood across all boundaries – now worldwide – because it has discovered a means to absorb
the most varied cultural influences yet find the shared, binding elements
behind diverse colourings and tones.

Pina Bausch has always insisted, quite reasonably, that her work cannot be judged as choreography. Her dance theatre is not a technique; it
embodies a particular attitude to the world, an ability to look at people and their behaviour with unswerving honesty and precision without
judging them. It shows people as they are and not as they should be. It
does not establish ideals which must be striven for, and certainly doesn't
set itself up as a moral authority. A "work in progress", continued from
piece to piece, it sees itself as an inexhaustible exploration of happiness,
working through trial and error and retaining its humour even in failure.
It holds steadfastly to the hope that humanity's right to happiness and love
can be met, that if we push doggedly through and beyond all blunders and
tragicomic dalliances, we shall arrive at a place where we can be entirely
at one with ourselves whilst in and of the world, without need, desperation, loneliness: without the limitations of convention and without the
absurd distortions of self-tailoring.

This attitude is as relevant now as it was thirty-five years ago when,
together with its choreographer, the company began its journey of discovery. Alongside her new productions Pina Bausch has continually revived
older pieces, which lose none of their emotional force and physical directness. They speak the same, no less radical language and espouse an alternative, ideology-free approach. They provide a model in which the process
of human development is a permanent process of individuation, a type of

self-development as far removed from egotistical self-empowerment as it is from collective credos.

The value of such a model in a time of worldwide migratory shifts and cultural warping cannot be underestimated. It shows not only that dance possesses a unique language for the political and social, but it also posits a societal orientation which takes individuals as its starting point and places them in an open and thoroughly flexible relation to others. No ideological corset or dogmatic higher authority is needed, only a tough persistence that never tires of examining which elements of our daily behaviour bring us closer together and which widen the distance between us.

That, even over such a long time-span, this ambitious research project into human desire continues to unearth new finds – as fascinating as they are disturbing – is enough to justify its high standing. It brings the viewer back each time to a moment of unsullied creativity where the world can be experienced again as if never seen before, where decisions can be taken – hopefully for the better. Conceived as a monograph on the pieces, this book traces the development of the Tanztheater Wuppertal from its beginnings to the present day. Alongside specific chapters addressing the artist's creative approaches and working methods, its core consists of individual descriptions of the pieces, seeking to illuminate a particular aspect of the work each time (costume, stage sets, music, language etc). Each description is based on the premiere of the respective piece, which is usually refined afterwards, but always remains unchanged in its fundamental content. The book deliberately avoids any evaluation or comparison of the pieces in relation to each other, not least out of respect for an oeuvre which, even when judged by its own high standards, has its weaker moments, yet still rises high above the average.

Pina Bausch's work re-questions the fundamental nature of dance and the elementary problems of human interaction as if for the first time. It can only be understood as a whole, as a continuous, multifaceted, dazzling investigation into the principle of desire. This book thus addresses an oeuvre which probably represents dance's most significant encounter with modernism.

Clearly no-one can write a book without the help of other people, and I would like to take this opportunity to thank everyone who has contributed to this book's existence. My thanks go above all to Pina Bausch who, in interviews and many private conversations, has afforded me an insight into her work and into how she views the world. Our friendship has taught me a great deal, above and beyond the contents of this book. For crucial pointers and assistance with interpretation I am highly grateful to Ronald Kay, who undertook detailed discussions with me on the texts. In the course of my research Bénédicte Billiet, Claudia Irman, Marion Cito and Matthias Schmiegelt all proved to be patient and helpful collaborators. Grigori Chakov was always able to provide me with videos from the company's extensive archive when I needed them. Matthias Burkert was always able to raid his encyclopedic memory to answer my questions on the music and provide useful information. I am grateful to Urs Kaufmann for his careful examination of the manuscript for factual accuracy, and for his unshakeable humour. Last but not least I would like to thank the many members of the company for shared conversations over dinner and wine. They have ensured that, although hard work, writing this book has proved highly enjoyable.

This new edition is not only as up to date as possible, containing a description of this year's new production, it has also been expanded to include two new interviews, with costume designer Marion Cito and set designer Peter Pabst. My thanks go to them both for their willingness to offer insight into their work and for pleasant conversation.

*Berlin, summer 2008*                                                    *Norbert Servos*

## From the mythical era, from the here and now
What dance theatre is about

Pina Bausch not only created a new style of dance, although she certainly did that. She not only developed an entirely new genre, *Tanztheater* or dance theatre: her dance theatre revolutionised and redefined the notion of dance itself so that its influence now extends far beyond dance, into theatre, opera and film. The impact of dance theatre on the various artistic disciplines can be seen worldwide, from mere imitation to independent development and further refinement. In dance theatre, an art form has been established that has the capacity to absorb and reflect contemporary life. More open than almost any previous form of dance, it straddles styles and disciplines in a free interplay between every possible genre, whilst still nonetheless retaining its distinctive attitude to the world.

Although closely tied to reality, dance theatre also draws from the reservoirs of fairy tales, myths and dreams. But because of the way it is structured, the dimensions of so-called reality and unreality are so thoroughly interwoven that a clear-cut line can hardly be traced between them. It is certainly not the case that the dimension of "reality" can only be assigned to the waking state, nor that of desire only to dreaming. Dance theatre nonchalantly rises above such fixed categorisation. Conscious dreaming can say just as much about people, about how they really are, as does the collision of their desires with reality. The refinement of the spirit, the highest aspiration since the Age of Enlightenment, is sent in a new direction. While this was once necessary in order to free the mind from its dependence on superstition, it can now form new bonds. In dance theatre the borders between imaginary and real are blurred; heart and mind go hand in hand. It is as if Pina Bausch is acting on the words of Antoine de Saint-Exupéry in *The Little Prince*: "One sees clearly only with the heart."

With this adage, the project of modernity takes a new turn: that which the surrealists sought in their attempts to tap into the laws of the unconscious, and which the expressionists strove to set free using emotional colouring, is now revealed; it is felt directly at gut level whilst simultaneously lifted into the realm of conscious comprehension. In the poetic digressions of dance theatre, the world of the imagination is seen as equally palpable and powerful as the so-called real world. The capacity for imagination is granted an independent and extremely potent power. The principle seems to be that anything which can be imagined can also become real – in advance and in retrospect. A kind of freedom has been established, which allows a playful take on reality, is precise in its observation, yet is one where things can change at any moment. This freedom is not aspired to in a political sense, instead it is tested in playful but precise experiments. In dance theatre no-one knows more than the audience does – neither the choreographer nor the players – and no-one raises a finger to teach people lessons. We can only look together for navigable paths, feeling our way carefully and trying things out. Dance theatre seeks nothing less than the full-scale rehabilitation of poetry, not in the self-indulgent sense of *l'art pour l'art* but by bonding the real to the possible.

Behind this lies an unusually unprejudiced view of the world, which observes every manifestation of human behaviour. From this perspective, one could say that the world is, initially, everything that happens. But it is also everything which might yet happen. In approaching these two poles, the utmost care and caution are exercised. Nothing is stated too soon. Dance theatre uses a multifaceted, multilayered language of metaphors in which the nuances and resonances are more important than pure description and naming. Thus Pina Bausch talks repeatedly about "letting things be sensed" in her work. Her vision of the world resembles Plato's famous cave image: in the world of appearances only the images of ideas are visible, not the ideas themselves. Thus her players are essentially groping in the dark – along with everyone else. Only testing and learning what works and what doesn't, what brings us closer to happiness and what drives us further away, can shed light on the situation. A cautious approach should therefore be taken so that no potential solution is missed.

This is the point of the continuous tightrope-walk between consciousness and dreaming: the lines are systematically blurred to enable new possibilities to be reached which are beyond pre-determined conventions. In this process, the dream-like sequences and the alienating displacements and disturbances always relate to something familiar and already known in conscious thought. In this sense "dance is the only real language," to use Pina Bausch's own words. It refers to something that has "always been known" but perhaps never regarded in this light. Her pieces are not mere fantasies, they allow that which is already known to become apparent and ascend to the conscious realm of comprehension; they dig up treasure which has always been lying close to hand and did not need to be hunted for in a distant utopia. In other words, people already possess what they need to be happy, they just have to identify it.

This is a new position within the project of modernity; it combines an inquisitive, enquiring sense of reality with a principle of hope, no longer consigned to the future but to be found in the present. Several dead-ends are thus systematically avoided. In her work, Pina Bausch is not talking about being adrift in the world, or about the pointlessness of existence. At the same time she doesn't offer certainties or answers, let alone solutions. The balancing act which is undertaken is more delicate, on the one hand calmly contemplating everything there is, on the other putting inherent possibilities to the test. Thus the path into the future remains open and only resignation and any type of zealous fanaticism are barred. Even before the era of ideologies began its death-throes, Pina Bausch had started developing a type of theatre in which a different approach to the world becomes possible: sceptical and critical, certainly, but not despairing. On the contrary: moments surface again and again in the pieces testifying to the possibility of being at peace in the world, of feeling at home here. In this respect they are just like fairy tales. Dance theatre diverges strongly from the momentum of the 1968 and post-'68 movements. It does not seek to confront; it tries to get to the bottom of things. It does not teach; it engenders experiences. It does not try to change; it allows change to happen.

This is made possible because dance theatre positions itself beyond all dualism. Just as it refuses to accept a division into real and unreal, into dream and reality, visible and invisible, it also refuses the traditional division between body and soul, flesh and spirit. Pina Bausch's pieces are about the soulful, spiritual body, which exists exactly at the interface between these polarities. The resulting tension is always maintained and actively formed. And it is as if, in actively sustaining the tension, access to the self were gradually distilled, little by little, to reach that resource, both individual and collective, which alone serves to mitigate the existential solitude of the individual. Both the aesthetic, dream-like scenes and the hard, edgy moments exploit the resources of the collective unconscious. Yet the archetypes are presented in an absolutely contemporary guise. Thus the pieces are rooted deep in the history of human culture yet speak of the here and now. That they can be understood all over the world is therefore no coincidence and not due solely to the nature of the choreographer's genius, effortlessly bridging the past and the present. In rehabilitating the power of imagination and human fantasy and in taking this seriously, they achieve something more: they allow a potential future to be tried out first in the playground of the imagination.

One of the themes dance theatre has addressed most intensively is that of received ideas and conventional images, checking to see whether they hold up to scrutiny. However, this examination of social models clearly takes place through the eyes of choreography, and dance theatre gives insight into how this might be viewed in the future. In dance, we are given to understand, the power of imagination finds expression primarily as energy: physical, emotional and mental energy, its concentration and clarity visible in every movement and gesture. In this sense choreography is the art of guiding and assembling these energies in a way that enables them to be experienced and grasped by as many people as possible. A choreographer will always see reality as a dynamic structure, a weave of reciprocal change and influence, in which defining, determining and deactivating are in fact the arch enemies of everything which lives and moves.

Although the energy of choreography may be neutral by nature, it is always expressed in a way that is seen and felt as polar: the polarities of life and death, dark and light, creation and destruction. Dance theatre operates at the centre of these polarities, avoiding all moral adjudication between good and bad. The ultimate abolition of these polarities is therefore neither necessary nor desirable. A different notion of happiness is being established here: rather than pandering to the polarities, they are actively and productively given form. This is what the spectators of Pina Bausch's pieces are sometimes challenged or invited to do, sometimes with a little wink. Because dance theatre measures the world of imagination against living reality, it creates a friction from which sparks of insight can flare. Such direct, unmediated personal experience no longer rallies at an unfair world; it engages with the motives determining all our actions. The mutual interdependence of spiritual outlook and physical bearing, of emotional balance and mental understanding that has always been upheld in the traditions of the East, is clearly endorsed by dance theatre. The idea that while the spirit might be willing, the flesh is weak is a Chris-

14

tian myth. In physical reality all fundamental constants have already been determined and intelligence is wholly dependent on sensual perception. The old antithesis of clever spirit versus ignorant flesh has been abolished.

In entering the dreamtime of poetry, the dance-theatre spectator is entering a time other than historical. For the first time, they have the chance to step out of the terrible continuum of history and consider themselves and their condition in a new light; the dreamtime of poetry is not tied to linear, literary progression. It roams freely across the various levels of time, sinks a plumb-line down to the world of the archetypes and brings them back up to light as new discoveries. Mythical time and contemporaneity are not mutually exclusive, they determine each other. The spectator is smuggled out of the familiar, known world and taken to a place where new decisions can be made.

It is no exaggeration to say that dance theatre aims squarely for a cathartic effect. It dissects the old body of societal conventions, smashes it to a pulp and reassembles the remains to produce a presentiment of new consensuses. Thus it could be seen to approach Antonin Artaud's idea of the "Theatre of Cruelty", which confronts spectators with the loss of long-held certainties, forcing them, in the words of Heiner Müller, to gaze into the whites of history's eyes, where all the unfulfilled wishes of previous generations lie, still waiting to be fulfilled. This is what produces an incessant sense of lack, which refuses to leave us in peace and continually forces us to try for happiness one more time.

For the spectator it is a case of allowing this deficit, this historical mortgage, to take hold of them, in order to emerge with a changed awareness and to understand the urgency and critical nature of the situation. The crisis which is thus experienced does not, however, cause resignation or depression, quite the opposite: it challenges us to actively take things into our own hands. It provides the courage Pina Bausch has spoken of, to grab back a hold on life and re-shape it. There need be no purpose other than to move ourselves into the life-giving centre of the conflicting forces and be in the world with all our senses. No metaphysics or esoterism are required, simply a precise sensory understanding and shaping of the present, but a present with overtones of the past and hints of the future.

This is not about overcoming a notion of history compressed into a ridiculous linearity. It is about positioning ourselves in the centre of all simultaneous opposites and striking incendiary sparks from them, which once more provides the motivation to engage actively with life. Dance theatre opens up a much wider context than the mind of the contemporary individual can ever imagine and urges us, in a friendly but insistent way, to take an active part. Interestingly this often succeeds through an unveiling of what seems highly intimate and personal. But because it is never private, always held up as an example, it is in no danger of falling prey to psychology. Dance theatre places individual experience in the wider context of a societal myth in which everyone can have a stake.

The process really is more important than the result here or, as Pina Bausch has expressed it, "the things we discover for ourselves are the most important." This should not be misunderstood as the elitist mentality of an artistic clique because this "we" refers to the spectators as much as to the players. The processes of living through and living out cleanse and open up the gaze to what is really important.

Thus in many ways dance theatre inverts familiar perspectives. It allows the flesh a spiritual dimension and reunites the mythical with the contemporary. So much humour, affectionately directed at human beings, finds its way onto the stage, that we occasionally feel a serenity that would only be possible were the choreographer looking back at life from its end. The things which, as Pina Bausch says, "we could smile about together" materialise only with an awareness of the time which has just ended. This is when human life appears simultaneously tragic and comic, insoluble perhaps but to be enjoyed with all the senses.

# The body's first-hand experience
How dance theatre speaks

> How do we first hear ourselves? Continually singing to ourselves, and through dance. These two things are still free of naming. They have no life as such, and nobody has personally given them form yet. When we come across them they possess the charm of the original beginning. But there is something else we have to get past first which fortifies their expression firmly and fully.
> Ernst Bloch, *The Philosophy of Music*[1]

When Pina Bausch took over the Wuppertal theatres' dance ensemble at the beginning of the 1973/74 season, it was a watershed in the evolution of the stagnating German ballet scene. Although other choreographers, such as Johann Kresnik in Bremen and Gerhard Bohner in Darmstadt, had already begun to break out of the restrictive expressive frameworks of both classical ballet and modern dance, seeking new forms appropriate to the times, it was the Wuppertal company under Pina Bausch which first succeeded in establishing the term "dance theatre" (German: *Tanztheater*) as a synonym for a distinct genre, which until now had only occasionally been used in the names of particular companies. Dance theatre, the fusion of both media, opened up a new dimension within both theatre and dance. As a statement of intent, the term described a theatre with a new agenda, in terms of both form and content.

The Tanztheater Wuppertal explored and broadened its unfamiliar playing field in the midst of a ballet culture which, apart from a few experimental centres such as Bremen, Darmstadt and Cologne, was content either to groom its classical heritage, grudgingly update it, or simply respond to the US import modern dance. The German tradition of *Ausdruckstanz* or "expressive dance", linked to names such as Mary Wigman, Rudolf von Laban, Harald Kreutzberg and Gret Palucca, had almost died out after World War II. Now aiming to create a political, ostensibly timeless theatre, *Ausdruckstanz* avoided confronting its provocative forebears, whose radical rejection of pointe shoes and tutus had demanded a new understanding of the body as long ago as the 1920s. Only John Cranko, with a classical background, remained the exception to this avoidance.

17

Now, with Pina Bausch, contact seemed to have finally been resumed, at least indirectly, to this all but forgotten revolutionary tradition – but without its *ecce homo* pathos, without its pan-humanity fatefulness, and in a wholly individual way. Bit by bit, the Tanztheater Wuppertal broke new ground in a way the *Ausdruckstanz* dancers had clearly sought yet failed to achieve: dance was being freed from the constraints of literature, disabused of its fairy-tale illusions and led towards reality. Trained at the Folkwang School in Essen under Kurt Jooss, with a philosophy of movement rooted in German *Ausdruckstanz*, and familiar with the US modern dance approach through study trips to New York, Pina Bausch achieved a unique synthesis of German tradition and American modernism in her early pieces, the most outstanding of which is probably the choreography to Igor Stravinsky's *The Rite of Spring*. The exceptional quality of her dance theatre can already be seen in these early works, though they still inhabit familiar territory. Her dancers unleashed a hitherto unknown energy onto the stage; their bodies told stories without pretence, unhindered by any heavy-handed meaning. Although, like the later Bartók interpretation *Bluebeard*, *Le Sacre du printemps* and the Gluck operas *Iphigenia in Tauris* and *Orpheus and Eurydice* still adhered to a plot, Pina Bausch had already gone beyond all previous notions of how a libretto might be interpreted. She did not simply turn source material into dance; instead she used individual elements of the stories as springboards, allowing free reign to her own powers of association. While other choreographers strove to translate music and stories into movement, dance theatre employed bodily energies as its immediate subject and medium. It conveyed its subject-matter by telling the story of the body, not by dancing literature.

There are early indications of the change that was to take place in the concept of choreography. As early as 1969, in the short piece *Im Wind der Zeit* (*In the Wind of Time*), with which she won the choreography prize at the International Summer Academy of Dance in Cologne, Pina Bausch provided a small foretaste of her undoubtedly enormous talent as a choreographer within the conventions of modern dance. The following year she officially abandoned "nice dancing". In angular, awkward movements *Nachnull* (*Afterzero*) described the aftermath of a catastrophe, in which the dancers appeared, transformed by their costumes, as skeletons.

In the subsequent year, 1971, Pina Bausch continued to follow this new, socially critical approach. As guest choreographer, invited by Arno

Wüstenhofer (director of the Wuppertal theatres), her first piece for a civic theatre, *Aktionen für Tänzer* (*Actions for Dancers*), had the dancers representing deformed figures. Pina Bausch created a grotesque dance of death around a girl wearing a shroud, laid out on an iron bed: an absurd marriage of Eros and Thanatos. The scenic and theatrical elements she was to increasingly integrate into her pieces were also first seen here.

Although Pina Bausch returned once more to the repertoire of movement established by modern dance in her critically acclaimed "Venusberg" choreography for Wagner's *Tannhäuser* (1972), as well as the two Gluck dance-operas *Iphigenia in Tauris* (1974) and *Orpheus and Eurydice* (1975), the mixture of emotional force and formal clarity which has distinguished the entire oeuvre of the Tanztheater Wuppertal was already apparent. Moreover, these dance-operas represented a totally new genre.

With *Fritz*, the short piece she made on taking up her permanent position at the Wuppertal theatres in early 1974, Pina Bausch ventured into the problematic world of childhood fears; a subject to which she did not return. The breakthrough into a new form, bearing the label *Tanztheater*, was to achieve worldwide recognition, and was first made with the half-hour revue *Ich bring dich um die Ecke* (*I'll Do You In*) in December 1974, in which her performers not only danced but also sang and acted. The revue format did not only provide the opportunity to introduce an element of entertainment, it was also itself held up to critical scrutiny. Pina Bausch came closer to what was to become one of her key subjects: the relationship between the sexes and their tragicomic efforts to seek happiness. That the popular revue genre proved highly suitable for an exploration of human interaction is the real discovery of the show. The poetic contrast between everyday reality and mass-media imagery was to become one of the determining motifs of the Tanztheater Wuppertal.

Thus the true significance of Pina Bausch's work lies in its expansion of our understanding of dance, freeing the concept of choreography from its limiting definition as an interrelated series of movements. Increasingly dance itself became the subject of interrogation, its received forms of expression to be taken for granted no longer. Dance theatre evolved into something which could be described as a theatre of experience, a theatre which conveys reality aesthetically, via direct confrontation, making it a physical fact experienced by the body. In shaking off the shackles of literature, while simultaneously rendering the abstraction of dance concrete, dance was made aware, for the first time in history, raising its consciousness and empowering it to take the means of expression into its own hands.

## Toiling across the plains: the theatre of experience

Pina Bausch's first ever dance performance in Wuppertal met with a sharply-divided, polarised reception. This new dance-theatrical innovation was not to be integrated into the canon of existing values and categories without a struggle; it was different from anything people had been accustomed to recognising as dance. Responses ranged from astonishment and bewildered respect to brusque dismissal. The disturbing newness of Pina Bausch's works clearly called for a new way of thinking about dance, as was demonstrated by her succeeding pieces ever more clearly. Having stepped over the boundaries between genres, erasing the demarcation lines which traditionally separate dance, spoken theatre and musical theatre, her work fitted none of the normal pigeon-holes. The pieces stood at odds to theatrical convention, generating a friction which, initially, almost no-one would accept as productive. Their reception thus consisted of an interminable process of assertion in the face of critics very reluctant to change their established models of assimilation or their firmly cemented habits of perception. On the one hand, there was a genuine readiness to acknowledge the imagination, inventiveness or even genius of "Bausch the artist". The content of her works, on the other hand, was seen largely as remaining mysterious and inaccessible. The distinction made between (talented) person and (hermetically sealed) work became a recurring feature of the pieces' reception. As the Tanztheater Wuppertal became increasingly popular, this provided the arguments for the pieces' simultaneous attraction and repulsion.

One reason for this disturbing effect lies in the montage approach, which has developed into the guiding stylistic principle of dance theatre. The freely associative interconnection between scenes – which do not seem to be tied to any storyline – to the psychology of the protagonists or to causality thwarts all our usual decoding strategies. A piece can be neither accessed in all its individual parts from one overall viewpoint, nor can a line be drawn around it, allowing individual elements within the circle to gel into a clear "meaning". Both content and form are too multi-layered, enmeshing themselves within the pieces to form a synchrony which can barely be comprehended in a single glance.

It is equally pointless to simply list the scenes in chronological order. Nothing of what occurs on the stage is easy to reconstruct using language. We can describe it but must be content with approximations. The complexity of everything comprising the living theatrical process cannot be pinned down with *one* meaning. Because Pina Bausch's pieces do not operate as "fables" in the Brechtian sense, nor consist of systematic variations on one theme, any coherence is first produced during the process of reception. In this sense they are "imperfect": they are not self-contained works of art because in order to unfold fully they require an active spectator. The key lies with the audience; their degree of identification and personal experience is examined. They need to – and must – be placed in contrast, in relationship, to the events onstage.

It is only when the corporeality (the physical awareness presented) on stage correlates with the physical experience of the spectator that a "coherent meaning" is produced. This is not related to the spectator's concrete (physical) horizon of expectation, because the activity onstage may disappoint or affirm; it unsettles and thus paves the way for new experiences. Wholly distinct from literature, dance theatre, with all its physical, mimetic and gestural potential for creating form, re-launches theatre as communication via the senses.

Pina Bausch's works take our everyday societal, physical experience as their starting point, using sequences of objectifying images and movements to translate them and distance us from them. Experiences we have on a daily basis, such as bodily grooming, reining ourselves in or even tragicomic self-inflicted drills, are displayed provocatively on stage via repetition, duplication etc and thus made palpable. The point of departure is the performers' genuine, subjective experience, which is also invoked in the audience. Simple, passive reception of the pieces is therefore impossible. Because it both works and deals with undivided energies, this "theatre of experience" mobilises the emotions which give rise to form. It doesn't play-act, doesn't pretend "as if"; it *is*. As the audience is moved by this emotional authenticity, which confuses and delights their minds and senses, they are forced to take a stand to clarify their own positions. They are no longer simply consumers of inconsequential entertainment or witnesses to an interpretation of reality. They are involved in an integral event where they experience reality as it is happening through the stimulation of their senses. Despite this, dance theatre does not seduce us with illusions; it entices us to confront reality. It relates to the wider societal structure of affects, which can be localised in a concrete historical setting.[2] The theatre of the 1960s had toiled its way up the conceptual mountains; now dance theatre is "toiling across the plains".

## The art of goldfish dressage: how dance theatre speaks

It was only with the Tanztheater Wuppertal that a discussion about what realism might mean within ballet could even begin. This "theatre of experience" did not only change the conditions of reception by exploiting every one of the senses to involve the audience in the performance; shifting dance from the level of aesthetic abstraction to that of everyday physical behaviour is not simply a question of style – it also changed the very meaning of dance. Whereas dance had, till then, been a world of pleasant appearances, self-serving technique or the abstract handling of existential ideas, Pina Bausch's work returned the spectator directly to reality itself. Raising dance's consciousness also meant confronting it with the whole spectrum of real events. Dance has a particular capacity to narrate via the physical presence of the body and this was expanded and used to portray a reality determined by bodily conventions. Brecht must have sensed this potential when, in *A Short Organum for the Theatre*, he wrote: "For choreography too there are once again tasks of a realistic kind. It is a relatively recent error to suppose that is has nothing to do with the representation of 'people as they really are'. [...] Anyhow, a theatre where everything depends on the gestus cannot do without choreography. Elegant movement and graceful grouping for a start, can alienate, and inventive miming greatly helps the story."[3] Although Pina Bausch's theatre of movement does not convey its message through a story or Brechtian *Fabel* – and is, in fact, characterised by its rejection of literary narrative –, this does not prevent it from using the techniques of Brecht's Epic Theatre. Applied to individual actions and individual scenes, they are essential elements of realist (dance) theatre, for Pina Bausch just as for Brecht. Thus certain core ideas originating in Brecht's didactic theatre (though without its

22

stated aim to educate the audience) are echoed in the Tanztheater Wuppertal: the gestus of showing, the deliberate exposing of processes, the technique of alienation and a particular use of comedy have increasingly become its defining means of representation. Along with motifs drawn from the world of everyday experience, they aid what Brecht postulated as "the depiction of people as they really are".

Pina Bausch's principle of montage, borrowed not from spoken theatre or literature but developed from the popular tradition of her own medium, from vaudeville, music hall and revue, appropriates reality in the form of isolated details or situations. In this sense it parts company with any conventional story-line dramaturgy. Rather than allowing every detail to be interpreted perfectly, the pieces are loaded with multiple layers and a complex synchrony of actions, creating a broad panorama of phenomena. The pieces do not maintain the kind of consistency in which the meaning of each element can be deduced using the guiding thread of a plot; the structure of dance theatre relates more closely to the principle of music: playing around an idea with subjects and countersubjects, variation and counterpoint. The governing principle is the dramaturgy of revue-numbers, processing the motifs in a free yet also precisely calculated and choreographed sequence of show-turns.

This is fieldwork: plumbing the depths of bodily habits and emotions and drawing its finds up into the light of day. Thus a complex of motifs may be illuminated from various viewpoints and can be approached from different directions. In so doing, dance theatre abandons that position of certainty which rests on an interpretation of reality which is already beyond question. It doesn't pretend to know something when really it can know nothing. Instead it makes what it finds questionable, in the best sense of the word. In Pina Bausch's dance theatre we encounter material drawn from reality, almost unmediated, and can observe how it mutates in various constellations. Theatre appears in one of its original senses: as a site of transformation. But the transformations are not used to deceive the audience, like bad conjuring tricks, nor are they intended to console, nor to allow something to be forgotten. Dance theatre does not numb the senses, it sharpens them for "what really is". Theatre functions once more as a laboratory in which the choreographer lets the various reagents influence each other, conflict with each other, complement each other and fuse to generate new insights. The spectator is part of the whole process and is not – as in theatre based on entertainment value and spectacle – fobbed off with mere effects. Yet the Tanztheater Wuppertal's adventures are enjoyable events. The entertainment is fuelled by a curiosity, a hunger for experience and not by the affirmation of what has already long been known.

This hunger for experience is without morality. Where conventional story-line dramaturgy equips its characters with ethical values of some kind, with motivation either political or generally humane, dance theatre abstains from all judgement. It presents its findings, and what the audience then experiences is either a travesty or a validation of what they were anticipating. The fieldwork involves continually taking samples from daily life in order to put everyday forms of human interaction to the test, and does not start with pre-conceived opinions. It possesses the freedom of an experiment, allowing curiosity to re-emerge. Pina Bausch asks questions; her pieces reveal discoveries made on reconnaissance missions undertaken with her ensemble.

The exercises, and variations on a theme, are therefore not subject to any kind of stringent logic, and the usual links, based on the principles of causality, are absent here. There is no taut narrative thread running from beginning to end; the audience is not taken by the hand and led to a destination determined in advance by the choreographer. There is no psychological motor driving and determining how the people on the stage behave and why. The free associations of images and events form chains and analogies, spin a web of intricate impressions, with almost subterranean interconnections. If there is a logic, then it is the logic of the body (rather than of consciousness), following the principle of analogy rather than laws of causality. The logic of affect does not abide by reason.

Thus with the Tanztheater Wuppertal the usual differentiation between leading role and supporting role is absent. Where central protagonists appear, as in *Le Sacre du printemps* or *Blaubart*, it is as if they are made anonymous, their destiny standing for that of all men or all women. The audience can no longer identify with the personal history of individual people. They are therefore forced to seek suspense elsewhere in the piece, in a place in which they are not used to looking. Suspense is no longer produced in connection with a *dénouement* which relieves the tension, but in every single moment, via the juxtaposition of diverse means of expression and moods: through the contrast between loud and quiet, fast and slow, sadness and joy, hysteria and peace, solitude and tentative rapprochement. Pina Bausch does not explore *how* people move; she explores *what* moves them. And she does not tie these motives to the individual psychology of a particular figure.

This expands the field of vision to take in the bigger picture. None of the figures on stage take on representative functions, acting exemplarily. The individual and the societal are directly reflected in the panorama of passions. No interpretation is needed in order to understand the social conditions behind a figure on stage. The unresolved desires Pina Bausch's pieces deal with formulate themselves directly. The dancers do not initially appear as professionals performing a role; they exhibit themselves unshielded, showing their whole personality. Their fears and pleasures carry the insistence of authentic experience. While dance theatre describes the history of the body in general, it also always describes a good deal of the current, living history of the people on stage. While Pina Bausch makes use of theatrical tools from across various genres, the autonomy of the individual media remains intact. In a very Brechtian sense, the dissonances and friction between them do not fuse to become a "total work of art"; instead, "their relations with one another consist in this: that they lead to mutual alienation."[4]

However, in a theatre which appeals less to the spectators' cognitive than to their emotional faculties, Brechtian alienation has a different function. Since Pina Bausch's theatre of movement does not employ a story as vehicle to convey wisdom at "the heart of the theatrical performance", its goal can only be to convey a reality which is experienced personally.[5] Direct experience takes precedence over rational enlightenment. If Brecht's Epic Theatre aims to produce the "correct consciousness", dance theatre offers intense experience. It does not plan resistance for rational reasons; it stirs up a riot amongst the affects. If didactic theatre has its eye first and foremost on the social context, and sets out events according to a world view already acquired, Pina Bausch begins with internalised norms and conventions. In her theatre of movement the social conditions can be read directly in people's physical behaviour.

As with Brecht, dance theatre takes "everything from the gestus". Here, however, the gestus is concentrated within the sphere of physical activity. It does not support or contradict a literary message; it speaks for itself. The body is no longer a means to an end, it is now the subject.

Something new has happened in the history of dance: the body is telling its own story. When, for instance, a man wears a woman round his neck like a scarf, as a sign that she serves solely as a decorative object for him, the scene requires no further interpretation. Again and again in Pina Bausch's work we see the body constrained: we see the whole range of human affects in its posture, shoe-horned into conventions; but we also see its longing to transgress the restrictive boundaries of taboo. Alienation makes the ingrained inhibitions visible. Things viewed as unquestionable norms are distilled from their usual context and can thus be experienced anew. The alienated depiction of the everyday language of the body, frequently distorted, "allows us to recognise its subject, but at the same time makes it unfamiliar."[6] Things which have become second nature in daily life can now be perceived for the first time in the distance which is opened up by a new strangeness.

Alienation is often achieved via comedy, using cinematic techniques. A series of movements is stretched into slow motion or speeded up in frenetic slapstick. But no-one on stage is ever made the butt of a joke. The humour does not judge their real needs, it brings out something lost in the process of distortion. Thus the comic moments always have an undertone of sadness, turning the grotesque balancing act that is petit bourgeois etiquette into tragedy. The self-righteous logic of convention is broken and assumptions behind gestures discredited, in order to expose a loss and reveal a longing which must be preserved. The audience laughs as it recognises the reality of its own behaviour on stage. And unlike in mainstream theatre, it does not laugh at someone else's misfortune. Pina Bausch allows no detachment and brings real desires uncomfortably close. It can be highly revealing to see public and private, studiously separated in daily life, suddenly meeting in an unmediated moment: a couple stands at the front of the stage smiling cheerfully while behind each other's backs they are pinching, kicking and generally abusing each other. To put it in a nutshell, this silly-serious scene exposes the contradiction between hypocritical public harmony and the reality of private civil war. The smiling mask is not the true face. Dance theatre's findings constitute a comprehensive survey of received, blindly adopted ways of behaving.

Time and again in her pieces, Pina Bausch returns to the myths of popular culture, as perpetuated by Hollywood films, comic strips, pop music and related genres such as operetta and revue. From them she extracts

26

not only the basic choreographic elements for her theatre of movement (such as chorus lines, revue formations, the principle of repetition), but also takes their central themes of beauty, partnership and happiness at face value. However, the idealistic images do not stand up to comparison with reality, and they expose our internalised assimilation strategies as self-inflicted physical conditioning. The embrace, rehearsed demonstratively in the Hollywood manner, goes wrong. The partners' stiff gestures do not fit together. Popular myths do not live up to their promise of happiness. Silent, unspoken agreements are disclosed as ridiculous farces. Underneath, however, the real needs show through, the glossy surface failing to conceal them. With a nod and a wink, the audience is made complicit in the unmasking; by laughing together we shed the constraints with ease.

Along with the outside world, theatre itself is included in the reflection. The conventions of the theatre apparatus with its separation between active stage and passive auditorium are tackled physically: dancers racing to the edge of the stage or taking the performance into the auditorium, and addressed squarely on stage. "Come dance with me", the dancers beg the audience at the end of the eponymous piece.

The Tanztheater Wuppertal resists the pressure to indulge in superficial showmanship, in mindless entertainment. As with *Ausdruckstanz*, which eschewed complicated sets and costumes in favour of a stage design focussing on the body, Pina Bausch subordinates scenery and props to the overall message. The refined, poetic stage spaces (initially created by Rolf Borzik, now by Peter Pabst) resist passive, culinary consumption. They often possess a fragile beauty, such as the meadow of flowers guarded by tethered dogs in *Nelken*. These are tangible environments (the exact cast of a Wuppertal street, a larger-than-life-sized nineteenth-century room, a cinema auditorium), but a far cry from any kind of naturalism. They are poetic playgrounds (an actual meadow, an immobile painted sea, an island floating in water) which expand dance theatre's realism into a utopian reality: a real utopia. However, above all, these are spaces for moving in, their design delineating the dancers' potential for movement, making the sounds of movement audible (for instance through fallen leaves or water on the ground) or offering resistance to the body (using earth).

The costumes (also designed initially by Borzik and then, after his death, by Marion Cito) consist either of simple dresses and suits, high-heels and everyday shoes, or shimmering, luxurious evening wear. They are the typical clothes of men and women, worn when they meet each other playing changing social roles. Dance theatre examines the function of each and every piece of clothing. In the earlier pieces especially, Pina Bausch continually showed women as either man-murdering vamps or naive nymphets: embodiments of male fantasies, treading a fine line between self-alienation and self-discovery. "Clothes make the (wo)man", but above all we carry our flesh to market in them. Their function as a restrictive casing is often taken to grotesque extremes within Bausch's dance theatre: when a muscular man in a lurex miniskirt plays cupid with a bow and arrow, the social mask suddenly appears as an absurd masquerade. The childish fun of dressing up is at play here, alongside the precisely calculated dramaturgic fun of unnerving the audience. In dance theatre no-one is allowed to be certain of what they are seeing; it might yet mean something entirely different. Despite all the critical questioning, however, Pina Bausch does allow her audience, her dancers and not least herself the sheer pleasure of elegance. Beauty has always been an important ingredient of dance theatre, not as an end in itself but as a factor in human desire.

This is also evoked by the rich and varied range of music from around the world, newly compiled for each piece by Matthias Burkert and Andreas Eisenschneider. There are no rules dictating which styles may be combined. Jazz is mixed with folk, heavy metal with classical music. The distinction between so-called serious and popular music has long since been done away with. The music is chosen solely for its emotional content and according to whether it boosts the underlying tone of a scene, whether it is loud or quiet, fast or slow. Here, too, Bausch casts her net wide, respecting all cultures and all forms as fundamentally equal. Openness is the first commandment and the sole criterion for determining whether a piece of music tells us something, precisely and authentically, about the diversity of human emotions.

Openness and serenity are two key notions underlying dance theatre's basic philosophy, which firmly resist pressure to fulfil audiences' expectations and attitudes of dumb, passive anticipation, inviting them instead on a joint exploration of living inner worlds. Theatre, in other words, is not situated outside reality. Dance theatre fights the institution theatre embodies (with its continual threat of ossification), in order to re-animate it as a place for living experience. For this reason the boundary between rehearsal process and performance is also no longer recognised. Things created and constructed are blatantly presented as such. The actors/dancers explain the next dance sequence to each other onstage, deliberate over the upcoming scene, appear unenthusiastic or frustrated with their work, or step forward awkwardly and say: "I have to do something." In laying bare its manufacture and its techniques, dance theatre banishes all slick theatrical illusions. Theatre is thus re-launched as a genuine process for assimilating reality. It seizes on the contradictions of real life and broadcasts them live and direct.

In one scene a dancer tells the tragicomic story of how a goldfish is trained to walk on dry land, with the result that the animal, now alienated from its element, is finally in danger of drowning in water. In just the same way, so it seems, the process of civilisation has left human beings high and dry: their bodies in a reality which is like the wrong element.

## The upright gait: body language and the history of the body

In *The Philosophy of Music*, quoted at the beginning, Ernst Bloch describes dance and music as being among the first means for humans to affirm their existence, preceding literature. However, "they have no life of their own, […] there is something else we have to get past first which fortifies their expression firmly and fully." Perhaps dance had to take such a long journey in order to find itself, in order to take the means of expression into its own hands and return to its origins.

But the path travelled cannot only be measured using the milestones inherent to dance, to which dance historians generally like to refer. Ultimately it is futile to talk of technical issues when people are the issue. The Tanztheater Wuppertal severs the thread of continuity in an interpretation of dance history which myopically claws its way from one technical innovation to the next, as if the dancing human, of all things, were isolated from any other developments in society. If we want to understand the significance of Pina Bausch's work to the whole genre, we have to step back and look at the bigger picture. Dance theatre's achievement, making the moving body its subject, has more far-reaching consequences. Bringing everyday human behaviour under scrutiny means studying the overall history of the body, the development of a particular control over the body.

The sociologist Norbert Elias's analysis of the body's relationship to social, economic and societal structures is unique. Elias assumes "that the structure of civilised behaviour is closely interrelated with the organization of Western societies in the form of states."[7] "For the structures of personality and of society evolve in an indissoluble interrelationship."[8] Central for Elias is the development of human beings' "inner nature", which includes the whole gamut of human behaviour, the changes in their affect structure and their "drive life". He envisages the process of civilisation above all as "the structural change in people towards an increased consolidation and differentiation of their affect control, and therefore of both their experience [...] and of their behaviour."[9] He observes an increase in people's dependence on each other during the historical process, requiring an increasingly complicated self-control from the individual: this "change in human personality structures" is effected in dependence on "the long-term change in the figurations which people form with one another, towards a higher level of differentiation and integration."[10] Along with our subjugation of "outer nature" which – particularly through industrialisation – has become increasingly differentiated into distinct technical branches, he sees an accompanying increase in control over the "drive life" and bodily expression.

A clear indication of this change to affect structure can be seen in the differentiation within human social intercourse: an increasing refinement of table manners (such as the introduction of cutlery) along with lower shame and embarrassment thresholds. The changes in "social figurations", as Elias calls them, result in the accumulation and complication of everyday rules of behaviour. Drive desires are increasingly unable to find direct expression, subject to the growing codex of conventions. Over time the affects are subject to a differentiated network of control stages, which changes human psychic organisation decisively. Industrialisation and the spread of technology have evolved a complex regime of control over "outer nature", used similarly to control our "inner nature".

Individual and society form an inseparable whole, influencing each other reciprocally and are bound together by so-called "chains of interdependence". Thus human patterns of behaviour, in particular the mastery of affects, are formed by the pressure of wider social determinants. Highly

30

significant here is the problem of power monopoly. The increasing concentration of power taken from individuals and given to institutions –
and ultimately delegated to the state – is matched by a process whereby
outer constraints are internalised as self-constraint. The link between the
"outside" (state power) and "inside" (individual affect structure) is fear. It
transmits the overall structure of society onto the personal psychic func-
tioning of the individual.

Dance must be situated within the same reciprocal relationship. In
dance we see the influence of external conditions on people's psychic
constitution and how this is reflected in the body. When dance theatre
addresses conventional customs and behaviour, this is not just a question
of good taste, manners, decency and morals; it is tackling history in its
fundamental structure, as it has been written on the body. This unavoid-
ably sheds a different light on the history of dance.

The strict canon of rules governing ballet – its measured order – is a
symbol of the social order of its time, exemplifying the control demanded
by modern humans of their affects. Typical of this ideal is the *danse
d'école* with its predilection for technical perfection: the highly differentiated control of body and emotion which people in the industrial age
must subject themselves to. Classical ballet, however, reflects this physical
restraint with apparent unawareness. In dance theatre on the other hand,
this unthinking continuity is broken. The unfulfilled desires which the
march of history has left hibernating in the body are demanding their
rights. The dance of nice appearances is halted so that we can finally ask
what moves a dancing body, and why it moves.

Right here is where the potential of dance theatre lies: where control
over people abandons the parameters of language and rational explana-
tion, where the subjugation of "outer nature" accompanies that of "inner
nature". Alongside analysis of the big historical processes, for which spoken theatre is much more suited, comes the question of how they impact
on the concrete, physical sphere. Rational insight is joined by physical
understanding; consciousness finds an equal partner in *physical* consciousness. Desire, without which there can be no hope, is seen as a painful
absence, with the right to a home in the body. The ideals of the head
alone do not spur anyone to action. In dance theatre utopia is completed:
the upright gait. Bloch's synonym for human emancipation must be learnt
with the whole body and with all the senses.

# Notes

1 Ernst Bloch, "The Philosophy of Music", in: *Essays on the Philosophy of Music*, Cambridge: Cambridge University Press, 1985 (translated for this book by Stephen Morris).

2 In psychology the term "affect" refers to the expression and manifestation of emotions and desires. The sociological term "affect structure" was first used by Norbert Elias. He used it to refer to the dimension of humans' "inner nature", involving the transformations of physical behaviour and drive life, which relates to the "outer nature", the social and economic situations of particular societal forms: Norbert Elias, *The Civilizing Process*, Oxford: Blackwell, 1994.

3 Bertolt Brecht, "A Small Organon for the Theatre", section 73, in: John Willett (ed.), *Brecht on Theatre: The Development of an Aesthetic*, London: Methuen, 1964, p 203.

4 Ibid, section 74, p 204.

5 Ibid, section 65, p 200.

6 Ibid, section 42, p 192.

7 Elias, op cit, p xii.

8 Elias, op cit, p 456.

9 Elias, op cit, p 451.

10 Elias, op cit, p 451.

**Works**

## Frühlingsopfer

Pina Bausch's three-part Stravinsky evening "Frühlingsopfer" ("The Rite of Spring") picks up on the German tradition of *Ausdruckstanz* more clearly than any of her other pieces while also including the essential stylistic elements she was to develop and diversify in her later work. Soon after the premiere, the third part – *Le Sacre du printemps* – was presented on its own and, under the title *Frühlingsopfer* or *The Rite of Spring*, became one of the Tanztheater Wuppertal's most frequently performed and successful pieces. To date, it is the last piece (with the exception of the second part, which is more closely related to dance theatre) to have been choreographed from beginning to end in the traditional sense. It marks both an ending and a turning point in a process of development characterised by increased radicalisation in theatrical expression and the expansion of traditional notions of dance. It could be said that *Frühlingsopfer* marks the end of a phase of choreography in the narrower sense. It was followed by the gradual crystallisation of what the Tanztheater Wuppertal has come to stand for. Its distinctive stylistic traits evolved in the 1970s from the montage approach, the inclusion of speech, and the refinement of the artistic development of the 1960s. So it seems appropriate to begin a portrait of the Tanztheater Wuppertal with *Frühlingsopfer*, the piece which first brought Pina Bausch wider acclaim.

The first part, *Wind von West*, is set to Igor Stravinsky's 1952 *Cantata* and consists of statuesque variations on the subject of human relations. Existential pain and the impossibility of intimacy within relationships are the motifs expressed through dance. The stage is divided into four spaces by doorways delineated in the background and gauze planes stretched between them. In the second space there is a filigree, stylised table, also used as a bed: a symbolic object in the battle of the sexes fought by an estranged couple.

Time and again, the individual, in isolation and in outbursts of desire, is juxtaposed against the group. Restricted to a few expressive movements, the group incorporates the rhythm of the surrounding situation with its mechanisms of control. In one sequence, one of the women in the group collapses, but the rhythm of the dance continues unbroken. Men take hold of women and shake them like lifeless dolls. A woman and a man dance facing each other, almost in mirror image, yet separated by one of the dividing veils. They fail to touch, remaining in separate rooms.

The same idea of separation characterises the relationship between individuals and the group: the two never meet in the same space. Alongside the recurring group-dance interludes, the various delineations of the space constitute a further tension-producing choreographic and conceptual element. The group, ruled by the dogma of its remorseless life rhythm, and the individual, who remains under its influence despite all attempts to break away, form poles of tension which represent, along with the attempts at intimacy thwarted by spatial separation, estrangement and personal rigidity. These poles determine the dynamics of both form and content within the piece.

The question of how male and female roles are determined is also first outlined here. Power comes from the man, for whom the woman is material available to use as he pleases. But the consequences of the gender-role dictates are not felt by one side only. Isolation and the impossibility of intimacy are a painful reality for both sexes, even if the power is unevenly distributed.

The second of the three pieces, *Der zweite Frühling* (*The Second Spring*) tackles this subject with Chaplinesque humour. We see into a petit bourgeois dining room, where a distinguished, grey-haired couple is eating supper; in the background are amorous "memories", largely those of the man: the bride, a Virgin Mary incarnation of pure innocence; a vamp, the embodiment of seductive lasciviousness; and her self-assured man-eating relative. These three stereotypes, along with the husband's younger doppelganger, present the spectrum of male fantasies within which all the woman can do is adopt one of the clichéd roles desired by the man. This leaves her no room for an individual feminine identity. *Der zweite Frühling*, too, derives its dynamic from a dualism: the frozen ritual of married life on the one hand, and memories – the man's desire for a marital second spring – on the other.

The use of music also demonstrates this. During the slow-motion dinner, he tries to approach her. As soon as he comes too close, a grating, clock-work music starts up. She swiftly twists out of his embrace and with quick little steps hurries off to her "housewifely duties". Through such cinematic scenes a kind of slapstick comedy is created, showing middle class life in the form of a tragicomic silent film. An historical quotation

36

has the same effect, when the man-eating vamp appears in a red, flowing, Isadora Duncan style dress and makes a mockery of the male fantasy with her over-exaggerated posturing.

Fantasy and reality are not strictly divided here. Just as the man's attempts to get frisky are continually interrupted by the "clockwork music", memories suddenly mingle with daily life. The seductress has a sweet tooth and scoops cream out of a bowl with her finger; the bride climbs over the married couple's chairs while they are eating. The resulting comedy serves to establish the Brechtian alienation effect, exposing internalised constraints and chauvinistic male morality.

The closing image is in the same mould. Once all the masculine powers of seduction have failed and the memories calmed down, the idyll is restored again: man and wife sit opposite each other holding hands across the table, a picture of sorry resignation.

The choreography of Pina Bausch's *Le Sacre du printemps*, the third and final piece of the evening, basically adheres to the original libretto, although without referring to pagan Russia. The war of the sexes does not arise from the worship of the earth; the separation is a reality present from the outset and forms the piece's *mis en scène*. The action focuses wholly on the sacrifice of a young girl. The only scenery is a layer of earth (peat) covering the stage, transforming the space into a timeless, archaic-looking arena, a battle ground of life and death. Like many future sets, this stage environment creates a "physical" field of action for the dancers. The earth is not only a symbol relating to the piece, it also directly influences the movements, lending them an earthy weight and recording traces of the violent sacrificial ritual. Thus *Le Sacre du printemps* writes history once more in the earth using bodies; by the end the once-smooth surface is a scarred battlefield. The earth sticks to the women's thin tunics, is smeared on faces, clings to the men's naked torsos.

There is no "as if" in Pina Bausch's dance theatre; the dancers are not acting out increasing exhaustion when they dance against the resistance of the ankle-deep earth: the exhaustion is real. The energy demanded of the dancers by *Sacre* is clearly felt by the audience. The effort is not hidden under a smiling face, and it is audible in their heavy breathing. The forcefully sensual presence achieved by the players through their unrestricted bodily exertion authenticates the story empirically and allows us to experience the sacrifice vividly.

The first scene shows one of the women lying on the red dress in which the chosen victim must later dance to her death. She is drawn into the dances of the group of women, from which one or another repeatedly tries to escape. Men and women form themselves into the magic sign of the circle and begin an earth-worship ceremony, in a language of movement borrowed from ethnic dance. Despite this reference to pagan invocation rituals, the piece does not share the atavism of the original. Pina Bausch adopts the basic forms of an archaic, patriarchal society, but transposes it into the present.

Thus the earth-worship comes across more as a community ritual after which the sexes return to their customary separation. Men and women are characterised very differently, using a vocabulary of movement strongly linked to *Ausdruckstanz* (the men, for example, via aggressive leaps). Here too, however, both sexes are entranced by an overpowering, compulsive rhythm.

Panic and horror take over as the time approaches for the victim to be chosen, shown when one of the women repeatedly picks up the dress. This "test" occurs several times, making it clear that anyone can be the victim, that it is indicating the fate of all women. The figures divide according to sex. While the men stand waiting in the background, the women draw fearfully into a tight circle. One after another, they emerge from the circle and approach the leader of the men in order to receive the dress. He is lying on it: a symbol of his power to decide on a victim.

Again the circle of women dissolves into a dance, then closes up again. One of them steps out, picks up the dress, which is passed around the group until the leader identifies the victim. This is the sign for the group to begin an orgiastic fertility rite, celebrating the rising rhythm of coitus. But this, too, happens as though under duress, its violence more closely resembling rape than an act of pleasurable release. After the victim has been presented to the anxiously staring group by the leader, she begins her dance of death under their fearful gaze.

The three parts of the *Frühlingsopfer* evening are three variations on the same motif, treated with a different choreographic approach each time: the first part more statuesque, the second forming a counterpoint through tragicomic, cinematic means, and the third as an existential investigation of the subject. The central theme is the antagonism and the estrangement between men and women. Here the accent clearly lies on the woman, shown as object and victim.

However, the sacrifice ritual retains an unavoidable fatefulness. In her version of *Le Sacre du printemps* Pina Bausch focuses all her expressive means on the bestial suffering the female victim experiences, brutally executed as if it were a matter of course. The piece stands as a metaphor for a world which mercilessly claims its (mostly female) victims. In this respect, the attitude of *Le Sacre du printemps*, as of her other pieces, is to state the facts. Unlike the dance theatre of Johann Kresnik, the aim is not to reveal social contexts. The Tanztheater Wuppertal seeks to confront us uncompromisingly with suffering and to draw the audience into the action with all the emotional power of dance.

Thus the newness of this interpretation lies not only in its departure from atavistic ritual, turning to contemporary subjects such as the war of the sexes and alienation; its radicalisation and emotionality are also new. Instead of the usual abstraction or omission of individual fears and desires, the radical experience of feelings becomes the starting point. The spectator is forced to take a stand. Like no other choreographer, Pina Bausch has made daily experience – not simply her own personal experience – the point of departure for her work. While pieces made in the wake of Brecht's didactic theatre all too often end with the trite formula "unfortunately life's not like that", Pina Bausch's theatre of movement targets the affects, which only a determined rationalist could claim are blind.

Increasingly concrete and close to everyday life, yet full of poetry, this theatre of experience uses associative montage to create a language which stirs deep emotions. It stirs up a riot among the affects and for the first time lends rational insight the physical substance to render it effective.


## Die sieben Todsünden


The first step in this direction is the two-part Brecht/Weill evening which Bausch compiled and which comprises *Die sieben Todsünden der Kleinbürger* (*The Seven Deadly Sins of the Petite Bourgeoisie*) and *Fürchtet Euch nicht* (*Don't Be Afraid*), a collage of the most popular songs from *Rise and Fall of the City of Mahagonny, Happy End, The Threepenny Opera* and the *Berlin Requiem.* The dancers perform simultaneously as actors and singers; the divisions between the genres are lifted and the various dance-theatrical means of expression integrated.

Brecht wrote the text for *Die sieben Todsünden der Kleinbürger* in the spring of 1933 in Paris, already on the run from the National Socialists. Having initially escaped to Switzerland, Kurt Weill invited him to Paris to write a libretto. The company Ballets 1933 had just been founded, directed by Boris Kochno, and Weill had been commissioned to write a piece for them. The premiere took place on 7 June 1933 in the Parisian Théâtre des Champs-Élysées with choreography by George Balanchine. The stage sets were designed by Caspar Neher, and leading roles were played by Lotte Lenya and the dancer Tilly Losch (the wife of the founder of Ballets 1933, Edward James). The piece was not an initial success; the breakthrough was achieved only in 1958 in a second Balanchine production for the New York City Ballet; the first German performance, which came as late as 1960, was choreographed by Tatjana Gsovsky.

The piece features a female singer, a female dancer and a quartet of male singers, representing the family. It describes the journey of two sisters, Anna I and Anna II, from Louisiana in the south to the big cities of the USA, as they tour to raise the money for a small house back home. "One of the two Annas is the manager, the other is the artist; the first, Anna I, is the saleswoman, the second, Anna II, the goods," is how Brecht describes them in a libretto stage direction. All the money the two Annas earn is sent back to the family: father, mother and two brothers. Anna I is the alter ego of her dancing sister and follows her everywhere like an admonishing shadow. She knows the rules of the marketplace and what you have to do to sell yourself; for women selling means, first and foremost, making their bodies and their youth available. Anna II – in contrast – represents the natural desire for happiness, constantly thwarted by the need to sell herself. Anna I has to continually prevent her sister from committing one of the seven deadly sins, thus jeopardising their profits. A member of the petite bourgeoisie living under the conditions dictated by the capitalist market and aspiring to acquire property cannot afford to live a natural dignified life.

In the dichotomy between the two Annas, Brecht shows the contradictions inherent in a societal system which forces the individual – who wants to be good – to be bad in order to survive. Brecht uses the definition of the seven deadly sins established by the "scholastic" Peter Lombard (ca. 1100–1169) according to which sloth, pride, wrath, gluttony, lust, avarice and envy all lead to eternal damnation. But what the Christian moral code identifies as vices, Brecht presents as virtues. As long as we are ruled by the laws of the marketplace, where one person is a salesman offering up another as goods, there is no room for such "virtues".

Unlike Brecht, Pina Bausch does not aim to emphasise social conditions in her production. She focuses on the destiny of women who have to sell their flesh. Anna II is a product bought largely by men. Her body and her youth are the only assets she can deploy in order to acquire property. The exploitation depicted here is that perpetrated by men against women. The social conditions affecting both sexes are acknowledged but remain vague.

The stage, open right to the fire walls, evokes sleaze. The ground is covered with an accurate cast of a real street, lit by a chain of dim neon lamps. The dominant colours are black and grey. Props are limited to the absolute essentials. Instead of remaining hidden in the orchestra pit, the accompanying band sits at the back of the stage. This conspicuous placement of the musicians and the demonstrative arrangement of the spotlights in the foreground are clearly not an attempt to generate illusion. The stage is a site of openly displayed, played-out reality in a wholly Brechtian sense. This is also a means for Pina Bausch to avoid presenting the familiar songs in an atmosphere of blissful nostalgia.

Her *Die sieben Todsünden* (*The Seven Deadly Sins*) does not, however, have the character of a Brechtian parable. While in Brecht economic realities turn natural human desires into mortal sin, Pina Bausch shows the contradiction between individual self-fulfilment and the wider pressure to conform. While Brecht reveals moral asceticism to be an instrument of inhumanity, Pina Bausch's Anna is faced with the choice between individual creativity and self-sacrificing toil for her family.

This shifts the conflict into the area of personal choice. The social context recedes behind the private. Anna II is basically a woman who has not learned a trade and has nothing to sell except her body. As a woman she is subject to the terms of a reality represented by men, and by her sister as her alter ego. She is forced to adapt to male fantasies in order to be able to sell her sole product: love.

For Brecht, however, the story of the divided Anna serves as an example of the social status of the petite bourgeoisie, from whom the prevailing social conditions require a rigidly enforced morality. Sin is now defined as being too slothful to do wrong, too proud to sell yourself, or succumbing to wrath after witnessing injustice in the everyday struggle to survive: all bad for business. The simple enjoyment of physical pleasure is described as gluttony, and selfless loving is condemned as fornication because it does not involve goods which generate profit. Greed, in so as far as it reveals deception, and envy – of those who are happy – are also both unforgivable sins for the petite bourgeoisie.

Pina Bausch sets her piece in the atmosphere of a run-down revue theatre. Anna I, the manager, who knows the rules of the male-dominated market, tarts up her sister for her role as sexual object. She combs her hair violently into place, forces her into a slutty dress and high heels, and presents her to the paying, male world.

In Baltimore a row of men wait patiently, carefully take their jackets off before raping Anna, one after another. In another city one of the johns first takes her measurements before assuming possession of his wares.

The second Anna's initial carefree naivety gradually gives way to a dogged, forced smile. Under the watchful eye of her sister, who knows how best to present her to a press photographer – dumb but sexy – and who succeeds in thwarting her unprofitable love affair with "Fernando", they finally achieve their goal: the house in Louisiana. By now, however, Anna II has lost her love of daydreaming and all her desires.

However, it is her refusal to submit to being a whore that repeatedly allows her to slip out of her marketable role. In contrast to Brecht, Pina Bausch is not focussing on social injustice but on the barriers denying the individual a happy life.

This continues to be her central motif during the second half of the evening. A line from the Salvation Army chorus in *Happy End* runs through the loose sequence of twenty-five scenes like a leitmotif: "Fürchtet euch nicht, fürchtet euch nicht […]" – "Don't be afraid, don't be afraid / No corruption will lead you astray / God will take you in his right hand / He will show you the virtuous way / don't be afraid, don't be afraid." It is sung by a young man in the role of a suburban Casanova and frequently paraphrased. *Fürchtet euch nicht* is another variation on the theme of a young girl whose romantic notions of love collide with reality.

The individual scenes are linked by a freely associative revue-dramaturgy, and it is here that Pina Bausch first consolidates this as her particular dance theatre style: a theatre of movement, allowing a motif to be developed and illuminated from various angles without a stringent plot. Revue becomes, simultaneously, the dramatic means and the subject.

Linked arm in arm in a chorus line, the company carry out their revue formations with a brutal, stubborn intensity, charge furiously to the front of the stage and flirt, winking, with the audience. The confrontation is direct and energetic, yet the situation remains unresolved; Pina Bausch's revue troupe moves as if in a parade of past-time glamour poses, but simultaneously convey a wholly primal delight in dancing.

It is as if, in its accentuation, the entertainment industry model of dance, seen a thousand times, suddenly acquires an elemental vitality again. While the girl troupes of the 1920s executed a mechanical geometry, Pina Bausch releases a joyful energy into that hackneyed form, leaving the mindless maths of disembodied dancing machines far behind. The restrictive boundary is crossed with ease. In the subsequent pieces, the techniques of the revue – thus transformed – become a potent stylistic tool for the Tanztheater Wuppertal's work. Pina Bausch did not, however, extract this form, as frequently claimed, from the theatre but from the (popular) tradition of her own medium: dance. Her pieces continually uncover the rousing, explosive power latent in music hall, vaudeville, cabaret and revue, which in classical dance has long since congealed into an unapproachable virtuosity.

Despite the delight in dancing displayed throughout, *Fürchtet euch nicht* does not avoid being critical. The schoolgirl dreams, replete with clichés and fuelled by the glamour of popular music and showbiz, do not stand up against reality. The glitzy world distorts the real needs and exploits them; it does not take them seriously. Two worlds are brought to light here: the world of individual experience and the world of theatre with its pressure to perform; this later becomes the overriding subject of *Kontakthof*. In *Fürchtet euch nicht*, Pina Bausch returns to the techniques used in *Zweiter Frühling*. Comedy can always capsise into tragedy.

The song of "Surabaya Johnny", who wanted money not love, crescendos into an aggressive peal of laughter, full of despair and anger. "The Ballad of Good Living", which contains the motto "the only good life is a rich life", shows petit bourgeois life as a comedy film: two older women in black dresses with lace collars perform an elegant gestural dance of mutual hindrance and consolation. Holding hands they skip daintily across the stage, smile coyly at each other and smooth out their clothes, always concerned to keep up appearances.

To the sounds of the "Sailors' Tango", living female dolls are placed around a hobby horse as if on a fairground carousel. The aim here is not to interpret or illustrate the texts; the images contrast with the songs, juxtapose their own associations against them.

In between songs, with his saccharine "don't be afraid" the young beau attempts to coax his chosen targets into a gentle seduction. He is the incarnation of all romantic pop heroes: two-faced. When his seductive powers fail him, he uses force to take what is not given voluntarily. Each girl is then integrated into the troupe of whores.

Pina Bausch expands the "Jealousy Duet" between Polly and Lucy from *The Threepenny Opera* into a quartet. Four women lie on their expensive furs – objects used to demonstrate male wealth and macho potency – and argue about their pecking order.

These scenes are broken up with group-dance interludes. Towards the end the group dances to the "Useless Song" in slow motion, the men joining the women, in drag. They have all long since become whores, with grotesque costumes and garish make-up. No-one can withstand the pressure to turn to prostitution. Despite any initial misunderstanding that there might be a feminist bias to the piece, Pina Bausch insists that even within the imbalance of power between the sexes, the conflict cannot be simplified into a relationship between aggressor (man) and victim (woman). She remains interested in the fortunes of men *and* women.

## Blaubart. Beim Anhören einer Tonbandaufnahme von Béla Bartóks Oper "Herzog Blaubarts Burg"

In *Blaubart* (*Bluebeard*) the formal techniques initiated in *Frühlingsopfer* and used as the stylistic basis of the Brecht/Weill evening grew to be the essential choreographic instruments: a genre-bridging theatre of movement. This mixture of elements from dance, opera, theatre, pantomime and film now asserted itself as the art-form called dance theatre.

For the first time the programme notes did not use a description such as "dance opera" (as of the choreography for the Gluck operas) or the label "ballet" (*Le Sacre du printemps*). This time the evening is described simply as "scenes". This implies something fragmentary, similar to the Brecht/Weill evening's revue form, and the rejection of a traditionally choreographed, flowing structure. There is no interpretation or adaptation of an opera in dance form, as with *Iphigenia in Tauris* or *Orpheus and Eurydice*.

While in classical dance, music often has an underscoring role, as an aural accessory to the dancing, in *Blaubart* it becomes a meaningful part of the content, an essential element of the production. Its function is of equal value to that of the other dramatic elements, and the full title is in fact: *Blaubart. Beim Anhören einer Tonbandaufnahme von Béla Bartóks Oper "Herzog Blaubarts Burg"* (*Bluebeard. While listening to a tape recording of Béla Bartók's opera "Duke Bluebeard's Castle"*). A tape recorder is the dominant prop, set on a trolley with a spool leading the cable up to the ceiling. Because the music is integrated into the theatrical action, the significance of the tape recording rises above and beyond mere technical necessity. It is a player too, rolled around and used choreographically to demarcate the space. Music and action play equal roles in the unfolding dramatic multiplicity.

Pina Bausch uses the opera's libretto as a foil for her concept. In Bartók the lovely Judith arrives at the legendary enchanted castle of Duke Bluebeard. She is given a set of keys opening seven doors behind which she discovers a torture chamber, an arsenal of weapons, a treasure chamber, a bloody garden, an enormous kingdom and a sea of tears. The seventh room, which Bluebeard opens only at Judith's insistence, contains the finely dressed, murdered bodies of the Duke's former wives. Judith

45

acknowledges the fate awaiting her, surrenders herself without resistance to the Duke's sadism, lets herself be dressed and crowned and goes calmly to meet her end.

Pina Bausch rips this fable out of its fantastic milieu and places the symbolism of the seven rooms in the everyday present. The subjects of her production are the antagonism between the sexes, the desire for love, the inability to understand each other and the flight into empty conventions. Along the way she demonstrates the constant ambivalence between tender violence and violent tenderness.

The Duke is now just a man called Bluebeard; his castle a large, white, empty room in a fin de siècle building, with a corridor in the background and tall windows with shutters. The white floor is covered with shrivelled, brown autumn leaves which record the dancers' actions, absorb their traces and make the stage scenery tangible through sounds and smells, much like the earth in *Le Sacre du printemps*.

The action is determined by the music. At the beginning Bluebeard sits by the tape recorder, listens to the first bars of the opera, stops the tape, rewinds, begins again, pauses and repeats the procedure, allowing himself to wallow in memories. As in Samuel Beckett's *Krapp's Last Tape*, where the lonely Krapp recognises the futility of his life while listening to recordings of his own voice, Bluebeard searches in violent desperation for the vestiges of tenderness, affection and love he once experienced. While the tape continually plays the same excerpt, he rushes over to Judith, lying immobile on the floor with open arms, throws himself on top of her, rapes her and, gasping, drags her a few feet along the floor. The woman meekly lets it all happen.

In Pina Bausch's production, the symbolism of Bartók's opera becomes a concrete world of direct images, focussing on the hopeless lack of understanding between man and woman. But the woman is not simply a victim; she grasps the role allotted her like a weapon. The man is not simply the ruler, master and winner by virtue of his gender; he is also a prisoner of himself, failing pathetically to match up to his own intimidating self-image. This is enacted by the male dancers, trying to impress the women with body-builder poses, hoping to be admired and adored. Left alone, however, Bluebeard has only a naked baby doll, which he prostitutes himself in front of, posing in smug narcissism. He lassos women with a bed sheet, spins them around in circles, puts them on a chair, piling two or three bodies on top of each other, filing the objects of his desire like a pile of documents. With all his strength he presses his hands on the head of a woman, forcing her to kneel: an act of wholly physical, brutal suppression.

Sexuality is reduced to its animal essence; the violence reaches its high point in the sexual act. Without the guise of harmonious union it remains simply a power struggle in which bodies crash against each other, the opponents pulling, pushing, hitting and tormenting each other.

Exhaustion is followed by a renewed search for contact: the game begins again. Couples seek security and support from each other, but the stroking hands grasp thin air. Dancers slip out of their partner's embraces, fall to their feet and are literally trampled on. Others try to cling to each other but fail, arms hanging limply from their bodies. An attempt at leaning on each other ends with a painful fall. The players climb high up the walls and grip tightly, seeking safety, or sit on the floor, leaning against the wall in exhaustion, only to be dragged back to the middle by the others and spun back into the group.

Peer pressure is another dominant theme in this piece. The dancers continually seek out a quiet corner, a window seat, in order to enjoy a moment of undisturbed privacy, but they cannot escape the desperate, compulsive struggles for love and happiness

The juxtaposition of groups and individuals, who doggedly struggle to live out a little individuality, is a recurring motif of almost all Bausch's early pieces. The crowd is ruled by the pressure of conventional rituals, which leave no space for the individual. These rituals are shown in *Blaubart* through incessant repetitions of the same movements and formations. It seems to be impossible to break out of this drill of normality, repeated exactly, down to the smallest detail. The dancers chase frantically around the stage, hit the walls screaming, discovering the boundaries, the constriction of the human emotional world.

In between, there are moments of apparent togetherness and peace, which then keel over into latent aggression or resignation. Bluebeard sits by the tape recorder, the women crowding around him, monotonously cooing the "thank you" from Judith's aria and touching him, their fingers tracing the shape of his face, his shoulders, taking possession.

The wounds received in the battle for happiness affect both partners equally. They assail each other with questions and demands, wanting to know everything, wanting to explore and discover, thus denying the other any privacy; they ultimately control each other. Soothing gestures escalate into vehement defence, swift flight or aggression. Affection flips over into violence. Pina Bausch makes the unpredictable ambivalence of emotion a central subject of her work. We can never be certain of what is happening, but the hope always remains that things will turn out better in the end.

In *Blaubart* women demand to be more than just objects of lust and sometime consumer goods. Bluebeard resorts to self defence: he puts mountains of clothes on Judith, piles all the roles of her predecessors onto her, rendering her immobile. He reinstates his mastery, winning a Pyrrhic victory in the pitched battle of the sexes.

The subject matter of *Blaubart* is not the main reason the piece stands out so strongly within Pina Bausch's work, since this recurs in various forms in most of the pieces; it stands out because of to the way in which it develops dance theatre.

More consistently than in the Brecht/Weill revue Pina Bausch reaches across the limits of conventional theatre and uses expressive means from every genre. She combines the individual elements to form a hard-edged dramaturgy of contrast, which does not weave dissonances into a harmonious whole, instead letting contradictions crash against each other. Loudness contrasts with quiet, fast with slow, light with dark. In switchback leaps and falls the audience is subjected to emotional highs and lows no choreographer had risked before.

No-one who is attempting to get to the bedrock of emotions can still indulge in "nice dancing". In *Blaubart* the dancers run, jump, fall, crawl and slide, driven by their inner needs and conflicts. They repeat the actions, nine, ten times, right to the very limits of endurance.

Their language is torn and truncated too, sounding alternately silly or destructive. The dancers scream, moan, groan, gasp, giggle, laugh and screech, and when they do utter words or fragments of sentences they speak to themselves in a monotone as if absent. When distress and mutual misunderstanding are so great, language, it seems, no longer aids communication.

Music can no longer provide harmonious coherence either. The composition is shredded, shattered into short sequences. As the incessant repetition grows unbearable, music becomes an instrument of torture. Only the finale, Judith's realisation of her imminent end, runs without interruption fifteen minutes.

Bluebeard has now put all the clothes on her and pulls the lifeless doll-woman down onto his belly. Lying on his back he drags her, panting and desperate, round the room, through the leaves. He claps his hands, and the group repeats the gestures, poses and movements of the piece once more but in static images. Just as the stations of someone's life are said to flash before them in their dying moments, in Bluebeard's hour of greatest need and loneliness he is reminded of the seven chambers in his castle. The clapping and panting echoes on for a long time; a man who has reached the outermost extremes of loneliness has become a murderer out of despair.

Thus in Pina Bausch's oeuvre *Blaubart* is one of the most uncompromising and impressive variations on the theme of the opposed sexes who are unable to reach an understanding or genuine intimacy. Without mercy, Bausch plays out the conventional behavioural schemata, aspirations and notions of happiness, then lets them flounder in the hopelessness of an unbridgeable lack of understanding. Like no other piece it leaves the audience baffled and uneasy but acutely aware of how things stand.

Dramaturgically it represents a further step towards an idiosyncratic theatre of contrasts, using free association and montage and focussing on the constant ups and downs of emotion. Although *Blaubart* contains vestiges of a Brechtian fable, extracted from Bartók's opera, the traditional narrative structure − of introduction, climax and conclusion − has been dispensed with. The tension now results from the continually changing, combined and contrasted atmospheres, no longer leading towards a climax which releases the suspense. Already, in the following piece *Komm tanz mit mir*, the fable is reduced to a minimum and in later pieces gives way to an open series of scenes.

While Judith and Bluebeard, mirrored and multiplied in the actions of the group, stand for all men and all women, the audience can no longer identify with one continuous character on stage as they are used to doing. Instead, this unmediated experience forces them to look back at themselves. Pina Bausch does not make a moral judgement of the events. She displays what everyone knows, exaggerates it and dislocates the all too familiar almost to the point of becoming unrecognisable. Nearly two hours long, without an interval, *Blaubart* is a radical challenge to conventional ways of watching theatre. There is no escape for the audience. They must draw their own conclusions.

## Komm tanz mit mir

*Komm tanz mit mir* (*Come Dance with Me*) begins before it has started. While the spectators are finding their seats, a dancer wearing a heavy overcoat and a black hat pulled right down over his forehead wanders calmly through the aisles, another hat dangling from a long fishing rod behind him. Curious and bemused, the audience waits to see what will happen on stage.

For the time being, this is hidden behind the safety curtain. Only a small doorway allows a glimpse into the white room behind. Women in colourful summer clothes and men in thick winter coats hurry past. They take each other's hands, begin circle dances, sing the children's rhyme *Hoppe, hoppe Reiter*. At the edge of the stage in front of the open door, a man in a white suit with sunglasses lies motionless in a deckchair, watching everything. Like secret voyeurs, the audience gazes with him into a bygone children's world, a world full of secrets and discoveries. The door slams with a bang; the safety curtain rises and frees up the view into a white room, its floor rising at the back into an enormous slide. The ground is grubby with skid-marks, its centre covered with birch twigs, branches and whole trees: a bizarre winter landscape, an enchanted childhood scene like an illustration from an old fairy-tale or a drawing from a yellowed songbook. Unlike the only slightly alienated, largely realistic stage sets of *Blaubart* or the Brecht/Weill programme, *Komm tanz mit mir* is a poetic world of associations, of wishes and dreams from times gone by. An atmospheric melancholy lies over this winter scene, with its chopped down forest and the sloping slide covered with the traces of failed attempts to ascend.

Against this background Pina Bausch proceeds to blur the restrictive boundaries defining dance and theatre: a player mingles with the audience, a dancer speaks, an actor dances. Significant here is not that each crosses into a foreign métier but the genuineness and intensity with which they perform. The actor's hard, angular movements and the dancer's unpractised voice create a different kind of authority and reality. In an interview, Pina Bausch named honesty and precision as her most important criteria. Here, precision means more than technical prowess, and honesty is derived from the patent directness of all players. They no longer present the audience with the perfect mastery of their art; they divulge themselves as they are, with their strengths and weaknesses. This brings them closer to the audience: up close and personal.

In *Komm tanz mit mir* Pina Bausch eschews the homogeneity and unity typical of most pieces even more radically than before. She montages individual images and scenic sequences to form a varied medley of songs with constantly changing moods. As in the Brecht/Weill programme the dancers sing the songs themselves, while being chased through the felled winter woods, pulled, hunted, carried, feeling their way forwards, finding and then running away from each other again. The melodies are distorted, rushed, stretched. The lyrics cover the same age-old themes: love and death, happiness and pain. But behind the pretty tunes Pina Bausch reveals the true horror and the dire states of need. Desire, she shows us, is painful; unfulfilled love generates hatred, and death is not a peaceful farewell. The struggle for happiness fought between the sexes is a merciless mutual assault.

The men pick up the branches and hit the women; one is forced up the slide with a forked branch, others flee frantically through the trees, fall and cry. In this inhospitable landscape the performers genuinely do risk scratching their arms and legs, being hit by a branch, falling or injuring themselves climbing the steep slide. What the audience sees is real, scarcely acted at all.

It is about power, about ruling and being ruled, and beyond that about the hope for intimacy, peace and happiness, which must not be abandoned. This hope is, however, continually disappointed, and the mutual misunderstanding is perpetuated in reciprocal humiliation, injury and lonely despair.

Pina Bausch demonstrates this in the most simple and persuasive way conceivable, by continually translating figures of speech visually and dramatically. Thus a man piles countless hats onto a woman's head or stuffs her into coat after coat: capping, coating, cushioning and cocooning his love, but the intended protection is a burden, is a suffocating affection.

One of the women defends herself from the men's intrusive attempts at protection, stands on a chair and furiously knocks all their hats off. Another lies like a collar round a man's shoulders, a decorative accessory of male vanity and a willing victim. The women continually change their clothes, change identities at will, seeking to appear attractive and desirable.

As in previous pieces the group reflects the fight between the protagonists: in this case the dandy in the summer suit and his partner. Like a leitmotif she constantly coos the eponymous children's rhyme "Come dance with me". The more hopeless this wish seems, the more strongly she insists: "Come dance with me / come dance with me / I have a white dancing pinafore / don't stop / don't stop / till the pinafore is full of holes." She tirelessly repeats the verse; at first tenderly, flatteringly, childishly pleading, begging; then louder, demanding, stubborn, commanding, and finally furious, shrieking, raging, screaming. Yet the man remains impassive and cool. The black-clad dancers link arms with her and bring her to the front, dancing in a broad revue line-up, then quickly abandon her again. Angry, she lapses into a dance of rage and attempts to break through his indifference with storming, stamping rhythms. As soon as he approaches her, threatening and demanding, she retreats behind her children's rhyme, unsure of what she wants and how.

Dance does not achieve togetherness, and language fails too. When both parties speak to each other at all, it is not *with* but *at* each other, in grating, imperious tones. Even a conciliatory request for forgiveness such as "it was my fault" degenerates into a noisy argument over prerogative, about who has the right to apologise. The power issue amongst the sexes is inflamed by language and escalates till both retreat sulking and bewildered into their respective corners.

Nevertheless, undeterred, she tries again and again to induce him to dance. He answers by issuing blunt orders, dictates her movements, demands, "make me jealous" or "say, I love you". She repeatedly obliges him, fulfils his wishes till, going absurdly over the top, she bosses herself around. When nothing has helped and she has made herself completely ridiculous, she explodes obstinately, shouting his own words furiously back at him. Nothing changes. The man's mask remains impenetrable. She stuffs her dress to give herself an enormous bust and bulging hips, applies conspicuous make-up and purrs lasciviously "sometimes I feel like a …". She takes his dream image of a seductive pin-up girl to a grotesque excess, but nothing helps. Man and woman are both prisoners. She wants him to like her, to love her, even if she has to go to absurd lengths to mask her true face; he can only see the woman as a carbon copy of normative ideals of beauty. Neither of them can escape this world of illusion. Only from childhood, from a few relaxed moments of melancholy, self-absorption does a hint shine through of where happiness might lie: in the serenity of being able to remain effortlessly true to oneself and to be loved for it. But no-one has reached this point yet. That is something to look for in the future.

Pina Bausch discharges her audience after an hour and a half's unbroken performance with the challenge: Come dance with me!

## Renate wandert aus

"Operetta" is how Pina Bausch describes her dance evening *Renate wandert aus* (*Renate Emigrates*), offering a hint as to what the piece deals with: the clichés of the mass media. Hackneyed behaviour, stereotypical roles, normative aspirations and cravings are the themes; their source is pulp fiction, comic books and melodramatic romantic films, a dream world of princes, princesses and carefree abundance. In the world of the mainstream media, the common man's heroes are always handsome and sought-after, successful and desirable. Should any little misunderstandings spoil the idyll, the various absurd, tangled imbroglios make amusing stories. Inexplicable "coincidences" of fate drive the plot till at the end the pair that is destined for each other comes together, gazes remorsefully into each other's eyes and swears eternal love. The genre guarantees a happy ending; all conflicts are suddenly resolved; the power of "eternal love" melts away all problems. Big emotional gestures ensure big profits and colossal success. Despite the best cultural efforts, cheap romances and doctor-and-nurse novels are the unofficial market leaders, unacknowledged in any bestseller lists; films like *Gone with the Wind* and *Doctor Zhivago* break all box-office records. "All our feelings tell us to believe in a happy ending," the filmmaker Alexander Kluge once said. And it seems

53

that the majority of people can only cope with everyday life bathed in the reflected sunlight of such dream worlds, however unrealistic their hopes may be; for without hope a person dies.

Pina Bausch therefore takes the desires and longings behind the popular myths seriously but dissects the false promises with unwavering precision. Cleanly and with a great sense of humour she distils the genuine, inalienable needs out of the clichés, along with whatever she can redeem from everyday life. The intact dream world of Hollywood heroes functions only for as long as it avoids collision with any kind of reality. As soon as the stereotypical notions of happiness are held to account within daily life, however, the beautiful world of illusion collapses leaving behind a bewildered morning-after feeling. Where opera deals with real emotions, operetta echoes them in kitschy miniature. Superficially entertaining, it minces and trills its way through a world of illusion and illusory conflicts. There is barely a trace of the anguish or emotional power behind the mask.

Thus *Renate wandert aus* tells of unrequited love, of flawless heroes and happy fairy-tale couples. But the dream royal couple ends up like bored petit bourgeois slumped in front of the television. They shuffle in apathetically, their crowns askew, squirm around on the sofa in positions they have already adopted thousands of times before and gaze disinterestedly around them. It is like a children's game which stopped being fun a long time ago. The grandiose dream has given way to a speechless, lifeless emptiness; the attempt to replicate grand gestures has solidified into empty posturing. With great difficulty the women totter across the stage on high heels, maintaining a tortured smile, while they fold their hands behind their heads and try to look as seductive and relaxed as Marilyn Monroe. This is hilarious yet also a sad and pathetic attempt to appear desirable and loveable. It doesn't work; the effort required to look like a perfect pin-up remains all too visible. Men as well as women continually make desperately funny attempts to match up to the dominant popular images and fail just as consistently.

The main figure, a girl called Angela, gives a friend practical instruction in how she should move if she wants to appear erotic. The lesson degenerates into military commands and bodily drills, till the friend collapses in exhaustion and Angela asks her triumphantly if she is happy at last. They have so utterly internalised the ideal images of their popular

54

heroes that Angela breaks down in hysterical despair when she suddenly discovers a mole on her body. Compulsive cleaning, seen later in the *Macbeth* project, is seen here too, as imaginary dirt is continually brushed off clothes.

But where violent power struggles previously drove the partners together, a complete lack of understanding now dominates. The idealised visions of the "dream factory" have shifted the relationship between men and women into an unreal world of dreams. An elegant lady speaks incessantly in Swiss dialect to her partner, who trots bored and wholly disconnected behind her. In the end, contact with the dream man occurs only in fantasy. A dancer shakes the hand of an imaginary opposite number and says a friendly "good evening". Angela talks repeatedly with her much-admired boyfriend Dick, who never actually shows up. Despite this she chats to him, invites him home, tells him what she has been doing. Another girl continually reads from a non-existent love-letter, claiming stereotypically: "I love you, I love you, I love you."

The men are dream beings; they wear white angels' wings on their jackets. According to the girls' wishful thinking they are all innocent as the wind-driven snow, with no intentions beyond gallantly kissing their hands. But as soon as they attempt to fly, standing on a chair and pathetically flapping their arms, they fail pitifully. When they actually appear as real beings, they exude nonchalant John Wayne ease – legs astride, looking cool – or an air of gentlemanly elegance, in dinner jackets or shiny suits. Men and women each make the other prisoners of their warped fantasies, neither letting the other escape. Dressed as a thirty-something himbo, an actor sings to one woman after another "I will dream of you every night": empty promises.

The women are either *femme fatale* man-eaters or naive girlies, too dangerous to approach, or too stupid and credulous. Like toys they let themselves be carried around and set down decoratively as required. In a partner dance they stand on the men's feet and let themselves be carried around the room like luggage but in correctly-held poses. They form a circle and are assessed by the men according their market value. At the front of the stage one of them shows off one dress after another as if on a catwalk, seeking to be loved and admired.

However, appearances can barely deliver what they promise. Well-behaved, as if in a dance class, the men and women stand opposite each other. The teacher and his ladylike, affected partner, demonstrate the correct techniques for fluttering eyelashes, sighing and kissing. Everyone practises alone first, earnestly going through the required moves. Then, at a sign from the teacher the pairs approach each other with optimistic smiles. Unfortunately the theory doesn't work in practice. The perfect loving embrace, à la Hollywood, ends in a tragicomic wrangle, a grotesque cat's cradle. The elegant chivalry only works when there is no living human to disrupt it: when an aging beau finds himself alone on a beach courting empty, discarded women's clothes.

As soon as someone finally gets time on their own, they are stormed by the rest of the group. One dancer, hoping to enjoy a moment of solitude, is ambushed by the ensemble with cheerful "happy birthday" squeals. The scene passes over him like a ghost train and leaves him behind, completely distraught.

Privacy is barely allowed, everything is forced into the open. While the others jump gleefully up and down on hastily wheeled-in sofas and armchairs, one player remains excluded. With a deeply embarrassed look, he bobs along with them tentatively a couple of times.

There is always the odd dancer who tries to keep hold of a little piece of individuality, to escape the marketplace of vanities, but there seems to be no way to be spared the rituals of convention. It is as if this desperately cheerful group cannot understand that behind their idols' promises of happiness lies nothing but emptiness. Stubbornly they still insist that there must be a key to contact and intimacy.

The space in which they unflaggingly seek fulfilment is a fantastic ice landscape: lovely to look at but cold. In front of an interior wall with doors and windows, two glacial cliffs loom above the stage, as tall as houses; on top of them stands plush furniture from a *fin de siècle* apartment: sofa, armchair, wardrobe, dressing table and wash stands. Interior and exterior space seem to have been swapped; the coldness of inner alienation grown disproportionately large in the cosy confinement of the furnishings. And as if to remind us we are in the theatre, an aluminium ladder stands conspicuously in the middle of the stage as if forgotten. In this space too the fortune seekers have left traces of their expeditions: clothes, shoes, plastic flowers, toys, chairs, parasols, handbags, paper aeroplanes. Like the costumes, the colourful scenery plays out the whole spectrum of a lurid, Technicolor film. The props are simple, everyday consumer commodities

56

(a washing-powder box, hinting that a soap opera is being acted out here) or carefully preserved trophies of childhood days. Angela continually uses them to build her own little world, speaking with "Dick" on a pretend telephone made of two plastic lovers' roses.

This world is gaudy and garish, caressed by shallow tunes from films and musicals (*Gone with the Wind*, *South Pacific*), dreamy string compositions and romantic pop songs (*Ich werde jede Nacht von Ihnen träumen*, *Ich bin ja heut' so glücklich* – I Will Dream of you Every Night, I'm so Happy Today). It is a fairy-tale world and yet in the show-turn dramaturgy – its contrasts this time relatively unobtrusive – the empty promises of the popular myths are unmasked with humour.

In spite of the brutal honesty, this occurs in *Renate wandert aus* with a relaxed exuberance, with winks and flirts to the audience. A smiling dancer pushes her way through the stalls, handing out chocolate and sweets; another continually presents new clothes at the front of the stage, climbs down from it, gets help undoing her zip, asks how she looks. It is an affectionate invitation to join in with the search for happiness, to find out together where the real contact begins and a deeper intimacy will succeed.

To this end *Renate wandert aus* does not economise on glitzy imagery, as if in gratitude for the hard work endured on this difficult expedition. For a moment the stage is filled with countless bunches of flowers. Then the room empties; music plays. There is no-one to be seen, just a sea of flowers in the middle of the ice.

## Er nimmt sie an der Hand und führt sie in das Schloß, die anderen folgen

Described simply as "a piece by Pina Bausch", this evening's complete title is a stage direction from Shakespeare's *Macbeth*: "He takes her by the hand and leads her into the castle, the others follow." With its untypical length, the title puts the spotlight on dramaturgical conception but also directs us to the point of departure from which the piece arises. Just as the playwright's working instructions are usually unknown to the audience, the piece also brings to light aspects which are usually kept hidden. In her *Macbeth* paraphrase, Pina Bausch adopts only a few motifs of the original and tracks them down in the reality of everyday life. Using the montage approach, combining fragments and quoting from familiar set pieces, she constructs a dense, atmospheric visual parable on the Shakespearian material.

The piece could be seen as a key work, if that kind of notion were at all applicable to Pina Bausch's dance theatre. For just as the individual elements of one piece cannot be combined to form a single, whole meaning, neither can an individual work be described as self-contained.

Pina Bausch's *Macbeth* is the culmination of various stages of experimental work, in which individual elements were constantly tried out, developed further or indeed thrown out. We cannot therefore talk of a consistent narrative development in the traditional sense. The plot does not pivot on an author and his identity, garnering his expressive means around a particular core idea and then constructing his work. Instead the working process is characterised by free structure and openness to experience and experiment. In principle Pina Bausch's entire oeuvre can be seen as an endless "work in progress".

*Macbeth* represents a rejection of the culture industry's usual presumptions and pushes beyond the boundaries of theatrical conventions. The players consist of four dancers who act, four actors who hardly speak, and a singer who, instead of singing, mimes and speaks. None of them is required to demonstrate the skills they originally learnt. Only the most basic element of dance remains: everyday communication via bodily signs.

Pina Bausch begins with the precise observation of human bodily language and transmits this onto the stage in complex series of activities, many of them occurring alongside each other. Concepts which till now in the dance tradition operated only at the abstract level of artistic expression are now formulated clearly and tangibly. The simple but seldom exploited realisation that inner processes can be read in the body's behaviour becomes a formative principle. Alienation effects play an important role again here; texts are spoken and sung lying on cupboards; children's songs, lying on the arm of a chair. Time seems to have been halted so that the gaze can focus on the important details. Individual scenes and various positions are singled out, doubled, slowed down or speeded up.

The arching structure of suspense used by conventional narrative dramaturgy is abandoned for good. The action is no longer orientated around a climax, nor are the individual developments aligned towards a dénouement. Thus Pina Bausch's dance theatre does not offer solutions, not even apparent ones. Her pieces are increasingly less inclined to follow a tightly strung narrative thread, instead developing in cyclic curves that carry the moving, visual stories along in an endless spiral. The *Macbeth* drama can and should be applied imaginatively to the audience's own daily life; the piece provides the opportunity. The situation is not elucidated via didacticism, but through the identification of every spectator. Thus the individual images are not connected according to the laws of causality; multi-layered associations override any linear narrative drive or continuity.

Only a few fragments and original quotations are left from the Shakespearian original. They serve as reference points for the various associations with contemporary life. Instead of the parable about the hunger for power, its images and roles now part of theatrical history, an actor tells the story in instalments (oblivious to chronology) as a comic-book fairytale. She performs the same ritual every time; sitting provocatively, her legs crossed, she applies lipstick, does a muscleman pose and rolls her eyes effusively as she describes the bloody deeds. Shakespeare's protagonists are shrunk to initials, now known as Knight B and Knight D.

Pina Bausch's piece seems to do the reverse of the usual techniques adopted for updating a theatrical classic and rendering it relevant to the times; the piece *is* present day life, in which Shakespeare re-appears as an historical quotation, as proof we are in the present, or as a still-relevant reminder of something past. Thus Macbeth is confronted with the history of his own role. The "high tragedy" slips into the trivial and a visual symbol is created for the piece's openness towards the audience, its inclusion of them.

The battered, torn, once-imposing furniture forms a chaotic inventory: club chairs, canapés, chaise-longues and cabinets in styles from every era. The familiar period drama atmosphere is parodied and paraphrased in the consciously kitsch, trashy colours of a pink bedstead, a violet confessional chair and a green shower cubicle. The props are not accessories, they are each shown to have a direct function: the armchair which demands an upright posture, the chaise-longue as battleground for petty marital wars, the glass cabinet in which the individual body can be displayed and cautiously explored.

The same is true of the dresses and suits, frequently changed, sometimes on stage, which have no decorative function either. They are always a direct part of each person, whether they underscore their identity or conflict with it. As a symbol of the hollow flow of time, water flows throughout the performance into a large pool at the front of the stage which gradually fills. The rhythm of the piece is set by sharply spliced music. Lethargic tango decadence gives way to the resonating commotion of insistent piano rhythms; in between come quieter, lyrical passages, historical quotations (such as from Giuseppe Verdi's opera *Macbeth*) and modern pop. The music is awarded the status of equal partner, given its own function. When the piano rhythms suddenly cut in, the players break off whatever they are doing, leap onto the chairs and sofas in a hectic game of musical chairs, or fight like children over the toys strewn across the floor. The power struggle is staged as an infantile performance in the nursery.

The constant swings from comedy to tragedy and vice versa, a significant element of other pieces too, becomes the dominant stylistic principle of *Er nimmt sie an der Hand und führt sie in das Schloß, die anderen folgen*. Behind the peaceful, sometimes amusing events lies a paranoid nervousness which can break out at any moment. The security of the everyday is revealed as a mere appearance of stability, an equilibrium which can slip at any moment. With the piano music the conventions are switched on. In jumping on the furniture everyone hopes to adopt a posture which will obscure insecurity, fear and guilt: body language used to conceal, yet betraying everything.

In her re-working of *Macbeth*, Pina Bausch abolishes all roles and redistributes them equally among the players. The motto "anyone can be Macbeth" applies to the actors as well, even though only one actor actually memorises the remnants of the *Macbeth* text, and only one actor is actually assigned fragments of the roles of Macduff and Lady Macbeth.

The guilt motif is taken up right at the beginning, expressed in a collective nightmare. In the twilight of a dawning day, with the red light of a juke box in the background, we see the players lying among plastic flowers and toys on the floor, on armchairs and sofas in a variety of sleeping positions. While the light filling the room gradually brightens, as if in a nightmare trance the figures begin to moan and twist, escalating into ecstatic convulsions under the hellish hallucinations of guilt and despair, before sinking back, a while later, into inertia, exhausted.

Pina Bausch often takes Shakespeare's text literally and conveys it in simple persuasive images. "Out, damned spot! [...] Will these hands ne'er be clean? [...] Here's the smell of blood still. All the perfumes of Arabia will not sweeten this little hand." These words are translated into a genuine cleaning compulsion. People are continually washing their hands and stepping into the shower; in a fit of cleaning hysteria one of the women tries to clean the garden gnome Tony.

The story is also anchored in childhood. Fighting over toys, singing nursery rhymes, playing cowboys and Indians or the childish suicide game, in which an actor with a colt cigarette lighter in a wild-west stance parodies the cinematic cliché of the determined hero, all point towards the underlying motifs of the events. The unconditional demand for appreciation and affection, originating in childhood, escalates into violence and unrestrained lust for power.

In the *Macbeth* project too, the story is not dealt with explicitly; wider themes and problems come to the fore instead. The piece uses confrontation techniques similar to the surrealist avantgarde. Provocative repetitions in compressed or stretched movements make it impossible not to engage with the themes addressed.

The figures portrayed seem familiar from previous pieces. As a sign of general disorientation, a man standing on a chair tests the direction of the wind, holding up his moist index finger to every corner of the stage. Again, with a helpless "help me hence", women are carried and put down elsewhere.

Once more a simple Brechtian "gestus of indication" dominates, translated into physical terms. The fact that the woman is a mere instrument to the man becomes clear when an actor lays one of the living dolls on the piano and plays it by pressing her lifeless fingers on the keys. Another drapes the woman over his shoulder like a decorative accessory while casually talking to an acquaintance using silent gestures.

Alienation between couples returns too: the elderly pair already familiar from *Zweiter Frühling* return, this time embroiled in an increasingly cynical love-hate relationship; the youthful romances appear in fro-

61

zen poses; another couple is so busy making hand-wringing gestures of embarrassment they never achieve intimacy.

The causes of the alienation lie in the internalisation of conventions, exposed in yobbish self-bullying. "Sit down and relax, breathe deeply, enjoy a smoke, keep your suit clean, say, good evening" or "sit down, relax, walk to the wall, run your hands through your hair" are among the commands, all underlined with brusque gestures.

The dimension of conventions also includes those of the theatre world, the constraints of production and the expectations of the audience. This is made clear when a dancer comes to the front and says: "Jo, you're on, smile." Or when all the players sit on a row of cinema chairs facing the audience as if reversing the situation in the theatre. While they swiftly swap places, they gather more and more of the strewn objects at random, demonstrating the state of a society which exhausts itself in material acquisition.

The pressures of convention are written literally on the body of each and every player. Whether at the press of a button on the music box a player repeats ballroom dance moves with a dumb expression and an imaginary partner, or a sudden, high-pitched giggle is retracted immediately with an apology, or everyone nervously sniffs themselves for body odour, perfect conformity requires complete control over the body. Only those who succeed can be certain not to stand out.

Despite this, the bodily signals which escape conscious control betray the real situation. The piece's gestural repertoire is gathered together once more in a scene where the actors/dancers cross the stage at a diagonal: the embarrassment and inner tension are revealed when scratching itches and biting nails; in the hysterical self-tyranny of sniffing all over one's body; the sinking into brooding boredom and empty waiting; but also a wink and an invitation to the audience to join in with the game. *Macbeth* at home: an everyday drama.

## Café Müller

Barely a month after the premiere of the *Macbeth* project in Bochum, the four-part evening *Café Müller* was premiered in Wuppertal. For the first time since the performance of Kurt Jooss' *Großstadt* during the 1974/75 season guest choreographers also contributed to the production. Alongside Pina Bausch, the evening included new pieces by Gerhard Bohner, Gigi-Gheorghe Caciuleanu and Hans Pop (a member of the Wuppertal company). All four contributions to this evening were separate, independent productions but did not have individual titles, all falling under the overall title "Café Müller". Of the original four-part evening only Pina Bausch's piece is still performed, mostly combined with *Le Sacre du printemps*.

The non-committal nature of the title and the trivial choice of the name are part of the overall concept uniting the four works. The choreographers had decided on a common outline structure for the contents of each work, with various fundamental elements which could be combined freely: a café, darkness, four people, someone waits, someone falls over, is picked up, a red-haired girl enters, everything goes quiet.

Pina Bausch's forty-five minute contribution starts from a very personal vantage point. Like an overview of her choreographic development, it brings together forms of dance from her earlier work, in the manner of the Gluck operas and the new theatre of movement which began with the Brecht/Weill pieces. Thus it seems consistent that for the first time since *Yvonne, Prinzessin von Burgund* (1973/74 season), Pina Bausch herself dances again.

Unlike in the last four pieces, the music is not altered, doctored or juxtaposed within a montage. The compositions, female arias from Henry Purcell's *The Fairy Queen* and *Dido and Aeneas*, are laments, revolving around the subjects of unrequited love, separation, grief and despair, and thus relating strongly to the content of the piece: loneliness, estrangement and the search for support within partnerships.

The scenery consists of a bare, dirty-grey room, filled with round café tables and dozens of chairs; in the background is a glass revolving door. Two female dancers in thin white petticoats and three men in dark, everyday suits thread their way through the tables and chairs which obstruct

63

the whole stage and prevent the dancers from making expansive gestures or forming a group. Thus the dancers are initially limited to slow turns on the spot, centred on their bodies, or to weaving limited paths through the room.

As in *The Chairs,* Eugene Ionesco's play, chairs become symbols and substitutes for human absence, signifying the void, the impossibility of making contact. They are also obstacles preventing dance, freedom of movement. But as soon as the dancers move through the room, one of the players – at the premiere this part was played by Rolf Borzik, Pina Bausch's set designer and partner – leaps up in panic and flings the tables and chairs aside, creating space to move, saving the dancers from injuring themselves. The scene is suffused with constant tension; we can never be sure whether he will succeed in pulling the chairs out of the way in time so that the self-absorbed dancers, their eyes closed, do not bump into them or fall over. It is as if the world in this strange café has fallen into a dream-rich sleep, while one person remains awake to protect the enchanted or cursed beings. Constantly on edge, he observes their actions, himself unnoticed by anyone.

The two female dancers, one at the front, the other almost disappearing into the greyness upstage, move with closed eyes, like sleepwalkers, absorbed in the inner world of their feelings, with no relationship to their surroundings. At times they move simultaneously, at times out of sync. They run their hands up and down their bodies, hit the walls, then sink, exhausted to the floor, seeking protection and support from the masonry. While one of the women hardly leaves the background, retreating to the protection of the half-light, the other dares to step into the room more often, along paths freed for her by the man. As if in a trance, she comes into contact with one of the other men; the couple claws at each other, tries to keep hold of each other, but one of the other dark-suited men splits their embrace and pulls them apart. The search for something to lean on begins again. The man who separated the pair puts them back together. He lays the woman in the outstretched arms of the man, who stands there dumb as she slips, powerless, out of his arms. She continually slips down, stretches up again, clasps him and slips down. Finally he steps carelessly over her and moves away. The second man repeatedly tries to join the pair, to place them in an embrace, to put her in his arms, but his best efforts are in vain.

64

In the middle of this situation, a red-haired woman bursts in, minces swiftly through the revolving door on high heels, runs around amongst the chairs, jittery and nervous, huddled under her coat and watching the events uneasily. She attempts to make contact and approach the others, but this closed community is far too wrapped up in itself. Subdued, she gives her coat and wig to the dancer in the background, who adopts the red hair and continues her lost dance unmoved. The others leave the stage.

The inability to communicate, estrangement between couples and the undaunted quest for intimacy and security are once more the basic themes, already dealt with by Pina Bausch in previous pieces. But due to the melancholy Purcell arias, a particular, dreamy sadness permeates *Café Müller*. Two worlds collide with each other; one seems bewitched by an evil spell (the two female dancers, the disconnected pair), the other is the "normal world". In the figure of the red-head it strays into the abandoned café and can make no sense of the self-obsessed rituals. She is the only one who notices the "set designer", following the paths he frees up but also finding her own ways through the labyrinth of chairs. While the others are wholly preoccupied with themselves, she wants and demands something else. Her vocabulary of movements, unlike that of the two female dancers, comes from everyday life; her outfit is provocative.

Her tempo is also noticeably different. While the "set designer" hectically shifts chairs and tables to the side and the female dancers follow their dreams in slow motion, she moves fast, but not at high speed. The various timeframes continually shift, overlap and meet each other.

In terms of subject matter too, *Café Müller* ties various threads together: dealing with loneliness and compulsive behaviour but also the search for another dance, another theatre, no longer obliged to serve a beautiful illusion, instead exploring the depths of emotion. The "set designer" literally provides the dancers with "room for manoeuvre", no longer behind the scenes but on the open stage. He does not assist the dancers by providing decoration, he clears the way for them. This might be what the solitary dancers with their sleep-walking motions are dreaming about.

# Kontakthof

Unlike *Café Müller*, *Kontakthof* continues the stylistic developments seen in the *Macbeth* piece, although it focuses more strongly on exposing the realities of theatrical production. Two dimensions fuse in this piece: a dance lesson situation where men and women meet looking for intimacy and affection, and the reality of the stage with its constant pressure to show off and market oneself. They are explored through a revue-like dramaturgy of successive show turns.

The *Kontakthof*, the German term for a courtyard in a red-light district, is now a large, empty room, again in a late nineteenth century style: a dance-hall with a small stage, otherwise containing only a piano, an automatic rocking horse and chairs along the edges. The place resembles the Wuppertal company's rehearsal space, a converted cinema; here Pina Bausch is establishing a link to her real working conditions, highlighting the pressures involved in making theatre and the audience's unspoken expectations, which the performers must be sure to meet. In *Kontakthof* reality and theatre meet, subjected to the same pressure. The *Kontakthof*, normally a meeting place for prostitutes and their clients, a place where the body is for sale, becomes a reference to the prostitution of dancers on the stage.

The piece begins with a simple presentation ritual. One after another individual players step to the front, followed by small groups and finally the whole company, displaying themselves in profile, from the front and from behind, stretching their hands out, running their fingers through their hair, baring their teeth, before returning to their place. Everyone tests their market value, the men as well as the women.

This motif is taken up many times. In one scene various players perform their absurd turns, leap at the stage walls while laughing hysterically, run round chairs, slam the piano lid, laugh till they are exhausted, till they throw up; every time the rest of the troop rewards the performance with lukewarm applause. The compulsion to perform escalates further, into an hysterical euphoria, behind which the need to be loved can clearly be felt. Whatever the players pretend to be, behind the façade Pina Bausch discovers the nature of their true needs and desires.

66

The man politely offers the woman his arm and accompanies her to the front of the stage. With a wholly matter-of-fact demeanour the couple demonstrates every kind of nastiness; they pinch each other, kick each other in the backs of the knees, poke each other in the eyes, twist each other's arms behind their backs, he pulls the chair from under her as she sits down. They smile throughout as if nothing was going on.

The lies behind apparently harmonious partnerships are revealed in the simultaneous display of the smiling, respectable façade and the openly sadistic games. The contradiction between public and private, concentrated into one moment, is made visible. As with the slowed-down or speeded-up repetitions, Pina Bausch uses a modified alienation technique to illuminate the situation.

A variation is offered by a scene in which a row of couples wearing human and animal masks skips across the stage hand in hand, glancing shyly at each other and giggling: a grotesque parody on the idyll of the twosome.

Accompanied by a deafening circus march and commentary from a Philippine dancer in his native language, the players parade along the front of the stage and enact their complexes: the imaginary double chin, disguised by sticking the neck out; allegedly big hips, or big, wonky noses, which have to be concealed.

Here too the disparity between the private sphere (the complexes) and its public display as a circus parade eases the tension through humour. The laughter the grotesque turn provokes is not only a reflex reaction to the comical gyrations on stage. The audience can also laugh about themselves. Everyone knows, all too well, that on the open market our bodies are goods, how strictly we are required to match the general ideals of beauty in order to compete in the marketplace, in our private lives just as at work. The ostensibly private sphere of the body is shown to be subject to the same public rules. The dancers' world is no different from that of the audience in this respect: both have to sell themselves to the best of their abilities.

Pina Bausch makes the commercial rules governing dance even clearer by showing how dance is taught: facing a man in the role of choreographer, parading along a diagonal, the troupe performs a repertoire of once-glamorous revue gestures, unenthusiastically and with increasing weariness. Only one of them breaks the line, complains at the others, wants to stop, then re-joins the ranks. For a moment, however, she defends the demands of the individual against the coercion of the group. Pina Bausch clearly shows how similar the worlds of art and daily life are, and always finds something "we can laugh about together".

As the players are no longer able to keep up the smooth illusion of a perfect stage show, they demonstrate how their art is produced. A man with a cigarette in his mouth holding a stage manager's book pops up from time to time to check up on the ensemble and the technical set-up. Our glimpse into the world backstage thus loses its voyeuristic character. There are even moments of complete bewilderment, as the group discusses the next number, the dancers walking back and forth explaining the next dance moves to each other. We have the feeling of watching a rehearsal, want to say: "They are trying out approaches to life here, but no-one knows the right path to happiness yet."

In order to get there, the players have to leave their hermetic stage world and connect with the audience. The audience is confronted with unexpected demands, asked for coins to put in the horse, forced to worry whether the dancer performing a balancing act on the narrow trim at the edge of the stage will tumble into the front rows. The ensemble repeatedly rushes headlong to the front of the stage, in a tango shortened to a shuffle, a couple quizes each other about their favourite things, talking across the others; there is a group dance of swinging hips. The players never tire of going to the border separating them from the audience and making them complicit in their search for happiness. They sit eye-to-eye with the audience while a "reporter" reads out accounts of their first love into a microphone. Then they turn round, their backs to the audience, and watch a wildlife film on the family life of the "ferruginous duck", themselves now spectators.

The music, from the 1920s and '30s, seems nostalgic, and yet *Kontakthof* addresses issues outside of any timeframe. It uses the empty formality of the dance lesson as an example of how the search for sensuality free from fear ends in failure, how firmly established the pressure to clothe all fears, embarrassment and loneliness in a mask of happiness is. One dancer tells the truth in a moment of calm: "I stand at the end of the piano as if I might fall. But before I do, I shout so that no-one misses it, and then I crawl under the piano and look out, most accusingly, and pretend I want to be alone, but really I want someone to come."

What the dance-class students seek is respect and affection. But this always goes wrong when they approach each other. The men throw off their jackets as they walk towards the women, already taking off a shoe in anticipation. Slowly couples get together, stroke each other's faces and arms, run their hands through the partner's hair, feel shoulders, chest and stomach tenderly, rub each other's feet and knees. But their movements become increasingly hectic and uptight, rising to an ever greater intensity till they are more like blows than affectionate touches. Affectionate violence and violent affection are established clearly here for the first time as central themes for the Tanztheater Wuppertal. The men run quickly from position to position, stand still, lie, sit, already poised in couples' poses. For a moment the women snuggle up to them, but then the partners jump up again, to try the same exercise with one of the others.

In another situation it is the group which prevents intimacy. One couple sits opposite each other across the distance of the entire stage, carefully removing their clothes and smiling nervously at each other. A crew of men interrupts them with a dance of embarrassed gestures. The couple gives up; they put their clothes back on and rejoin the others, marching in a circle. As in *Le Sacre du printemps*, the choreographic circle form symbolises the social group ritual, which no-one can escape from.

The couples sit next to each other as they would at a dance class. One of the dancers works her way through all levels of flattery, repeatedly saying "darling", in order to make her oblivious partner take notice of her, and as she fails, collapses into hysterical fits of tears. After a while the troupe starts singing, she tries to join in, still sobbing, but finally gives up. The scene is a tragicomic parody of the stood-up girl cliché. We can enjoy a smirk, but we also feel for her.

Two revue girls who dance across the stage holding hands in long pink lacy dresses seem to have walked straight out of the slushy world of Juan Llossas' songs. Mischievous and girly, they act exactly like the women extolled in the songs: "Oh Fräulein Grete, when I dance with you, oh Fräulein Grete, I belong to you. The sweetest, loveliest creature there is, whoever meets you is smitten forthwith." "My beautiful vis-à-vis, I am in love with thee. You two seem so lonely, you and your glass only. If I might be allowed, could I add to the crowd?" This is how women are serenaded in Llossas' songs. In hard contrast, Pina Bausch stages the true relationship between the sexes.

A woman in the role of a man-eating seductress poses around in front of a man, accompanied by the text of the easy-listening song *Blonde Kläre:* "Blond Clare, do me the honour, it would be so grand. Your presence makes me dream of nuptials, that you must understand." He follows her from behind a control panel, grasping wildly at the air. He interprets her self-confidence as a come-on. The scene is later repeated in a similar way by the whole group. Sitting on chairs, a horde of wild gropers stalks towards the women to the sounds of boogie-woogie. The women stand pressed against the wall and flinch at every imaginary touch in the distance, moving closer to each other. An absurd dance of carnal desire, a misunderstanding of love. The way the men imagine the women only places them in a straightjacket. This is seen when the women walk in a circle displaying pinching, tight lingerie and vertiginous high-heels: uncomfortable instruments for controlling their appearance to fit male ideals of beauty, while we hear a woman's cries of pain amplified through a microphone at varying pitches, high and low.

The men's attempts to console a woman, standing lifeless at the centre, escalate to an almost unbearable insistence. In relations between the sexes, anything well-meant ultimately goes wrong and degenerates into a fight. Women and men stand in separate groups opposite each other. Commands are shouted over from both sides: "Cheek, back, stomach, knee, shoulder, hand, feet." With each part of the body named, the group shifts together and inches a step back, before carrying on as before. Increasingly fast and aggressive, the commands wage a war of attrition, rise to a screaming duel, then ebb away again.

Pina Bausch makes the differences between the sexes all too clear, as well as the problems men and women have with each other, without resolving them. Her pieces leave unanswered questions in their wake and an unspoken demand on the audience to turn things round and find the key to happiness together. Only then is it possible to escape the coercive rhythm of life expressed in *Kontakthof* as a dance marathon. The couples dance to wild boogie-woogie rhythms till they are exhausted, till the men are simply carrying the women around like lifeless dolls. Every so often, however, one of them slips out of the line, simply breaks ranks, or laughs themselves, literally, to death.

Things could change thanks to these few isolated people and their individuality – convention and group pressure notwithstanding.

In 2000, twenty-two years after the premiere, Pina Bausch conducted an unusual experiment: in rehearsals lasting a whole year, she restaged *Kontakthof* with senior citizens from her chosen home Wuppertal. The twenty-five "ladies and gentlemen over sixty-five", as the subtitle describes them, are not professional performers, certainly not dancers. Despite this the experiment succeeded and has opened up a new dimension for the Tanztheater Wuppertal.

Even at the time of the premiere, Pina Bausch wondered what it would be like if the same players were to perform the piece in their old age. With over-sixties, would the meaning and atmosphere change? Or would the piece retain the same strength? As twenty-two years after the first performance most of the players had ended their dancing careers, Pina Bausch gave *Kontakthof* to the senior citizens of Wuppertal. The choice of this piece is particularly fitting as the scenery and the nostalgic music seem to stem from the youth of the now mature performers. And the cautious courtesy of the dancing lesson, the main subject of the piece, remains familiar to the older generation from personal experience.

One calculated alienation effect deployed in the original production is dropped: there is no contrast here between the nostalgic music and a youthful cast. However, the "ladies and gentlemen over sixty-five" reveal a particular verve and youthfulness in their version of *Kontakthof*, bestowing an astonishing timelessness on the piece. The advanced age of the players not only exposes the emptiness of conventions further, it underpins the subject with the serene gravity of accumulated life experience. This is retained not only in the dramatic action but also in the quieter passages. Age is its own fountain of youth it appears. And quite incidentally, in casting people of this age Pina Bausch transgresses further deep-rooted taboos: that eroticism and tenderness continue to be an issue even in later years is accepted without question in this *Kontakthof.*

## Arien

*Aktionen für Tänzer* (*Actions for Dancers*), the title of one of Pina Bausch's earlier pieces, would serve equally well to describe *Arien* (*Arias*). In a performance over two hours long, without intermission, this is the keyword for a series of densely atmospheric mood images, *tableaux* filled with melancholy and angry despair: a race against time or against the rituals and prescribed patterns for behaviour restricting the individual. "To show everything people do to each other or have done, at different times," is how Pina Bausch described the point of departure of this theatrical expedition. On the subject of arias she said: "When someone stands alone like that and sings, isn't that something very lonely, someone standing quite alone, and then this singing?"

The figures' actions evoke self-affirmation; the attempt to objectify themselves as time, quickly or slowly, flows on. The actions are of two kinds: consoling themselves for the existential void of a subjectively experienced nothingness, and also trying out new possibilities, even if this simply means exhibiting their own inability, the endlessness of their search.

An important tool for self-affirmation is memory. Behavioural patterns, gestures and actions from various times and various social conventions shift into each other and intermingle. Time as the differential between past, present and future is abolished, as is the distinction between reality and fantasy. The dimensions flow in and out of each other, fusing into a complex scenic process of acted imagery, driven dramaturgically only through the ups and downs of moods, through the tightening and easing of tension.

Much is conveyed only in the atmospheric concentration of mood. The piece does not deliver a concrete "message" which can be grasped. Pina Bausch continues to dismantle conventional aesthetics.

The stage is opened up right to the firewalls, so wide that even the walkways and lighting galleys can be seen. The length and breadth of the usual performance area is covered by an enormous lake, which deepens upstage to form a swimming pool, although we discover this only later. The opera has gone under, has sunk. The arena of the Colosseum in Rome could be flooded in a similar way to stage sea slaughters, which is suggested later when a small frigate crosses the operatic ocean, playing war games and splattering spray.

The water changes the bare, unadorned room, which reappears reflected in its surface. It makes it harder for the dancers to walk or run. Their smart clothes soak up the water, stretch and cling to the bodies. While their glamour is diminished, the elegant pleats of the evening dresses and the sharp cuts of the suits spoiled, the bodies are revealed all the more clearly. Nakedness lies under the costume, under the second skin worn for show. In the water the people on stage become more vulnerable. When they then pause for a moment, their uncertainty is disturbing.

The water is a force opposing them. When they become tired from all the hectic running, we see clearly that what they are doing is hard, physical work. The water can also be enjoyed of course: clothes flung off for a bathe or an airbed blown up for sunbathing. It can be enjoyed in solitude, in intimate moments of self-affirmation.

On both sides of the stage are dressing tables, in between are spotlights. Two mirror screens stand in the front corners of the stage. The dancers prepare for the performance accompanied by slow jazz music: get changed, do their make-up, walk around, smoke and chat. This relaxed changing-room scene begins the piece. Pina Bausch does not so much take the situation of the "theatre within the theatre" as the subject of her work but more as a prerequisite. The play can now evolve effortlessly out of the naked stage reality presented. One player practises a boxing champ pose in front of the mirror; another discovers an incipient beer belly while getting changed.

Pina Bausch: "There is nothing you can read which hasn't already happened. The most unlikely things; everything exists already, is out there." And what could be more "unlikely" than a flooded opera stage across which people move as if this were entirely normal?

Through this dreamy scenery a very convincing model hippopotamus plods in, like melancholy given form: clumsy, gentle and delicate, apparently unmoved by the now excessive activity around him, but a testimony to the "unlikely" things which lift the elementary desires on the stage to a poetic, utopian reality.

At the centre of the piece are classical Italian arias sung by Beniamino Gigli as well as excerpts from Beethoven's *"Moonlight" Sonata*, Rakhmaninov's préludes and Schumann's *Scenes from Childhood*. If the jazz sounds at the beginning, along with songs by the Comedian Harmonists, stand for the present, in the bare, black stage space the arias become a swansong for the once glamorous institution of the opera.

The production and activity contrast with this harmonious singing. Lined up diagonally, figures stand and lie in the water, brooding grimly over the emptiness; they move slowly through the landscape, changing their pose from time to time, like statues of grief and exhaustion reflected in water.

A man in a bright, checked 1920s suit commentates on the events. A woman, making herself up in front of the mirror, delivers a monologue of questions: "What is your opinion of arias?" The figures stick firmly to their poses, even when a woman attempts to shake them out of their lethargy by splashing them with water. They make a sad, forlorn image.

The mirrors are an important instrument in the attempt at self-comprehension. As important behind-the-scenes props in the theatre, they stand for the role of theatrical action itself: holding up a mirror, offering assistance in viewing reality – which is sometimes painful and alarming. Couples drag each other in front of the mirror many times, abandoning each other to the mercy of their reflections. One player jumps back from the mirror in horror after catching a glimpse by chance.

A deeply unsettling feeling emanates from *Arien*. An atmosphere of disaster lies over the piece, which explodes in screaming hysteria, then lets the dancers sink back in on themselves again. Behind this lies a grief which is deeper than sadness: a despair born of helplessness. The figures balance over an abyss of broken and breaking forms, which seem to slip out of their hands. When laughter is heard here at all, it sounds like a desperate protest, like someone attempting to make themselves heard in an ever more inexplicable world or trying to pre-empt others laughing at them. Only occasionally do they succeed in taming the bewilderment into a tight form, as in the children's singing game, *Jetzt fahrn wir übern See*. The dancers sit in a circle of chairs and sing the rhyme, clearly and calmly. The song is shortened by one word every time it is repeated, and anyone who carries on singing the deleted words at the end has to drop out. The rules of the game, which everyone sticks to, reflect an intactness which the adult world seems to have lost. *Arien* shows once more the extent to which dance theatre must struggle to find a form, which also means a certainty about the world, a way of understanding phenomena, and shows that nothing is self-evident. The dancers plunge into the stage from the sides, each alone, spiral around their own centres with wide, expansive arm gestures, lost and frantic; only once do they all come together for an accelerating cancan, a form which binds them together.

Moments together as a couple are always precarious. While a dancer carries a lifeless, doll-like woman across the stage in an embrace, the others shout his name, as if he were in dire danger. The action in *Arien* continually runs the risk of falling into an abyss, constantly dancing at the edge of a chasm. In between, everyone listen intently to the void. Painful as it is, the grief resulting from the desperation brings self-realisation.

This grief can tip over at any moment however. Out of a silent, slow march of paired figures wearing black, a childish competition develops. The men begin a playful long-distance spitting contest. The group begins to move; some stand at the front of the stage and begin a verbal game where everyone in turns says a word to create a nonsense sentence. Gradually the action subsides; suppressing laughter, the players turn round, start playing other games which all have one thing in common: every so often someone has to drop out because they are too slow. Finally the group breaks up.

Another situation involves a dinner party. The hostess welcomes her guests: her best friend with exaggerated affection, her arch enemy with barely concealed aversion. The guests make their way to the table. The hippopotamus shuffles over and, despite subtle hints from the hostess, will not go away. The group becomes impatient and disperses. Women standing on chairs are carried to the mirrors, where they continue their superficial conversations over the heads of the men. A man shows off evening dresses, adopting a series of effeminate poses.

Gradually the polite celebratory atmosphere mutates into a gaudy children's birthday party. The dancers smear their faces with make-up, inventing crazy costumes. One proudly reports that he has been offered two film roles. Another repeatedly recounts the desirable attributes he has acquired: graduation, stocks and shares, clean, tidy, hard-working etc.

In one of the very first scenes, the situation in the theatre is reversed. The dancers scrutinise the audience and tell absurd stories, make jokes or read out stories from the tabloid press, about the latest record in rolling peas for instance. Then comes the ritual of being spruced up. The women sit at the front of the stage and meekly allow the men to dress them up.

To the sounds of *Eine kleine Nachtmusik*, they frantically pile clothes on them, make them up, decorate them with colourful scarves, bows, rings, braid, bracelets, equipping them with accessories, till each man has created his type. The result is a gallery of grotesque puppet-beings: fairy-tale queen, diva, baby-doll etc: a testimony to the male image of women and a response to the expectant attitude of the audience.

Pina Bausch also dares to disconcert the audience right in their midst, however. While the ensemble has its back turned to the audience, reciting incomprehensible texts over their shoulders, one of them suddenly appears in the auditorium about to jump off the upper circle. Suddenly there is panic on stage: "John, don't do it. Man, what are you doing? Come down!" After a lot of hesitation, "John" calls off his attempted suicide and lets the others talk him down.

The ensuing calm is short-lived. Soon after the women have been decorated, the group begins a tired, forced laughter, which slowly crescendos, finally escalating into shouting and screaming so that it no longer has anything to do with humour, only with fear, desperation and rage.

Things which appear amusing are constantly revealed to be shallow theatre, intended to obscure the real chasms. Just as individuals get through life on a daily basis thanks to such comedy, the theatre also serves up its audience with tired entertainment. In fact, dance theatre insists, something very different is at stake.

In *Arien* the means and motifs of dance theatre appear formulated in their full complexity. As such they also determine the following pieces. It becomes increasingly clear that Pina Bausch's dance evenings constitute the continuation of one single story, examined from different angles each time. They aim to form questions; the audience has to find the answers themselves. In the actions – apparently chaotic, actually calculated – our fears and needs, otherwise carefully buried, are pushed to the limit, towards a long-sought, much-needed solution.

## Keuschheitslegende

Soft violin music from the loudspeakers creates a mood of romance. The stage and stalls are brightly lit. Onto the stage, again opened right up to the firewalls, this time expanded into the backstage and wings, the floor painted with a static sea, steps a shy little minx. Fumbling nervously with the hem of her skirt, she suddenly lifts her jumper up: "Wanna look?" Nervous and curious at the same time, she squats down, mimes doing a poo, wiggles her hips professionally and announces with childish pride: "Finished!"

This first scene presents the basic situation and outlines the subjects and narrative framework of the dance evening, named after the popular novel *Keuschheitslegende* (*Legend of Chastity*) by Rudolf Georg Binding. Infantilism and professionalism, childhood and adulthood are the twin poles between which love is tested, sought, lost, prevented and imagined – the desire for intimacy and safety stemming from childhood versus its suffocation in the conventions of adult life, in which everything depends on perfect self control. This dichotomy determines the piece: on the one hand feeling curiously forward, discovering one's own and others' bodies; on the other taboos, the constraints of decency and internalised feelings of guilt, which make the couples continually back off from each other.

These poles are never immediately juxtaposed, just as they are not limited to particular age groups. At the negative pole, fears determine the action; the positive expresses the wish to straddle the boundaries of taboo and the desire for a fear-free sexuality.

Thus *Keuschheitslegende* acquires a dimension not shared by the preceding pieces. While *Kontakthof*, and *Arien* are characterised by the battle of the sexes, alienation and isolation, we now witness the delight that comes from overcoming the constraints of convention. It is no longer left solely to the spectator to engage heart and head and find a possible alternative to the melancholy presented on stage.

This dimension becomes apparent when, accompanied by deafening strip-show music, the whole ensemble rips their clothes in a side-stepping dance and flings them off in a wide arc, or when, in the final scene, everyone holds hands and dances a grotesquely skewed Charleston towards the front of the stage, singing along to the tune. The brightly coloured armchairs, sofas and canapés, distributed all over the stage and set on casters, are used for wild journeys across the stage. At such moments it becomes clear what dance theatre can also be: a joyful transgression of taboos, imparted along with an invitation to join in.

Nonetheless, the piece deals with the same issues, continues the same endless, fragmentary story, exactly as Pina Bausch once formulated it in interview: "Essentially it's always man-woman issues or relationships, in other words our behaviour, or our desire, our inability, our impotence; the only thing which sometimes changes is the colour."

In *Eroticism*[*], Georges Bataille wrote: "The human spirit is prey to the most astounding impulses. Man goes constantly in fear of himself. His erotic urges terrify him. The saint turns from the voluptuary in alarm; she does not know that his unacknowledgeable passions and her own are really one. […] But man can surmount the things that frighten him and face them squarely." This also sums up the message of *Keuschheitslegende*.

The fear of admitting things to ourselves, of acknowledging the overwhelming desire to be loved, is a constant factor in Pina Bausch's work. This fear continually manifests itself as a tension in which well-meant affection frequently tips over into violence. The pivotal point lies at the place where convention and desire clash and the rules of decent behaviour betray desire. The fear can only be overcome if we look the reasons for it "in the eye", and this is exactly what the Tanztheater Wuppertal attempts with each new piece.

Vulnerability: a man in a black suit stands at the front of the stage with his back to the audience. Another man marks the vulnerable points on his body with white chalk and explains how best to hurt him.

Abandoned: the little girl left alone by her parents, suddenly runs to the door in a panic, can't get in or out, screams louder the more scared she gets; the guests assembled for the evening are unable to console her and eventually get on with their business.

Communication technology: sitting in ever more grotesque positions on a chair, ringing a telephone number which is always engaged.

Shame: a recurring gesture – the players hide their face with one hand, turn from the audience, afraid to show their faces.

Masculine myth: in utter desperation a man sings the German hit *Ich*

---

[*]  Georges Bataille, *Eroticism*, London: Marion Boyars, 1962, p 7.

*brech' die Herzen der stolzesten Frau'n* (*I break the hearts of the hardest women*) in a breathless staccato between laughing and crying.

Chasing after happiness: the women lie in the armchairs as if asleep. Through the loudspeakers, we hear Gustaf Gründgens singing of a "little glimpse of happiness". The men lose coins and search for them under the armchairs and the women's skirts, only to lose them again straight away. The women do not move.

The peaceful, melancholy *tableaux*, which exhibit the utmost vulnerability, are counterpoised with scenes in which desires are tested against the behavioural codex of western culture. Language in the form of quotations from classical as well as popular literature which are translated into action; the instructions, however, found to be useless. While a woman reads from Ovid's *Ars amatoria*, the subdued ensemble, seated in a circle of armchairs, is instructed to put their strict love-governess' lecture into practice. The "art of love" turns out to consist of stale, old-hat tricks, resulting in attempts at physical contact resembling grotesque acrobatic displays. Ovid reads no better than any modern sexual self-help manual. The boundary between high art and banal literature seems fluid: both are inadequate when it comes to love.

As if it were the most ordinary thing in the world, highly realistic crocodiles move among the manic happiness-chasers, dangerous, slow mythical beasts from another time, promising to outlive the worries and problems of the humans. With a dream-like logic they slot into the theatrical activity, lending the piece a poetic, imaginative breadth.

Like a leitmotif, fragments of Binding's novel are repeatedly spluttered out in a raunchy torrent. The book ostensibly tells the story of a girl called Evchen and her holy encounter with the Virgin Mary and the naked baby Jesus, to whom Evchen generously gives her shirt and is rewarded with the double-edged "gift" of eternal chastity. At a subliminal level, however, this work of popular fiction is richly garnished with steamy, repressed innuendo.

Binding's story can be taken in two ways: as a parable it describes the effect the "heavenly gift" of chastity has on Evchen's life, barring access to pleasurable bodily experiences. At the same time the holy and the obscene come together as one in the tract – unintentionally – but precisely in the sense meant by Bataille. The obscene is the necessary counterpart to the repressed bourgeois morality.

Pina Bausch responds to this with a stream of "dirty" children's rhymes along the lines of "milk, milk, lemonade, round the corner chocolate's made". Various "come-on" rituals are put to the test; the women try to attract the men the way they would an animal: they make enticing "here, kitty" calls, waggle the hem of their skirts or tease them with a ball tied to a piece of elastic, as if trying to amuse their favourite tomcat.

The woman with the cigarette lighter trick ("You wouldn't have a light, would you? Thanks, that's lovely.") turns up here of course, as does the red-light-district girl, cooing into the microphone: "Come on in, come on in, everything's squeaky clean, so clean you could eat your dinner off it!" This smacks of bourgeois mentality at its finest: filth and cleanliness, pornography and decency.

Pina Bausch also plays with genres here: vaudeville, music hall and cabaret atmospheres are interspersed with the etiquette-manual aspirations of bourgeois morality. The poles become relative and cancel each other out. We skip across the borders with playful ease; there are harsh drills and absurd tricks, both on this side and that.

Invisible balls are juggled, crabs ceremonially eaten in the correct manner; the hidden erotic undertones behind the actions are blatantly highlighted. We hear cheerful swearing in the local Ruhr dialect, see domestic strife fought out on moving sofas. One player tells the story of the arduous process of training a goldfish so that it could walk on dry land, with the animal, now estranged from its natural element, left in danger of drowning in water.

This fatal circus trick is a metaphor for the human condition: alienated from their erotic impulses by a centuries-old cultural tradition hostile to their drives, humans have become frightened of their impulses. The resulting tension has reached breaking point – wanting to and yet not wanting to (or not able to) – as enacted by one of the women. First getting one of the men excited, she then pushes him away with a furious "don't touch me".

As in earlier pieces, along with the ensemble scenes, *Keuschheitslegende* includes consistently maintained individual roles: the stage manager who, with narcissistic self-love rubs moisturiser over his body; the eternal loser who only dares stick his neck out once, as a shy child-molester ("I'm your nice uncle ..."); the hilarious contortion specialists. However, the real protagonists in the piece are the women; in the world of social drilling exercises they are left the least room for manoeuvre.

The women are restricted to the role of the petrified little girl, vulnerable and delicate, or its opposite, that of the seasoned seductress, who converses confidently with the audience, munching sweets. However, the roles are not clearly delineated, also revealing the potential for play within the ways that women are tailored and moulded. Only the *grande dame*, the evening's experienced hostess, is granted an identity approximating a classical role.

Like the players, choreographic formulas also recur each time, increasingly reduced by Pina Bausch to basic patterns for choreographing the space: the diagonal, along which the dancers swap roles to highlight gendered behaviour (the women in jackets, the men in feminine finery); the circle as a symbol of closed convention; parades along the front of the stage to confront the audience, advances on the stage edge, the dividing line between the players and the audience.

Despite all the radical confrontation they contain, Pina Bausch's pieces are always a charming, affectionate flirt with the audience. In *Keuschheitslegende* the dancers throw sweets into the auditorium, pass a telephone around, play with water pistols, address individual spectators and encourage them to join in. This does not resolve the issues raised, but the pleasure derived from play provides the strength to persevere.


## 1980


Named simply after the year it was created, the second production of the 1979/80 season continues the exploration into theatre's scope begun in *Kontakthof* and *Keuschheitslegende*. Pina Bausch brings the outside inside; the stage, again open right to the firewalls, is covered with real turf, filling the whole space with a damp meadow fragrance – a further example of how much dance theatre is about an all-encompassing theatre of the senses. In the place of the moving crocodiles from *Keuschheitslegende* or the hippo from *Arien*, we now have a stuffed deer transfixed in an idyllic pose. Inside and outside have been swapped round: the stage space takes the form of a natural playground. What is nature and what is art? The boundaries blur and merge into one another.

In almost three and a half hours, the company, with the addition of a conjuror and an elderly gymnast on the parallel bars, parade the familiar Bausch subjects. They include children's games and childhood hollow. *1980* continues to tell of the search for the original motives behind the ossified codes of behaviour, shrivelled to routine formulas. Like an archaeology of the everyday, it attempts to unearth and bring to the light of day the living body with all its impulses. In repeated sample tests the ensemble examines the material found to see if it holds up.

In this field work of bodily communication Pina Bausch treads very carefully. It is not just brash confrontation with conventions, an amusing and revealing exposure; a genuine need also seems to be hidden in every polished ritual. Thus *1980* also maintains a delicate balance. In the montage, much that is deeply familiar seems suddenly new, unknown, revealing hitherto unnoticed potential to the spectator.

Dance theatre raids everyday life as if it were a typesetter's box of letters, then rearranges the symbols of communication in surprising new ways. The familiar is made questionable, in the best sense, and thus given the chance to reveal unexpected liveliness or its bewildering contradictory nature. The hierarchies separating the significant from the supposedly insignificant, detail from leitmotif, no longer apply. Banality exists alongside solemnity; personal memory becomes mixed with group ritual.

This principle is also followed in the choice of music, which sticks to the tried and tested collage of popular and so-called "serious" music. Renaissance songs in English lend the atmosphere an overall gravity, interspersed with the chirpiness of the Comedian Harmonists, film soundtracks such as *The Wizard of Oz*, or the reverberant stateliness of Edward Elgar. In this piece too the changes in atmosphere within the music set the tone for the varied atmospheres of the scenes, underscoring or conflicting with them. The means and subject matter of dance theatre have been established; what now changes is the "key" of each piece and its particular emphasis.

In the hundred minute-long first part of *1980*, the emphasis is on childhood memories and children's rituals. In the first scene one of the dancers sits alone on a chair, ladles soup into his mouth with childish enthusiasm, saying "pour maman, pour papa, pour la tante Marguerite …" each time he swallows a spoonful. The ensemble arrives on the scene, this time via the auditorium, clothed in festive evening wear, striding along with sweeping gestures as if they were draping a shawl around their shoulders. While till now the company has mostly approached the audience directly, almost aggressively, or engaged in flirtatious conversations with them, they now reveal a generous charm. As so often, the dance consists of ritualised everyday physical gestures, magnified to revue-like theatricality or seen in intimate close-up.

A select clique meets for a party yet does not feel at home on this skewed playground. The festive entry is juxtaposed with a solitary birthday scene in which the birthday girl, in the absence of any guests, sings *Happy Birthday* to herself. In another scene someone sticks matches between his toes and lights them. Loneliness and abandonment drive people to bizarre rituals: a declaration of love, coupled with a display of jealousy, is directed not at a person but at a chair – someone's relationship to human beings has obviously gone wrong. When the assembled company meets for a festive polonaise it becomes an image of wishful thinking.

*1980* is about taking leave and about loneliness, about grief and death. It was Pina Bausch's last collaboration with her stage and costume designer and long-term partner, Rolf Borzik, who died on 27 January 1980, shortly before the premiere. The piece spans the arc of a whole life, from birth via childhood and adolescence up to old age and finally death. What it means to grow old can be understood when we compare the movements of old people, such as the gymnast on his parallel bars, with the younger dancers, or when Judy Garland sings two versions of *Somewhere Over the Rainbow* in immediate succession: one at the age of sixteen and the other a much later recording, her voice now shaky and spent.

In this very personal piece, Pina Bausch examines the relationships between beginning and end, growth and decay, youth and old age from all manner of perspectives, thereby going through an extended grieving process. The theatre becomes a site of contemplation in which feelings such as grief, often buried under formality, can be experienced again.

While language, here allowed a more important role than in other pieces, seeks to lie or tell a different story, the intonation and posture of the player reveal the true feelings. One after another the guests take leave of their host, uttering various hackneyed formulas, but with such reserved solemnity that the goodbyes are more reminiscent of condolences. What language attempts to hide, the body betrays.

Pina Bausch lets opposites clash openly and thus reinstates authenticity of feeling. We realise that familiar phrases all too often function solely as alibis. Exaggerated hysteria seeks to hide fear and insecurity, but actually betrays itself with every word spoken. In actions derived from daily life and exposed for what they really are, superficial affirmations are exposed as empty shells. Saying things in order to deny emotions simply means acting out learned scripts, as absurd as the request "would all passengers please leave the ship, we are now departing", delivered in a selection of languages by a dancer pinching her nose. The voyage undertaken by the Wuppertal ensemble in *1980* brings the restricted and restrictive formalities of everyday life to light.

The laughter, which the party guests rehearse in the form of exercises till it becomes compulsive, cannot disguise the grief and fear. The sense of absence and lack central to the piece suggests where the search for happiness and restored sense of understanding might begin.

The nostalgia for lost childhood reawakens the desire for happiness; a woman remembers being dressed by her father, other players speak openly about the childhood fear of burglars, let themselves be rocked back to sleep, be tapped gently on the naked bottom to the sounds of a lullaby, or casually sing *Mamatschi schenk mir ein Pferdchen*.

It is as if such moments stem from a fairy-tale time when wishing still worked. Things which bifurcate in adulthood must once have been one and the same – as in a sequence in which a girl runs round in a circle waving a handkerchief like a flag and saying "I'm so tired", till she does in fact have to stop from exhaustion; message and reality are one.

The piece uses quiet moments to contrast with the noisiness of official occasions: the dancers stand close together, wipe tears from their cheeks in small, swift gestures, clap their hands soundlessly and repeat the process till it becomes a silent gestural dance of mourning.

Where feelings become overpowering, dance begins, deployed by Pina Bausch more powerfully again in *1980*, but always in isolation, restricted to an individual dancer who dances entirely for herself in the background as if trying to recall a lost movement. In these intimate moments individuals find solitude; at one with themselves through movement. The short dance sequences, which are interspersed throughout the piece, separate

84

from the larger formations, reach their climax in an elegant, poetic solo, in which the dancer's only partner is a fully-functioning lawn sprinkler. Soon enough, however, the momentum of the movement cuts out again. That which breaks down in language also breaks down in dance. There is no form obviously available for that which Pina Bausch seeks to express in her dance theatre. It must first be dug out again, from under all the encrustations. The solo thus also seems to be reminding us of the tightly choreographed early pieces.

Other reminders of older pieces are also woven into *1980*. The king from *Renate wandert aus*, now naked, is lead through the scene with a paper crown on his head and soberly announces that he has been robbed. In another scene we seem to be meeting the couple from *Zweiter Frühling* again. A bank robber in a stocking mask stumbles disconcertingly through the desolate picnic party, his slow motion contrasting with the group's hysteria. Fantastic, unreal moments go hand in hand with genuine danger, when the men throw a woman around like a ball, or a man holds a woman by her arm and leg and swirls her round playing aeroplanes. And once again there is one person who doesn't fit in and, garishly dressed, plays the over-the-top belle of the ball, flirting with the audience in a vain monologue.

In the second part, the situation is further accentuated by quiz games and absurd feats. The performers are asked, for instance, to describe their home country in three words. Out come the usual clichés: Chopin, vodka and Nijinsky naturally stand for Poland; John Wayne, hamburgers and Cadillacs for the USA. From the far corner of the auditorium a dancer questions the ensemble members about their fears; the further back they move on stage, the louder they have to shout out their answers. Similar questions about the scars they have develop into a peculiar competition in which the pain endured is finally rewarded with flowers and trophies. An "applausometer" determines the ultimate winner. Situations from life are lined up to form a chain of compulsions. Thus a communal sunbathing session turns into a comical contortion show in which everyone exposes just one part of the body to the sun, carefully covering the rest from view.

Life is full of compulsions, of which theatre-making is just one particular variation. The comic caricature does, however, show how easily we could leave behind such complicated image-competitiveness. Laughter, which in dance theatre so often sticks in both players' and spectators' throats, provides genuine release here.

As if at an audition, the dancers are ordered to smile, jump, show a leg, respond to a word such as "dinosaur" or practise tongue twisters such as *Cottbuser Postkutscher*. This is a parody of the compulsion in theatre to show off, hardly distinguishable from that in everyday life. The parade of national characteristics does not leave out Germany; a hearty *Prost, prost Kamerad* evokes stuffy Teutonic men's clubs, and German football songs evoke the battle cries of the stadium.

The mood of this party crowd, so keen to adopt the right pose, swings between attempted theatrical festivity and loneliness, between undeterred, cheerful certainty and grief, moments of uncontrolled hysteria and self-focussed calm. The everyday vocabulary of communication is tested out, rejected, tried again, rejected again. In fact the aim does not seem to be to find a solution. The things which suddenly liberate unexpected vitality or prove valuable in helping people communicate are found incidentally, in the process of experimentation. Often enough the truth of a scene lies hidden in the material it uses from the start. It simply requires a particular approach to make it visible.

Refreshingly, Pina Bausch's dance theatre presents itself without stated aims. It does not seek to mean anything other than that which we experience directly in the constant metamorphoses on stage. The elements of the theatre (sound, light, movement and colour) are not a vehicle for a message beyond themselves. Nothing is represented via them; the reality of the body speaks for itself.

Pina Bausch's pieces feed from the reservoir of authentic experience, translating them into a system of easily comprehensible signs. The spectator enters a world of experience in which they are invited to participate in, not a didactic institution. The dramatist Heiner Müller accurately described the nature of such a theatre: "Only the increasing pressure of authentic experience can produce the ability to look history in the whites of its eyes, which could mean the end of politics and the beginning of a new history of mankind."*

---

★  Quoted in Horst Laube, "Die Geschichte reitet auf toten Gäulen", *Der Spiegel*, 7 June 1980, p 157.

## Bandoneon

It seems consistent that the only piece produced for the 1980/81 season should make the compulsions of the theatre its main subject. With *Keuschheitslegende*, the work of the Tanztheater Wuppertal had already reached the boundaries of what is possible within the institution of theatre. *Bandoneon*, named after an accordion-like instrument used in South American dance music, particularly tango, does not resolve the problem of theatrical convention either, but the piece certainly does not avoid the issue, placing it squarely at its centre.

"I have to do something!" With these words a dancer comes on stage, into an enclosed, high room furnished as a café, with many small tables and chairs and larger-than-life portraits of boxers from times gone by. A piano stands against the far wall; clothes hanging from hooks suggest that further guests are here. Through a high door in the right-hand stage wall, the only opening apart from the side doors, come the men in typical dance theatre dress evening suits and are asked one after the other what they associate with the word "Maria": the cue for a colourful mixture of evocative answers ranging from "marihuana" to "Mariacron", a type of brandy.

The women appear, less self-assured and taking up less room than the men, who now take their places at the tables, put on their jackets, remove them, and change places. One after the other the women, who are standing close together wearing smart evening clothes, come forward and, holding their noses, deliver their responses to the word "Maria". Only after this does the tango music quietly begin, playing at various volumes throughout the evening, sometimes rising to the level of blaring, distorted feedback.

Argentine tangos from the first two decades of the twentieth century fill the sparse room with that mournful desolation and erotic sensuality particular to tango. Their subject is loss, the absence of everything which an underprivileged peripheral culture lacks in a metropolis like Buenos Aires where the tango originated.

Tango, according to the lyricist Enrique Santos Discépolo, is "a sad thought which can be danced". Hellmuth Karasek writes that "because it comes from a world of repression and failure, from a reality whose ideals do not match the life lived, tango's attitude is melodramatic; it denies life, either lamenting it as a loss or conjuring it as a dream."* At the same time, however, "the erotic charge [...] which is strangely juxtaposed with the sadness and hopelessness of its texts [...] is also an expression of the anarchic attitude alive in tango."** Against this melancholic aural backdrop, with its oscillation between revolt and resignation, between melodramatic gesture and silent self-absorption, Pina Bausch's *Bandoneon* is an expedition to the very interior of desire. As in tango music, the banal is combined with the sublime; scenes from the world of the everyday are found beside operatic drama.

However, *Bandoneon* does not adopt the attitude of tango wholesale. The piece does not deny life; it pares life's impulses down to the roots. When, as in most of the previous pieces, the music directs us to the past, this is not in nostalgic reminiscence but rather as a reflection from a childhood which has remained painfully alive. It is not an anecdotal idyll that is being created here, nor is it about personal obsessions. It is more a promise (of happiness, of union), which, precisely because it remains unfulfilled, must be demanded all the more strongly.

Dance theatre performances are like an inexhaustible search for the key to happiness, undertaken again and again despite every failure. Dance theatre seems not to experience the despondency brought on by defeat; on the contrary defeat seems almost to represent a challenge. Childhood, to which the music refers, seems to be a secure place for the mission to help unfulfilled desires win their rights. Thus these aural spaces never emanate the stuffy comfort of recognition. They awaken a utopian hope, demanding that the constraints of (bodily) history be released.

When, in *Bandoneon* just as in *Kontakthof, Arien* or *Keuschheitslegende*, the dancers move with childish simplicity and openness, a little of the freedom that is possible – but usually obscured by convention – can be seen. When a couple dances a peculiar and subdued tango, the woman astride the man's shoulders, facing him, and then continues to dance on the floor; sitting entwined with each other, this is about the relationship

---

* Hellmuth Karasek, "Ein trauriger Gedanke, den man tanzen kann", *Der Spiegel*, 14 June 1982, p 192.
** Ibid, p 192–3.

between the sexes which has been frozen into ballroom dances, and at the same time about an obstinate resistance.

While the company, lined up along the walls, measures out the space, individual rituals take place. A husband and wife undertake a silent slapping duel; someone demonstrates acrobatic tricks with a hat; unnoticed by the others a woman lies screaming on the floor. Later the group watches her scream: what was originally a genuine crisis has now become a role.

Alone in the tango café a male dancer puts on a tutu, walks shyly towards the front of the stage, baffled and embarrassed, finally succumbs to the pressure to do something and begins some slow *tendus* and *pliés*, which he repeats in various locations. Later the company follows his lead, carrying out the ballet exercises in everyday clothes.

More uncompromisingly than in other productions, Pina Bausch subjects the audience to punishingly longwinded processes, confronts them with an undisguised helplessness in the face of expectations based on pure spectacle and entertainment. This is about individual fears but also about how to cope with them, and not be taken over by them. It is about joy, the ability to be happy, which most people last possessed wholeheartedly as children. And it is always also about the impossibility of dancing "prettily". More even than previous pieces *Bandoneon* is a series of pictures illustrating dance and dancers, a view of the ballet studio and the people in it.

Dancers' reappraisal of their personal histories – their dance careers – is a motif running through the piece. One dancer grooms another brutally and forces her to smile the whole way through. When she fails to master her pain and hide it under a smiling façade, as required in ballet training, the mistress of the school for pretty appearances dunks her head in a bucket of water as punishment. Another reveals that his ballet teacher held a lighted cigarette under the soles of his pupils' feet to force their legs up higher. Painful muscle stretches are demonstrated, in which one dancer sits cross-legged while the other stands on her legs, the entire weight of the body used to force the joints apart.

Exposing this torture reveals how highly dubious this artistic quest for ethereal weightlessness is, seeking to make the people on stage disappear behind a stupendous mastery of the body. In the large, inhospitable room the training exercises and dance rituals are isolated into absurd acts of self-conditioning. They leave bewilderment in their wake, as seen in the dancer with his worn-out tutu or like the vacuous exercises the ensemble carries out with grim, unenthusiastic expressions, to the beat of excessively loud music.

It seems only logical to reap the rewards for such suffering immediately; in a clapping sequence all the women give every single man a round of applause, all the men applaud every woman individually, all the men applaud all the women and vice versa. Theatre is revealed to be a grotesque show of strength, a display of muscles and expertise, behind which the genuine needs and desires must stay hidden. Theatre, *Bandoneon* demonstrates, is like life. Both are ruled by a ruthless competition of repression, illustrated by a practical introduction to fouling techniques slotted in after the applause sequence, as if we were in a sensation-hungry football stadium, not in a theatre. In order to keep up his image, one dancer has to hold the bridge position for a marathon length of time, to the point of exhaustion, for which he receives only lukewarm applause from the others. Something must continually be produced, even when no-one really wants to.

Pina Bausch does not just display this pressure to produce a show, she also interrupts the flow of the piece for many minutes, as if stopping time. A dancer comes to the front with a piece of paper ready to read something out, but has to wait till a long piece of tango music is over before she can finally recite a poem by Heinrich Heine. Such interruptions create something resembling a staged peace, a pause for contemplation, in which the tensions between stage and auditorium increase and can be made a conscious experience.

About an hour into the performance, the stage sets are taken down; stage hands spend nearly fifteen minutes removing spotlights, tables, chairs, pictures, even rolling up part of the floor covering. What remains is a wholly unadorned room, about as cosy as a railway station waiting room, in which the piece then continues. During these fifteen minutes the entertainment apparatus of the theatre is halted, although this is not an intermission. Other than a group of dancers practising leapfrog exercises, nothing happens. It is a moment of self awareness, a radical stop, in order to determine, with all our senses, exactly where we are.

Individual desires mingle with this confrontation with the medium of theatre. Moods vacillate. At one point the whole company plays suicide, whereby each dancer, while listing their personal reasons out loud, ties their scarf into a noose and jumps from a chair. At other points everyone breaks into childish cheers ("La mer!") and leap for joy. Melancholy alternates with unsullied enthusiasm. A woman on stage is admired by another in the auditorium, then suddenly insulted. With the theatrical gestures of an opera diva, another woman constantly sucks at a lemon as if addicted, to the applause of the whole troop. A further woman sings an aria to a living mouse in a box.

As is mostly the case in Pina Bausch's dance theatre, these poetic, surreally dislocated actions take place with utmost simplicity and as if they were a matter of course. Thus a smartly dressed lady, sitting alone at one of the tables, carefully eats a tulip. Such moments assert a kind of solitude which is more than self-absorbed loneliness; it is intimate time spent with oneself, an escape from the sudden outbreaks of hysteria or the wider constraints on behaviour. Something fantastic takes root with these unbelievable actions, positioning itself at odds with the business and the bustle of everyday life. Individuality resists appropriation by any form of institution, whether it be the theatre, ballet or simply peer pressure.

Favourite dishes are listed, the delights of relaxation with a trouser button undone after a substantial meal are dwelt on, or the pet cockerel is remembered, which mother slaughtered and cooked and the child then ate all on his own out of grief, in order not to have to share any of it.

Although *Bandoneon* is driven almost entirely by tango music, not once is a classic tango danced. Pina Bausch does not make any concessions to nostalgic expectations here, instead turning the melodramatic extroversion of the tango inwards. The partners find themselves in strange poses, simultaneously radiating abandonment and tragic intimacy. Tango is danced kneeling or gently leaning together in endlessly slow turns. The couples' dances are awkward or frozen. The women sit astride the men's folded arms and let themselves be carried in this exhausting position as if spellbound, or wrap themselves around the men's hips desperately looking for a hold, then slip powerlessly off again as if seeking protection which the archaic twosomeness of the ballroom dance cannot grant them.

Only once do the pairs break free, parading along the front of the stage with wildly gyrating hips, releasing the sensual vitality of dance which has become typical of other pieces. Between moments of calm and outburst, affection must be tried out like a new experience; the dancers hold their calves, feet, shoulders against each other, comparing, approaching, feeling the way very cautiously towards each other.

"Do something!" demands one of the dancers of the audience in the second half, turning their expectations back on them. *Bandoneon* is a further stop along the way in a quest with an uncertain end. Pina Bausch and her dancers assert their helplessness and bewilderment in the light of a theatrical convention which insists on its right to entertainment. With stubborn resistance they bring their refusal into just this theatrical machine, still looking for a humanity which can only exist beyond the businesses, institutions and mechanisms.


## Walzer


The dancers balance tiny folded-paper ships on their outstretched hands, and, laughing shyly, cross the stage from either side in a parallel formation. The soundtrack to this cautious procedure is a blaring recording of the ship welcoming station at Schulau, near Hamburg, where incoming ships, described according to their size, freight and capacity, are greeted with noisy national anthems.

A dancer steps up to the microphone with the words "and then Pina said …" and goes on to describe the tasks Pina Bausch set her ensemble during rehearsals. The parallel, crossing formation breaks up. The dancers begin constructing boundaries around themselves using flotsam and jetsam lying around on stage: plants, stones, scraps of paper. Others make Morse-code hand signals from the side of the stage: rudimentary, truncated communications. Language in *Walzer* (*Waltzes*) is often reduced to minimal signs and simple naming. Gradually the dancers' individual actions converge as they lie down in a large sail-shaped formation.

Arrival and departure; travelling to transcend boundaries (which the militaristic anthems reinstate immediately); nationalistic pathos and the desire to fence off a little private happiness. The national anthems recur throughout the first half of *Walzer* – alongside vocal and musette waltzes from Brazil and France, while the dancers form patterns of prone bodies, uncannily reminiscent of corpses. When the childishly earnest dancers again hold their paper ships out, accompanied by the national anthems, it is as if they are trying to circumnavigate the deadly beautiful geometry of this large form with their fragile toys.

The motto of this piece might be: war no longer starts, it only continues. And it is perpetuated by and entrenched within personal relationships, which it has frozen into clichés. The everyday battle lines are drawn not just externally but also internally: parade grounds of convention, rubble heaps of unexpressed emotion. But there is the potential to resist – not with political agendas, but with poetic subversion.

In a series of dry-swimming dances, carried out under continually changing orders, the company traces paths into past and current centres of political crisis (to Hiroshima, Belfast, South Africa, Afghanistan, and also to Munich), all the while smiling enticingly at the audience. A national anthem soon drives them from the stage. Cautiously, with uncertain smiles, they re-emerge from their hiding places, holding their hands up as if threatened, and slowly begin twirling to the sounds of a waltz.

The pretty form turns out to contain terror: movements danced with bated breath. Moments hang in the balance, leaving us uncertain. The poles of life and death fuse into a living death – or a sudden lust for life – breaking through in the midst of danger. *Walzer* is largely fuelled by a savage grief, fighting to survive.

The piece in fact eschews any kind of artificiality. Lighting has long been reduced to simple, austere effects, limited mostly to varying degrees of brightness which create clear contrasts. In *Walzer* the stage is equipped with only a few necessary props: chairs, used by the whole ensemble in moments of calm, a table, a piano and above all flowers. Everything reminiscent of conventional theatricality is abandoned in favour of a concentration on the essential, with any decorative trimmings pared away. Theatre is a place of experience like any other. The people who work here report on events from their own world of experience, they present themselves as they really are. They stand in a row, with sunken heads raised only to state their respective Christian names and nicknames, as if this were an inspection. When the names of former colleagues are mentioned, who no longer belong to the ensemble or have died, this becomes a journey into the past too. Memory is something which must be preserved. Each performer shows us an object – a clock, a rifle, scissors, an old model railway – and recounts its history. They describe pearls of wisdom and rules of behaviour drummed into them by their parents; they

93

quote expressions from autograph albums, intended to lend an uncertain future a hint of stability, and describe what they first wanted to be when they grew up. All this takes place with a modest gravity which can still be rendered surprisingly ironic via comic exaggeration, as a dancer emphatically states her chosen careers: "archaeologist, nun or spy". The personal history of each individual is presented as an element of the larger, wider history of which it is part. And this history is always also one of dancers in a_theatre.

The confrontation with the institution of theatre leads to an even greater openness in *Walzer* as Bausch addresses her own working methods and discloses the rehearsal procedures usually so carefully concealed. "And then Pina said …" is a core, recurring phrase in this production. The dancers demonstrate the answers they have found to the choreographer's questions. They also show how these answers, taken from their store of personal experience, have taken on a form which elevates them above the merely private. The company approaches the audience with open hands and lays their cards on the table. The external pressures and the constraints of theatrical production are countered with an exposure of theatre's inner workings. *Walzer* therefore reads like a statement of the ensemble's intent – an ensemble which like no other is based on personalities, and, perhaps for this very reason, comes into conflict with the theatre business. Individuality refuses to fit neatly into the institution. Thus the Tanztheater Wuppertal's work is a rare example of a "march through the institution", seeking to change the system from within. Not letting itself be worn down; instead defending and maintaining its distinctiveness.

Living and dying: war and peace; the big themes and how individual lives fit into them or resist them. Between these poles, the succession of generations and our relationship to the family acquire a new significance. If in earlier pieces the family was often a place where a catastrophic lack was experienced, where we were indoctrinated into prejudice and disempowered by rules, now it is seen more as a valuable heritage where something is salvaged against the passage of time. The relationship to our own origins is enriched with an almost affectionate heedfulness.

For almost fifteen minutes the stage is transformed into a darkened cinema, and the women lie in the men's laps, their legs spread wide to watch a film. It documents a gentle childbirth, with the new-born baby learning to breathe and finding itself in the world, lovingly stroked and massaged by the doctor. One of the dancers lifts up her skirt and paints a foetus in an amniotic sac on her pregnant stomach. With a child's toy she then imitates squealing baby cries, treating all motherhood mysticism with irony right from the start. No indulgent maternal happiness is conjured up here; the birth evokes the magic of a primordial beginning.

In any case, the various atmospheric elements in *Walzer* create a diversity which prohibits sentimentality from ever getting a hold. Killing, hunting and chasing recur frequently, used in contrast with other motifs. The feelings experienced by an animal caught in a trap are investigated: the group barks at each other like a pack of hunting hounds; the men lay the women's lifeless bodies in a neat row in order to assess the "kill" professionally.

In the middle of an elegant but boring party, a woman demonstrates all conceivable means for killing insects like an over-enthusiastic advertising saleswoman and deploys them against the men. When her best efforts achieve nothing she concludes that you could still put your underpants on your head: war on insects played out as hysterical close combat in the living room. Later the same woman nails her colleague's dress to the wall with icy precision and tapes her hair up. Her task completed, she scrutinises the audience severely as if looking for the next victim. Latent competitiveness and rivalry force their way into the open.

These isolated tragicomic moments are linked by small dances, for which Pina Bausch has again found a simple choreographic formula: the ensemble typically slips into a polonaise, snaking in a long line through the room, sometimes hand in hand and led by a woman in the role of compère, sometimes simply in a line – tiny bodily gestures formalised to music or energetic revue dances which wind through the piece like garlands. Caresses for an imaginary partner weave into a gentle medley of intimacies: stroking faces, tickling, ruffling, tousling.

Alongside this there is dance theatre's familiar, basic form: ensemble dances demonstrating strength and solidarity, disappearing into the depths of the room before returning, hand in hand. The steps for a ballroom dance are outlined with chalk on the floor, numbered and rehearsed in numerical order till the art has been mastered and the dancers can move freely and relish the moves. These interwoven dance passages radiate the alluring charm first seen in *1980*, very different from the angry runs which characterised earlier pieces.

The investigation of romantic clichés is also pursued further in *Walzer*. Led by a trainer, his voice amplified by a microphone, the couple learns the "farewell kiss". Standing more than a meter apart they suck and slurp towards each other till their lips meet with an explosive bang. The procedure is practised repeatedly.

The microphone, a prop Pina Bausch has often used since *Kontakthof*, fulfils the function of a zoom lens in a film; it distils something which would otherwise evade perception. The "school of seeing and of the senses" draws our attention to details.

The kissing exercise has a pendant in the form of an upstage sequence where a women is kissed lovingly by a man, faints in melodramatic bliss, then gets up only to be kissed again and again as if addicted, and as if each time were the first.

With great difficulty a couple crawls towards each other; we are genuinely unsure whether they are the survivors of a catastrophe, or if this is simply a party trick. Then they exchange cheerful pleasantries, as if the positions they are lying in were perfectly normal. Happiness and danger are as close together as laughing and crying.

A dancer demonstrates what came to his mind in response to the keyword "danger" chosen during rehearsals. He throws a heavy stone in the air, watches it fall back down and gets out of the way at the very last moment. The dancers carry out acrobatic tricks, balancing acts in the quest for happiness.

Standing on a man's shoulders, one of the dancers lets herself fall to the sound of horrified screams from another woman, with implicit trust into the waiting arms of the group, her eyes closed and an entranced look on her face: she shows that she has enough trust in her own ability to overcome a life-threatening risk, and trusts the others to support her. The audience holds its breath as if in the circus, while the dancers gamble with genuine danger. After all, the stakes are high when betting on happiness.

Among the genuine highlights of *Walzer* are the showy solo numbers, woven into the piece using the same technique of contrasts. A woman lies on her back with her legs against the wall, plays the drunken wife who doesn't want to go home, pleads to stay for another little glass of wine and a cigarette.

Contrast: a woman in a long tulle dress measures out the room piece by piece in cartwheels as if dancing were an acrobatic show of strength. We see the effort gradually exhausting her.

A man, who is not a professional singer, stands at the piano. The group stands and stares in a silent choir formation. In a good but unsteady voice he sings "I love you as you love me". Happiness in love seems uncertain when the voice singing its praises lacks all professional confidence.

Contrast: a woman sits all alone in the large room. To the sounds of Édith Piaf singing *La Vie en rose* she draws her hands extremely slowly across her face: an image of desperation and abandonment magnified in painful clarity by its slow motion. It is as if her face ages under her hands or discloses its real age.

A dancer in a blue one-piece bathing costume and high heels comes on stage furiously, shows off her toned muscles making the audience feel flabby, then demands a table, a chair and an apple. In the scene, built up in front of our eyes, she eats her apple aggressively, continually making it clear that she doesn't need any help. But at the end of her bravura, hate-and-jealousy act, targeted at her colleagues, the theatre and herself, she breaks down into tears and in a stammer begs for entertainment, company and music.

How can we maintain our independence and still be loved? How do we reconcile the desire for privacy with the desire for intimacy? And how can the theatre deal with such contradictions?

While such scenes fully accentuate the dancers' personalities and performing abilities, the last thing they represent is an attempt to show off technical virtuosity; they lack the necessary surface gloss which is evoked, if anywhere, in the women's shimmering dresses, from all styles and periods, and the elegant suits worn by the men. Under this socially acceptable outer skin, however, dance theatre explores a disturbing, rebellious world of emotion, constantly threatening to collapse.

In *Walzer* there are continual allusions to passages which cannot be completed because the main player is ill. The final scene consists solely of a recording of the pianist Wilhelm Backhaus' last concert in which he breaks off during a sonata and announces a change to the programme, playing Schubert's *Impromptu in A flat Major*. The ensemble sits on a row of chairs throughout and simply listens, now part of the audience themselves.

*Walzer* probably goes as far as it is possible to go within theatre. It takes its place in the continual chronicle of events which the Tanztheater Wuppertal updates from piece to piece. It not only reflects the state of play in the outside world, it also reflects on its own status within the culture industry. Its edgy relationship to the industry is mirrored in its relationship to itself. The fine line the company treads with each new piece is an achievement wrested from its own threatened exhaustion.

## Nelken

*Nelken* (*Carnations*)* marks a key change in Pina Bausch's work. The happiness dance theatre has been fighting for seems to have edged within reach. The stage shows a magnificent sea of flowers, with thousands of carnations inserted into the ground, creating a sense of tranquil gaiety: a variant of the playing field of real grass which provided a sensually tangible space back in *1980*.

A dancer enters and takes his place on a chair he has brought with him. One by one the entire company follows and sits in a horseshoe-shaped formation. With operetic gusto Richard Tauber's voice sings out from the loudspeakers: "The world is beautiful when happiness tells you a tale." For a short while the ensemble continues listening as the song fades out, then the dancers stalk carefully through the carnations down into the audience, asking individual spectators to step outside for a moment, as if to discuss something personal or to exchange secret intimacies. On stage a dancer translates George Gershwin's song *The Man I Love* (sung by Sophie Tucker) into sign language.

The song runs through the piece like a leitmotif. It invokes the dream of simple pleasures in a happy twosome, of loving and being loved, of faithfulness, of a little love nest for eternity. *Nelken* begins without drama, tenderly and quietly and includes the audience in its loving intimacy right from the start. Love, pairing-off and happiness are the key subjects inves-

---

* Following its premiere *Nelken* was radically reworked. This description is based on the revised second version.

tigated here during the ongoing journey to the core of desire, but the atmosphere is noticeably gentler, brighter and more playful than in earlier pieces.

"For love is strong as death; jealousy is cruel as the grave." This line from the Song of Solomon is quoted in the programme and could stand as a credo for the piece, which dwells less on the everyday bars to happiness than the apparently all-conquering power of love. The underlying mood of *Nelken* is determined by a fantastic vision of happiness in which love overcomes all adversity. We are now cheerfully capable of the effort required for mutual understanding. The dancers repeatedly rush to the front of the stage with outstretched arms, radiating happiness and offering ample amusing clichés on the subject of love.

But the happiness retains an unnerving dimension, too, and does not lose itself in blissful self-indulgence. The sea of flowers the men and women romp around in, mostly wearing identical armless tunics, is guarded by four sheepdogs on long leashes. The games and dances take place in a forbidden Garden of Eden. The sunny meadow of carnations seems like a lost paradise of happiness and child-like innocence; it is extremely dangerous to sneak back in. We constantly get a feeling of what might be possible but is still far from being realised.

In the middle of this summery playing field Pina Bausch places dark, disturbing or mysterious images: a man and a woman shovel earth onto each other's heads with little toy buckets as if enacting a burial ritual; a bare-breasted woman, wearing nothing but her underpants, carries an accordion around her neck although she does not actually play. Only at the end of the first half does this silent musician get going, translating a story about the seasons of the year into a gestural dance which the rest of the ensemble takes up, accompanied by a piece of early Louis Armstrong.

*Nelken* searches for the reasons why the ability to be happy is so hard to reach and retain. These reasons are partly found in childhood, in our parents' see-saw childrearing techniques, laying the groundwork for all future emotional confusion with their alternate use of carrot and stick. A woman whines like a child, then responds to herself in parentally sharp tones: "Will you just stop it!" The desire for consolation is met with rough blows. Heartbeats are made audible via the microphone, a precise measure of inner emotion.

The dancers, skipping through the carnations like bunnies, do not fare much better than children. They are driven away but soon return. The joy of oblivious play cannot be suppressed.

Before we realise it, this tough struggle between playfulness and orderliness develops into a comic chorus line, bent double, in which the men literally dance the women under the table.

Like a tragicomic visual quotation from the *Three Graces* a trio of men in skimpy "Sunday best" dresses playing ring-a-ring-o'-roses explain to each other and the audience what they do when domestic strife flares up.

A man practises arguing, anguished gestures on another man, but the puppet-like, powerless imitations put any embittered attempt to start a fight into perspective; the usual dogged seriousness of such moments suddenly appears excessively dramatic.

Children's games are played, their unfair nature exposed when everyone suddenly turns on the ringleader, who, till then, had high-handedly set the rules. It is almost as if the Tanztheater Wuppertal wanted to restore a lost innocence, a state in which feelings can be shown again spontaneously and without fear.

Taking pleasure in our own vitality also requires an uninhibited attitude to our bodies. One after the other the dancers appear at the front of the stage and, smirking at the audience, pour streams of water from plastic cups, beginning a digression on the joys and quirks of peeing. Other responses are delivered into an interviewer's microphone. Dancers explain how they felt when they first fell in love, what situations they find exciting and how their body then reacts. Statements on the reality of the body again lead into dance. With a suggestive, even explicit, fondling finger emerging from interlocked hands, the dancers describe circling caresses.

An aspect of love is the ambivalence of emotions, the tenderness of violence and the violence of tenderness. In a painfully long scene, a dancer kneels on a chair, the naked soles of his feet pointing outwards, and is tickled mercilessly, becoming hysterical but at the same time suppressing his torment. He would dearly love to scream, but he maintains his composure, because the torture also involves pleasure.

Emotional expression is sometimes generated by force. In a virtuoso act, with only a fairground fortune-telling machine for company, a man chops a mountain of onions and dices them into tiny pieces. Other dancers come in, rub the onion into their faces and present their red, crying faces at the front of the stage: a classic theatrical technique for manufacturing unreal emotion. Dance theatre, however, looks for the true feelings behind the studied poses and gestures, looks for a place where they can be encountered genuinely.

But the players do not take themselves too seriously in the process. When the god of love appears in a lurex miniskirt armed with a quiver full of mischievous arrows, undermining all lofty notions of love, the joke is also on him. As *Nelken* was created in the Tanztheater Wuppertal's tenth year, for the final scene the ensemble groups together in a school-class photo format with serious expressions, in the middle a male "grandmother" with a wonky long-haired wig.

The core element of *Nelken* is a fifteen-minute sequence set to the slow movement of Franz Schubert's *String Quartet in D Minor "Death and the Maiden"* which draws together the ambivalences, discrepancies and tensions surrounding the subject of love and takes them to radical extremes.

All the players lie peacefully holding hands on tipped-over chairs arranged in a circle. A woman stands up and reads out an affectionate, concerned letter from her father. Suddenly everyone jumps up and runs to the front of the stage with outstretched arms offering love. But the outburst of joy is broken off as soon as it begins; the dancers turn round, fetch their chairs and sit in a row, swinging and rocking up and down, put the chairs back, run forwards again with words of love, form a row again. While this is going on two stuntmen begin stacking cardboard boxes into two monolithic blocks, watched by an anxious woman who, stammering helplessly and screaming, desperately tries to avert the impending danger. The bigger the blocks grow the harder it becomes for the dancers to get past them to set out their row of seats. Their movements interlock into ever more complex forms, they race up and down stage, switching between lamenting and beseeching gestures. Between the stuntmen's calm preparations and the group's hectic position-changing, the woman paces up and down, increasingly nervous and bewildered. She begs for help, but the dancers pursue their swinging and beseeching rituals, undeterred. Finally the stuntmen climb up to their elevated jumping positions. The group scatters for a moment, comes back together but their lamenting movements become gradually more tired and slow, while the woman's agitation increases to hysteria. The stuntmen jump – and land unhurt in the piled-up boxes.

The tension, tightened to bursting point, explodes; the row of dancers breaks apart amid protests. One man does a somersault from standing, cursing; another, in a long evening dress, is forced to perform classic showpieces by the group. Furious, and gradually left alone by the others, he shouts at the audience: "You wanna see something?" With pointed indifference but no less impressive for all that, he delivers his *jetés* and *battements*. Wuppertal *Tanztheater* derives its strength from sources other than circus-like, classical virtuoso turns. The fit of rage against the pressure to perform in the theatre is immediately counteracted. A man in a dinner jacket appears and, in the abrasive, self-satisfied tone of bureaucratic power, barks at the dancer in evening dress, still disorientated and breathless: "Your passport, please!" Monotonously and matter-of-fact, barely looking at him, he says: "Put some proper clothes on!" In the threatening stillness an atmosphere of absolute despotism steadily grows.

A second man is also required to show his passport, is instructed where to stand by a silently pointed finger and made to remove his trousers. A woman who arrives is also asked to prove her identity and ordered to pull her dress over the man's shoulders so that a ridiculous, hermaphroditic puppet is created, with naked male legs in socks. The other dancer has now exchanged his dress for a suit as instructed. With studied disinterest the border guard orders him to imitate a goat, demanding the animal "with sound", then a barking dog, a parrot and a frog. The helpless man follows the cynical official's orders assiduously.

In the face of the cold insolence of power the "protest at the opera" is struck dumb. While autocratic power asserts itself with utter high-handedness, theatre seems to be a site of artistic freedom, constantly under threat of attack from outside. At the same time the two worlds overlap; it is clear what the rejection of attractive appearances is directed against. The drilling deployed to produce this stylish, classical virtuosity uses the same means of intimidation as the contemptuous pose of power.

But Pina Bausch turns this scene around too. A droning Brazilian march breaks the oppressive silence. The company appears in a chorus line, the women in long dresses, the men in black dinner suits. They move forward, at a menacingly slow pace, thrusting their left hands away with their right, and drive the stunt men on in front of them, who demonstrate samples from the repertoire of staged fight scenes. Arriving at the front edge of the stage, they all suddenly sink into affected curtsies. The strict determination, which had promised solidarity and strength, changes over into the ceremonial. Individual dancers rehearse action scenes with the stuntmen, who make reflex reactions to the slightest touch, and the dancer wanders through the scene still pretending to be a dog: the coercion seems wholly internalised.

Then the stage gradually empties. A dancer orders another where to stand, then suddenly takes his leave: "If anyone comes looking for me, I'm in the canteen." Soon after he arrives with a colleague whom he introduces to the public, yelling aggressively: "She's still young and fresh; she'll be taking over from now. It'll be more fun for you and for me too." But then they both walk straight off again. He returns to explain angrily that she has pulled out after all.

Behind the refusal to deliver slick entertainment something else emerges: a chaotic muddle, which is also precisely calculated, in which the various dimensions rub together and cause friction. Rigid principles of order are set against an apparent lack of orientation; choreographic structures are transported via chaotic runs, as if the dancers were searching for a point in space, for a place where they could still dance nicely and peacefully. But in reflecting on the laws of theatre destructive moments of reality continually break out.

A deeply disturbing mood emanates from such sequences. The panic and hysteria driving the dancers releases the spectator back into everyday life unsettled, which is to say more alert and critical. In Pina Bausch's dance theatre, the things which, in the world outside, still follow their distinct, orderly routes, meet in a head-on collision, which stirs up contradictions. These are dances on the edge of a volcano, fuelled by reality, letting their contradictory impulses react with each other. But in the rollercoaster ride of polar energies and power, reality is threshed out into a recognisable form.

Dance theatre players do not claim to know more than anyone else, but they endure the tension, endure all conflicts till they are over, holding out for a better ending. They do not make claims, they show – by taking action. They learn through trial and error. Thus all experience in dance theatre is direct and physical, and the audience is invited to share it.

By the end the field of carnations has been trodden down. The Tanztheater Wuppertal dancers and their audience have opened a further chapter in the search for happiness. The journey continues.

## Auf dem Gebirge hat man ein Geschrei gehört

"Something which grows and grows and can't be stopped / Breaking something, because you believe something can be stopped that way / Signs for death and fear / Making a virtue out of a weakness / The calm before the storm / Everything will be alright again / Wanting to feel something at all costs / The desire to move mountains / A hint that things are getting better / Something broken and something whole." These are some of the keywords, subjects and questions with which the Wuppertal ensemble sets out in search of a piece again, seeking a direct encounter with the phenomenon of reality. The questions relate to the personal and general experience of the dancers and their choreographer, to the authentic material harboured in their bodies as experienced history, an inexhaustible wealth of finds for that archaeology of the everyday which Pina Bausch practises in her work, avoiding all preconceived interpretations. Fitted together in the pieces according to the laws of free musical composition rather than rational sense, particular subjects and countersubjects are always present in the catalogue of questions used in rehearsals: the coercive forms of conditioning, and the persistent hope for healing.

Following *Blaubart* in 1977 and the *Macbeth* piece in 1978 the single new production of the 1983/84 season also carries a lengthy title. Unlike the preceding pieces' titles, reduced to a simple signal, the biblical line "on the mountain a cry was heard" (Matthew 2:18) evokes the essential, underlying mood. It is taken from Heinrich Schütz's *St Matthew Passion* from which the piece quotes a passage: "On the mountain a cry was heard, much lamentation and wailing; Rachel was weeping for her children and would not be comforted; for that was the end of them." The verse refers to Herod's "murder of the innocents", but in using this quotation Pina Bausch is certainly not playing on religious references. What is retained, in the fragment used as a title, is the breathless announcement of a catastrophe, the causes and nature of which remain unstated. A tense uneasiness runs through the piece from the start, a panic and fear of an unnamed danger, which was already presaged in *Arien, 1980* and above all in the long Schubert sequence in *Nelken*.

104

The stage is open right to the firewalls, bordered at the back by a black wall of steel. The ground, rising gently towards the rear, is covered in a deep layer of earth which, as previously in *Le Sacre du printemps*, retains the traces of the actions and makes walking and moving difficult: a barren, windswept arena.

The company appears; the women in simple, 1940s dresses, the men in suit trousers and grey or white shirts; dark, subdued tones dominate. The dancers cling nervously to the walls, steal through the auditorium, constantly seeking cover, hiding from an invisible danger. Cautiously they feel their way forward. During this music-free opening we hear their steps all the more clearly, hear the moments of stillness when they hesitate, then scurry on, hear their speeding breath, till they vanish again. "Something which grows and grows and can't be stopped."

With naive, almost stubborn ease in the face of this nervousness, a man stations himself at the front of the stage. Clad in red bathing trunks, a matching bathing cap, sunglasses, pink rubber gloves, his nose squashed flat by a disfiguring red cord, he pulls balloons out of his trunks with demonstrative nonchalance and starts to blow them up: an image of imperturbability and a game which plays on the audience's tense feeling of anticipation. Something in the way he stands emanates tremendous alienation. His silent presence provokes and disturbs like a figure from Beckett.

Two more men join him, one sitting on a chair he has brought, the other standing next to him as if on guard. They watch for a while and are given a blown-up balloon. Slowly and cautiously one places the other's head down on the balloon, as if he wanted to see how much weight the trapped air could carry. While the grotesque man continues blowing up balloons unmoved, they quietly leave again.

A woman appears, bursts a balloon with the burning tip of her cigarette, runs in shock to the far corner and blocks her ears. Only now does the music begin; in a delicate voice, Billie Holliday sings *Strange Fruit*.

The two men return. One attempts to bed the other down on the balloons but they cannot support the full weight of a human body. When both men have gone, the swimming-trunks hunk bursts several balloons in a stubborn rage.

Two further men appear, carrying a woman in their arms, and help her walk up the wall, at ninety degrees to it as if it were the ground, while

Billie Holliday sings *Lover Come Back to Me*. The muscleman takes the woman off their hands, lifting her with unwavering confidence in his own strength and carries her through the room, while she continues her walking movements in the air as if in a trance.

Strong men, weak women? It is in the nature of the Tanztheater Wuppertal to ask difficult questions while unable to offer easy answers. The self-confident macho man has an opposite in another man who wanders through the piece like his helpless pendant. Sometimes he appears as a childish scary monster, sometimes as a hobbling hunchback of Notre-Dame. When the whole ensemble is stirred into a wild dancing frenzy by rock 'n' roll rhythms, he stands around shyly and attempts, unsuccessfully, to join in with the general gaiety. He seems to represent the ignored, hidden side of the all-confident masculinity.

Pina Bausch's balancing act between dream and reality is embodied by these two male figures in *Auf dem Gebirge hat man ein Geschrei gehört*, broadly identifiable as leitmotifs. The piece comes over as an ambitious act of remembrance. The bodily signs seem to have been recalled from an ancient cultural store put together from diverse elements reaching across eras and nationalities. The physical language of a lost happiness, felt in the sense of lack and of terror, assembles its signs from across all cultures. This lends the moving, physical images a ritual, archaic power, striving for timelessness. However, the present is reflected in this work of remembrance, because it draws on the collective stores of age-old images. The history of unfulfilled desires, which also tells the underground history of the body, provides the thrust from the past which drives the current desires to demand fulfilment. This need piles up into a mountain of debts which the present is always called on to honour. Thus Pina Bausch's pieces report on the current state of need but also of the desire which builds up and presses against it. This seems like the attempt, undertaken by any means possible and at any cost, to remember the lost or forgotten formula for happiness. The deprivation this research uncovers is spelled out in universal terms: floating between dream and reality.

The harshness of the introduction is sustained well into the piece. Clearly delineated entrances and exits characterise the dramaturgical structure, quite distinct from the almost imperceptible interweavings and tessellations of previous works. This makes the differences between solo and group scenes contrast all the more explosively.

Thus in the first part the entire ensemble is driven on stage when Mendelssohn Bartholdy's "War March of the Priests" from his incidental music to Racine's *Athalie* strikes up at a belligerent volume. The stifled fear of the beginning tips over into hysteria; everyone rushes about, groups form, capturing a man and a woman and pressing them brutally together in a kiss. Soon the hustle and bustle is reigned in to a rowing-boat formation, in which everyone leans into the oars with all their strength, as if it would enable them to leave this battlefield of unfulfilled desires and brutality between couples. A woman remains alone, thrashes around like a fish on dry land; two others come to her rescue, rowing over on a mattress. The couple is captured again, and the men inadvertently find themselves in the trenches at war together on the front. A man uses a woman lying lifeless in his arms to hit another woman with. But as soon as the music ends the scene ends, like an apparition controlled by external powers.

Accompanied by gentle Purcell string music a woman in a pastel dress appears, smiles mischievously at the audience, presses her bottom against the wall and performs a half handstand, several times and with childish pride: a timid trick appealing for love and acknowledgement.

To counteract the loud destructiveness of group pressure, which sweeps in as if it were a societal inevitability, Pina Bausch uses small, gentle solo and duo actions which evoke mute resistance or natural innocence. Thus two women in little girls' clothes come on stage holding hands and smiling and start to turn cartwheels, without letting go of each other's hands: a powerful image of togetherness which stands at odds to the pounding mechanisms of constraint. A certain child-like directness is retained in these scenes: a spontaneity which will not surrender.

This sisterly harmony is immediately contradicted. A man runs through the auditorium, around the stage, vanishes among the passageways behind the stage, reappears, runs on and, increasingly out of breath, sings the old Yiddish song of the burning ghetto, *'s brennt, brider, 's brennt*. The action underscores the text in the simplest way possible. Then the scene ends, carried into a dream-like sequence. A solo violin gently begins a Russian mourning song. A large man enters, wearing a black velvet leotard, his hands held up as rabbit ears, followed by a woman, cowering behind him in a black pinafore, accompanying him like a dancing echo. Insecure he asks the audience "Are you laughing at me? Why are you looking at me like that?"

107

Coping with vulnerability is a way to break the cycle of fear. Anyone who looks danger in the face is not so easily threatened by nameless fears. Showing yourself as vulnerable also involves strength, from which resistance can be drawn.

In the motif of the hunt, already investigated in *Walzer*, danger is given form. Language becomes significant during one long sequence, otherwise playing a lesser role in this piece. Offstage a recorded voice explains the finer points of foxhunting, rehearses the correct imitation of the sounds made by quarry, which the ensemble, fearfully lined up against the wall, attempts to follow. What initially seems comic soon changes when the instructor delivers a frighteningly perfect imitation of "the death-cries of a dying hare".

People treat each other as if they are involved in a cruel blood sport. Lined up in a tight row on the ground as if sleeping, a group of women is gently poked by a man, as if he were trying to wake or rock the women. Soon another man appears, tells one of the women to stand up, slaps her, stuffs an apple in her mouth and pushes her around in front of him. Another man arrives, pulls the row of women apart, hits some of them, throttles them, kicks them and insists that they call him "uncle". When the women refuse he flies into a genuine killing frenzy, screams that he wants blood, wants to kill, to see babies burn: an outburst of destructive, masculine rage arising solely from envy of the women's stillness and unworldly peace.

An unbridgeable chasm seems to hold men and women in two equally unreal and inhospitable worlds; in a furious hatred born of desperation and of the dream-spent slumber of latent possibility. The tension the gulf generates is released in the violence of the stronger sex.

The rough and ready arena easily allows itself to be converted into a bizarre landscape. Fog makes the bare expanse of earth appear like a moor. The company falls into a hectic little revue dance, crawling on the floor to the sounds of Gerry Mulligan and Johnny Hodges' *Back Beat*, tormented and cheerful at the same time. A woman in her knickers, her dress drawn up against her stomach, stands at the front of the stage, pulls her hair and screams. The curtains open and close briefly, slicing the fog, while the action continues uninterrupted, not to be halted by any theatrical conventions, till the stage finally empties, the players coughing as they retreat.

Quiet conversations and isolated actions can be heard through the fog. Then a man appears, drawing a woman along behind him, singing loudly as if she wanted to banish fear or to make a protest.

The first part ends with subdued calm. For a long time a woman stands at the front in the middle of the space. A man comes and kisses her tenderly on the mouth. When she fails to react he leaves in disappointment. Another man arrives and colours her hair grey, making her age gradually in front of our eyes. We hear Heinrich Schütz's chorale from which the title is taken. The bathing-trunks man, now wearing a dinner jacket and a white shirt, announces the interval. The woman is still standing in the same position after the interval. When a person remains immobile in one place for so long, the passing of time is thrown back at the spectator, becoming tangible because it is not filled by any entertaining diversion.

In the second half, of a similar length, two dimensions cross; while the often brutal group dynamic gradually frays apart, new approaches are tried out in small duos and solos.

One man leads another, holding his outstretched arm, and hands him objects or places them directly in his hand, as if his partner were blind or too tired or as if he wanted to touch the almost unreachable things from a great distance. As soon as he touches something, he breaks off his searching gestures, apparently satisfied. Minimal dance movements gradually develop, their broken gestures sticking closely to the body, without gaining momentum. Finally the pair creates a walking dance; they show their front and rear sides, exploring simple movements while Fred Astaire sings *Maybe I Love You Too Much*.

A man and a woman stand opposite each other. He attempts to touch her, but she shrinks away in shock. Perturbed, he examines the spot on his own body where he had tried to touch her, but still doesn't understand.

A woman runs her hand around her neck, along her arm, strokes and rocks herself as if asleep, follows where her fingers point, measuring the space in each direction.

A woman dances entirely by herself in a red velvet dress while a man follows her, vaulting in pursuit of a slip of paper: dancer and acrobat, each on their own, yet still forming a pair.

The "blind man" is led in once more. This time his helper fetches him a woman in a pink evening dress whom he can offload his exhaustion on to and touch. She sings him a song, about "great" Germany and "little"

Japan, a sailor and a geisha who come together in a happy ending, while they tug and bite at each other throughout.

The eroticism swings between greedy attempts to consume each other and tender moves towards intimacy. Loving is also about colossal hunger. The great searching movement seems finally to have led to a partner with whom a joint reconnoitre of desire is possible.

This tactile intimacy continually leads to sparse, economical, precisely deployed group scenes. The men pass like classical ballet princes through the space, which suddenly loses its weighty gloom. A Caruso aria accompanies them, and the arena is suddenly transformed into a bright playground of desires.

A little later the men fill half the stage with firs and spruces. A woman turns a variety of backward rolls through the sawn-down, flattened forest; another makes herself a bed from cushions and sheets, repeatedly calls someone who doesn't come and quite possibly never existed. Lucienne Boyer sings *Parlez-moi d'amour*. When the music comes to an end the stage is cleared again.

The group format gradually dissolves. The fog changes the interior space into a landscape once more. Finger signs, like shadow theatre, flow into a dance. The woman in the pink dress is bound in bandages, packaged into a static mummy. For a moment everyone meets for a polonaise in which they all attempt to shake each other off. A boat is slid swiftly through the scene. The curtains open and close as if the phenomenon formerly known as theatre has finally gone off the rails. Little groups form, as if milling around at a party. A man proudly displays his blow-up breasts. A woman stands in a bucket of water and shouts. Another man makes himself a human drum kit, playing bongos on their bottoms. Then the theatrical evening pulls itself together, having sunk into chaos, the revolt of bodily signs is replaced by an "orderly" presentation.

An orchestra of elderly gentlemen enters; they take their places and begin to play as if at a small town bandstand, off-beat and imperfectly. A dancer is stationed next to them, with a sunken head as if she is required to listen to the offering with humility. Then she sways past, carried by a group of men like a gondolier, returns and starts again.

The fantastic arrives to break the progressions of events. In the moment of calm the impossible becomes possible. The force of the "improbable" bodily images verifies its own reality.

The piece ends as brutally as it began. Mendelssohn Bartholdy's music, this time painfully loud, again provides the soundtrack for a variation of the hunting scene from the first half, which sees the men and women driven to the limits of desperation. The couple is chased again, forced to kiss, till they are wholly exhausted and stand facing each other gasping, tired and sorry, with kiss-damaged faces.

We are not left with a gesture of reconciliation at the end. The reality which has taken over the theatre has long since pulled the rug from under our feet. Happiness cannot be summoned by force.

War no longer starts; it only continues. In *Auf dem Gebirge hat man ein Geschrei gehört* Pina Bausch captures it in distressing, unnerving images, simultaneously vulnerable and tender. Fear, danger and despair are given unmediated form. The experience of reality presents itself on the stage as intimate physical experience.

The tendency already seen in previous works is pursued further in *Auf dem Gebirge hat man ein Geschrei gehört*. When the curtain closes in the middle of the piece it is as if the apparatus' mechanisms have declared their independence, which reads as a sign that guaranteed narrative progression will no longer be provided.

The repeated proliferations of hysteria bring the theatrical signs into thorough disarray. The bodily signs, released from the ordering structure of conventions, attempt an uprising. This happens as if in a fairy tale; in the language of moving images, everything appears possible. The onset of the fantastic opens the door for a chink of light which illuminates the gloomy scenery of the present for a bright second. Against the dark background desires are lit up, tangible and close.

And just as an ancient knowledge of the deepest motives is crystallised in the symbols and metaphors of fairy tales, the Tanztheater Wuppertal's pieces seek to be read as an iconography of the conflict between the constrictions of what is given and the breadth of what is possible. The inner and outer worlds, past and present, collapse into one and become a moment.

## Two Cigarettes in the Dark

In the previous season, 1983/84, Pina Bausch had only created one new production (*Auf dem Gebirge hat man ein Geschrei gehört*). In the place of the first premiere that season came the revived production of the Brecht/Weill programme "Die sieben Todsünden". Having paved the way for dance theatre for over a decade, by developing two new pieces per season, each filling an evening, each produced under pressure of time yet of the highest quality, Pina Bausch and her ensemble approached the next decade at a gentler pace. Uniquely within the history of dance theatre she began a complete reconstruction of her repertoire, recapitulating year for year, right back to the early productions *Iphigenia in Tauris* and *Orpheus and Eurydice*. This preserves the energy of the dancers, who are challenged by the Wuppertal working methods in a completely unconventional way – with their whole person. It also allows us to retrace the development of a very special oeuvre.

Clearly no-one is in a position to undertake such a retrospective unless their work addresses subjects which transcend the topical issues of the day. Very early on Pina Bausch defined her work by saying she was interested less in *how* people move, more in *what* moves them. This is a precise description of both the premise and the object of her choreographic research. In uncovering the motives behind human action and skilfully giving them form, she reaches a territory far removed from any theatrical fashions. The pieces' essence, above and beyond ties to a specific time, is their direct access to the emotions, beating a direct path, and the spectator experiences this just as strongly in the renewed encounter with older works. Pina Bausch's dance theatre does not simply offer hints; movements do not merely suggest something symbolically. The shudder of horror, the misery of grief, the outbursts of revolt and the ultimate reconciliation with a difficult world unfold with uninhibited *élan* in the fantastical spaces. Those who watch do not only understand; they experience, suffer, hope and fear at the same time. While in the coming years the piece-by-piece revival was to wrest the work from oblivion and maintain an impressive ready-to-perform repertoire for the company, the ongoing research continued in parallel. Pina Bausch continues to create her bigger picture, extended constantly in a single "work in progress". In the process she loses neither her uncompromising viewpoint nor her radical form.

*Two Cigarettes in the Dark* begins with an abrupt confrontation. A door opens, and a woman crosses the austere, white space, stands at the front of the stage and in a chatty tone says: "Come on in; my husband is away at the war." With a smile, she spins on her heel and walks off. Accompanied by the loud, sonorous sounds of Claudio Monteverdi, a bony, fragile dancer appears and twirls her arms around in an anguished dance, as if she wanted to escape from herself but cannot. Her strapless evening dress continually slips down under her breasts; the fancy outfit and the inner need are not compatible. The music cuts out, but as she tries to leave the room, a man blocks her way. There is a short exchange of more restrained blows, like a dry run, before he then beats the living daylights out of her.

Hardly any other piece is so unreservedly terse right from the beginning. The times, it seems, are harder. Fear is on the increase. Fear has become a personal, physical reality, putting an ever greater distance between people. Using only eleven performers, like *Danzón* later, *Two Cigarettes in the Dark* has left the sex wars behind. Instead an unfriendly chill predominates, which seems to shut everyone off in solitary isolation. Even the stage evokes a cool sobriety. Nature, till now used to transform the stage into a fantastic playground of passions, is confined to a broad space seen through three large windows: in the middle a jungle of plants, on the right a desert of cacti and on the left a "sea" with fish in it. The space, accessible via various doors, presents the elemental landscapes as if they were museum pieces from a forgotten era, and like visitors or exhibits in a museum, the players lose themselves in this curious vitrine.

One of them stands on a wooden block, like a pedestal, and enjoys a cup of coffee like a living statue. A woman's naked torso serves as a projection screen for a holiday film, the scene mutating into a circus arena where "the little girl" is groomed and house-trained like an animal. People put themselves and each other on display: showing how they want to be but aren't allowed to be, how they are but cannot cope with being any longer. Behind everything lurks a latent aggression, directed inwards rather than outwards; a piece played out, as it were, with bated breath. The performers mostly appear muted; when they attack each other it is out of resolute anger towards themselves. In a polite, conversational tone the actress who opened the evening recites Brecht's pornographic poem *On the Seduction of Angels* at the front of the stage like a festive ode. As she is about to leave she is stopped by a man who hits out at her with fake gestures before taking a cautious, repressed peek at her cleavage.

Danger looms large when a man with an axe tries to entice imaginary hens to the slaughtering block, and the company dances in with broken wing-beating movements. However, at any moment the intense fear may shift into fairy-tale reverie. A woman is drawn in, wearing a wide tulle dress and sitting picturesquely on a carpet. A slender, ascetic contortionist joins her: princess and fakir on the flying carpet.

The atmospheric peaks and troughs are intonated, as in earlier pieces, by the music: dark, droning Monteverdi chords heard in such isolation they resemble serial music, contrasting with a few soft bars from a late Beethoven string quartet. In between these extremes we are taken on a tour of musical history: from medieval love songs to Johannes Brahms, from Henry Purcell to the obtrusive jolliness of child star Shirley Temple. Unlike in earlier works, pieces of music are rarely played to the end. The atmosphere changes too rapidly: fragile self-absorption overtaken by icy solitude or fake frivolity.

Despite its brittleness, this smartly dressed party attempts to maintain its composure: two men in dinner jackets stand at the front but the champagne they pour themselves leaks out of one man's mouth and fizzes all over the other's face. Neither loses control; the desire for a little glamour and happiness is too great. A lone woman stages her own personal, racy coach ride, driving non-existent horses along, briefly reliving childhood happiness in her imagination. Another wraps herself in a cloth and lies on the floor, rocking dreamily to a mellow French chanson as if lying in a hammock, wholly relaxed. But the excursions into the private never last long; a loving couple that swirls through the terrarium jungle in slow-motion is summarily shot by the actress. Passions, openly displayed in public, are theatrical exercises, as with a couple that lies panting in an armchair; they kiss each other, then pant again – mere show.

The women are wracked by an unnamed pain, often paralysed. They are carried in like lifeless insects, put down, then carried out again. They lie as if dead or dead beat on an expensive fur coat, roll themselves up in a thick overcoat, are winched up on a rope and then carefully lowered back down into the room. They do not utter a word.

The men become helpless and self-conscious when faced with them. They turn into timid voyeurs, squatting dumb on the ground and gazing. But amongst each other they repeatedly end up in competition. One of them paints areas of his body for the others to kiss him on, and an intimate warmth seems to be developing, accompanied by gentle Beethoven string music. Suddenly he pulls a plastic bag over his head and drags the other man to the ground by the hair in a showdown lasting several minutes.

Many are thrown into an unbearable state of tension. One continually meanders through the piece like an absurd clown. His clueless to-ing and fro-ing accelerates into an over-exaggerated marionette dance. At one point he cooks soup in his hat in a grandiose, angular harlequinade, at another he shuffles around like an apparently harmless idiot, then suddenly grabs a dancer and abducts her. Throughout he succeeds in maintaining the inscrutable equilibrium between gravity and slapstick which has distinguished all the great comics from Buster Keaton to Charlie Chaplin.

Only occasionally does an affectionate approach succeed, for instance at the end of the first half. A woman begins to dance very slowly, accompanied by live Tchaikovsky piano music. A man follows her, holds his hands around her protectively, forming them into two flapping wings which play around her body. While the soundtrack changes to a gentle mandolin concerto by Vivaldi they move fondly and poetically through the room. Two women in long evening dresses arrive, stand at the front of the stage for a long time before making the polite, friendly announcement: "It's time for the interval."

While the first half operates with sustained, almost unbearable tension, Pina Bausch allows more room for humorous interludes in the second half. Motifs are repeated or juxtaposed with strongly contrasting images. Moments of silent bewilderment and solitude are set against outbreaks of *joie de vivre*. The silent voyeur sinks himself in the "sea"; a woman burns cigarette holes in her fine dress; a man ties himself to a chair — actions of grim self-hatred, although this was really meant to be a glitzy event. Smiling complacently a man makes party preparations, acts dressing-up and making easy small talk. As he tries to leave, the fragile dancer seen at the beginning drives him back angrily with a chair, sits down, stuffs her cheeks furiously in an attempt to look better, less skinny and vulnerable. For a brief moment an outburst of joy succeeds in breaking through.

Then the men slide towards the front as if on skis, their feet thickly padded, wearing swimming trunks and sunglasses; to the sounds of a Shirley Temple song a woman hops like a child left alone to play. A heavily stuffed lady loses her way in the museum, followed by a repressed groper who she attempts to keep at bay with commanding rebuffs but with little success. Finally he nails her felt slippers to the floor and simply leaves her standing there, nonplussed.

A long night falls over the scene. Accompanied by the soft tones of medieval music, four women in long evening dresses rehearse handstands with silent determination, but for no particular reason, and bounce balls around noisily. Men arrive carrying a board which the women glide down with utter concentration, love and joy as if it were a children's slide. Everyone relaxes, sitting on chairs around the walls, smoking and waiting, letting time pass. A waiter offers drinks but no-one is thirsty.

The scene livens up once more. With loud, exaggerated sound-effects the actress performs a drama of sexual jealousy between a drunken couple, then white blinds drop down, obstructing the windows to the landscape and shutting the party up in a sterile room with no way out. Bent double on the ground in a solemn dance, five couples crawl in to the rhythm of Ravel's *La Valse.* They rock and sway forwards, with great difficulty, hit the walls and turn round. The waiter brings champagne while the party guests sway towards their downfall. One of them rolls out of the ranks, grabs hold of the waiter tightly and drags him down. The dance breaks up against a wall and gets no further. In despair the couples crawl together, hold each other, still continuing to dance and finally fleeing the room to the last, distorted bars of the idyllic waltz. After this catastrophe an icy stillness hangs in the air for a moment. Then the actress enters, bare-breasted in a long blue skirt, with a fag hanging from the corner of her mouth and forks in hay, piling briquettes, as if she was re-establishing normal working life in peacetime. Exhausted, one of the dancers leans against the wall. A dark song by Hugo Wolf plays: *Alles endet, was entsteht.* For a moment it seems as if the piece will dispatch the audience with this sorry swansong, then things take a final unexpected turn; the lights are turned up, the title song *Two Cigarettes in the Dark* plays, and with a gentle swing the company approaches the audience with outspread arms wearing stunning evening attire. The party is going ahead after all.

## Viktor

The stage set shows an enormous grave, its sides many metres high. A gravedigger is beginning to fill it in. Music blares out, and a smiling dancer in a red dress comes to the front of the stage – but she is armless, like a damaged sculpture. The crowingly cheerful, interminable Russian waltz music makes her smile become forced, and her big moment turns into an act of helplessness: she is a damaged person, exposing herself for a long moment, silently enduring her yearning for happiness. A man enters, covers her with a coat and leads her off. Carpets are brought in, and a woman is rolled up in them. As if lying dead on the ground, a couple is married by another man. The music drowns out his words as he cautiously turns their heads to face each other for the matrimonial kiss, but the lifeless bodies roll apart again. Another man brings in an unruly woman who sings and plays a finger game, writing signs in the air. He places her on the ground, attempts to suffocate the gentle signs of life under a thick winter coat, embarrassed and touched. No talking in the mass grave.

The music changes to a melancholy Bolivian lament. To the sounds of sighing and weeping a sitting dancer in a black pinafore dress jerks to the front of the stage with a wrapping, winding arm dance. There a threatening, ghostly voice announces: "My name is Viktor. I'm back." She is dragged back and begins all over again, undeterred.

The scene changes abruptly. Accompanied by up-beat New Orleans jazz the men carry the women to the front, the women sitting with difficulty astride their folded arms. Suddenly the spectators find themselves at an auction. A woman reels off the "lots" at a rate of knots while paintings, vases and whole cupboards are rushed in and out. The wholesale sell-off has begun; society has hit rock bottom. Despite its longing for ceremony and glamour, *Viktor* confronts us with an explosive anguish right from the start. The shattered society has fallen into the pit and can only dream its way out with difficulty. This is a view into an alien yet familiar world.

Pina Bausch has always incorporated the experiences gained on extended tours with her company in her pieces. There is something fascinating about the exotic in the midst of the familiar, while the exotic in turn makes the familiar, personal cultural landscape suddenly appear alien. From the finely judged distance this creates, the known is encountered, as if it had never been seen before: completely anew. The riotous switchback moods are underpinned in this piece largely by Italian music. Folk music from Lombardy, Tuscany, Sardinia and southern Italy dominates, interspersed with works by Pyotr Tchaikovsky, Antonín Dvořák and 1930s dance music. Amongst the changing atmospheres the men and women continually take one more shot at intimacy.

They are rarely allowed to succeed. A couple kisses passionately. A second woman worms her way in, steals a few blind caresses before she is viciously attacked. The next man attempts to kiss her from the side, his mouth askew, but she responds with nothing but hysterical laughter. A third man holds her in an intimate embrace while pouring water on them both. Later he stands stiffly in his coat and hat beside a different woman, looking at her politely from a distance, not risking a word. Another couple joins them; she performs a handstand while he casually checks the firmness of her thighs.

But it isn't only women who are viewed coarsely as mere meat. A woman carrying a man in her arms like a baby is interested solely in his monthly income. Another proudly balances a washing basket on her head. A man turns somersaults over her arm, but she is unimpressed by the unusual trick. Something seems awry in the relationship when, accompanied by strange brass music, they walk leaning against each other at an angle, supporting each other yet not truly connected. A couple sits next to each other in an icy stillness. Angrily, she snaps at him: "You're so talkative and so generous!" She aggressively recounts the grandmother's tale from Georg Büchner's *Woyzeck*. "And she is still sitting there, quite alone," she concludes caustically. But nothing can penetrate his silence, and they both leave. It is only later, when the tragic dancer from the beginning approaches him, that he finds a partner. He undergoes a lengthy metamorphosis, first becoming a careworn old woman, carefully eating a meagre meal, crumb by crumb. Then he peals off his headscarf and coat and stands snoring in front of a microphone, moving only reluctantly to eat a few biscuits which are put in his mouth, before suddenly waking up, gazing for a while at the woman and finally leaving with her, cheek to cheek, smoking a cigarette. Only a cautious approach has any chance of success, not a sudden, amorous ambush.

In their solitude everyone dreams of their big moment, but they never pull it off. Either it becomes a grotesque performance, as with the semiconscious woman in front of a microphone on top of whom various men place books, twisting her mouth into a smile. Or it becomes absurd, as with the man in a dinner jacket who saws up wood with elegant gestures using a circular saw. The dream of wealth is no compensation either. A woman busily pulls her furs out of the fridge and checks them over. Later she sits alone, smoking on a chair, her back to the audience, unwilling to be looked at.

They are all wanderers, travellers, longing to break out of the prison of their loneliness. Laid out like a corpse, abandoned by everyone, a man lies in the huge grave. His wristwatch wakes him from the dead. He shouts out a clichéd travel report, then breaks down in tears: "I want to sleep, eat!" A passing wanderer simply looks at him, helpless.

The dancing too is full of this bitter yearning. A woman ostentatiously stuffs raw meat into her high-heeled shoes, straps them on and does a slow dance to an extract from Tchaikovsky's *Symphony in B Minor No 6 "Pathétique"*. Suddenly she stops. Only once, right at the beginning does the company come together for a tightly-danced polonaise. While a woman laughs exuberantly and cannot be calmed, the line of dancers winds its way into the stalls. Rudi Schuricke sings "You are so magical".

Towards the end of the second half the motif returns, but the scene develops into a lonely hearts' ball. To the sounds of a tarantella, a group of charming, elderly men enter and give their coats to the ladies, who are chatting and doing their make-up. A grotesquely disfigured "lady" in drag appears and does various turns. Then the women are each made to stand on a chair, gather up their skirts, display their legs and tie ribbons in their hair, in front of a man. Satisfied, he paints stocking seams on their naked legs. Suddenly the scene turns. Accompanied by a melancholy Russian waltz the men now sit at the front of the stage and make themselves up like the women, who watch them, baffled, then begin a polite couple's dance with them after all. The elderly gentle men enter again and stand in a row. For a moment harmony prevails. To the sounds of *Puttin' on the Ritz*, the ensemble starts an elated revue dance, advancing to the front of the stage where, like an extension of the audience, the elderly gentlemen are sitting. But the bizarre "lady" sullenly shoos them all back to their starting points; the fun isn't allowed to get out of hand.

The individual pleasure in the body, which tries to break out in dance, is continually bullied into submission. In the second part, after the interval, the cowering, diminutive mother takes control, a surly old woman. She stares sceptically at two women, who run their arms pleasurably around their breasts, heads, mouths and shoulders. While a man measures out the room with gentle pole vaults and another, dressed as a belly dancer, wiggles his hips, she swiftly commands a squad of women to enter, who then parade past with rigid, heavy steps, their arms swinging vigorously to and fro. She corrects them gruffly, sending some of them back. Thus dance becomes either a chore or a lonely passion. A woman dances devotedly while two men hold a piece of cloth in front of her, smoking disinterestedly. Tired, she stops and lights a cigarette and is then lectured by the old woman. All her cheerfulness drains away, like that of the woman who hops around in a childlike circle to the point of exhaustion. Frustrated, the female dancer reappears drunk, swears at the male belly dancer and shouts at the audience to get lost. Undeterred the old woman leads in her all-female line-up; then everything degenerates into wild panic. Everyone runs around like headless chickens to an energetic march composed by the man who provides the piece's title, Viktor. They balance as if above a chasm, hold out ropes, scream, reel and lurch. Then the scene calms down and suddenly it is as if in a dream.

A woman is turned into a living gargoyle, her mouth filled with water. Two men wash themselves under the fine jet, then a woman. A younger man takes a shy look up a girl's skirt: she smiles. He confesses, stammering, that he can't imagine his parents sleeping together. Another woman receives ballet lessons from a weary teacher. The young man watches proudly, secures her arm and leg in an arabesque position, sits down beaming in front of her, so carefree he fails to notice that he has arranged the girl as if on a crucifix.

The calm is short-lived. The omnipresent old woman muscles in again, training a woman to dance. Another woman shouts as if she wanted to give vent to the other's despair, her head pressed between two stones. In a comic number, a man gets nowhere when he tries to make an order in a café; the three lazy, lethargic waitresses see all guests as insubordinate nuisances.

As if demonstrating the opposite of such unfriendliness, the women sit at tables at the front a little later, spreading bread rolls which they hand out to the audience smiling sweetly. Schuricke sings "You are so magical" again. A cheerful, relaxed atmosphere takes over. The elderly gentlemen meet in the background for their regular get-together. The women make a stab at happiness, to a Fred Astaire song; they hang from long ropes, swinging in elegant evening dresses, laughing despite the physical effort: "I'm in heaven."

The dominant old woman cannot permit this happiness; in an instant the music changes. Now she drills the men who have to carry out the same sequence as the women and are sent back in just the same way. In an interlude reminiscent of early cinema, a grandmother is murdered in her bed; darkness falls over the picture and everyone leaves. The screaming woman alone remains, the only one to offer a sign of her despair. As if crucified on a clothes-rail, the woman is led to the front. Two men mark out a precise, circling dance on the spot, to a guttural folk song, moving their feet accurately back and forth. It is as if the iron rules of an archaic rural life upheld by the old woman now apply again, allowing no deviance.

The disconnected old couple appears again. In a nasty voice, she rattles off the grandmother's tale at him once more. But nothing rouses him from his silence. They sit beside each other dumbly; no-one comes to relieve them from their double loneliness.

Having reached its end, the piece starts from the beginning again. We hear Tchaikovsky's *Pathétique*, and the smiling, armless woman stands at the front. Carpets are carried in, the dead couple lies on the ground and is married, all signs of life in the singing woman are smothered under an overcoat. The auctioneer runs swiftly through the lots, the dancer begins her difficult, sad sitting-dance and is then dragged back again. There follows a moment of complete silence. The entire ensemble sits with her, and the Bolivian lament plays again. Their heads hanging, they all rock towards the audience, but only the dancer herself swings her arms, expressing the pain of everything lacking, dancing her grief for what is lost and may never – who knows – be regained.

*Viktor* leaves its audience with no apparent consolation. The human beings on stage seem to be on the edge of an abyss, their existence under threat, from an external inferno or from inner collapse. With every piece the dancers perform their delicate balancing act anew, as if they wanted to say "only that which withstands panic and terror, endures utter solitude will last. Only the kind of joy which rises from a basis of withstood grief is valid." It is as if each individual's existence must first prove itself against the vicissitudes of life, accentuated to the extreme, in order to bring its true substance to light. In other words, undergoing the suffering caused by an imperfect world is an exercise which ultimately gives strength. When everything has been undergone, when the illusions have worn off and we can look at ourselves and each other as we are, only then can we stand our ground invincibly. This is a kind of self-confidence which leads to genuine freedom, unsullied by appearances, masquerade or self-deception.

Thus the bedrock of grief from which Pina Bausch's pieces grow is not a cul-de-sac of despair. It describes a woundedness which must be maintained and withstood, which does not let up till it has reinstated the happiness of being entirely at one with ourselves. In order to achieve this, the people in the pieces throw all their energy into the fire of their passions. They understand how to surrender themselves completely, without exceptions. This leads them through and out of the malaise, but only if they are honest and precise. This is the wisdom of old fairy-tales; a trust is reinstated that will buoy us up in life. Thus dance theatre fulfils art's age-old task of taking a close look at a situation, formulating its basic conflicts and at the same time reconciling people to it by taking a calm look at everything that is – including all the sometimes frightening facets and all the possibilities.

This is what the continual flirt with the audience in dance theatre seeks: to establish an understanding of the needs and desires we all share. Pina Bausch has said in an interview: "I am a realistic optimist."

## Ahnen

The new production of the 1986/87 season begins aggressively with an unusual choice of music. Out of the loudspeakers comes the stubborn beat of punk rock. When the lights come up, the stage shows a desert landscape, a forest of enormous, prickly cacti: a maze of human fears and desires, entirely harmless – or completely dangerous. A sea lion lies motionless on a sandbank in the background, as if stranded or just sunning itself. A languid punk in a kilt and leather jacket leads people in and positions them for a group photo: a man and a woman, both wearing leopard skin evening wear and cat masks; next to them a conventional couple in 1920s dress, a man with a lettuce, someone with a stocking over their head – various people who have nothing in common with each other, as if they have wandered into the cactus forest by chance or are a random group of travellers.

The loud rock music is replaced by loud chiming bells. A man dances a small solo in which his finger, pointing out into the room, continually turns back towards himself. Darkness falls over the scene. A woman comes past with a large bell round her neck. A few men lift another man up onto a chair and carry him, standing, like a figure in a procession. A woman comes, demonstrates a short Scottish country dance and is carried back out on a stretcher. The music changes again, mixing the insistent rhythms of a Jew's harp with the ear-splitting sounds of a pneumatic hammer. Two men do a simple foot dance to the music on the spot, holding their ground in the midst of the chaos. One woman trots through the scene, another wanders around in a long red ball-gown, amazed, between the cacti. In the background someone sets up a building site on the sandbank, wheels stones in and begins building a house which will never be finished.

It is as if someone has plucked these diverse individuals from various milieus and eras and sent them together to a desert, challenging them to cope. They simply carry on doing what they normally do, with the result that nothing quite seems to fit. They proceed as if on a free-form building site: build things, knock things down, but no-one knows what the overall plan is. Thus this piece too reads like an interim report from an experiment where various characters are brought together and allowed to collide repeatedly until their Babylonian incomprehension is shown up in absurd juxtaposition and opposition. The piece's title, *Ahnen*, could refer either to unknown ancestors or dark premonitions; this is left open. More often than in other pieces by Pina Bausch, the mood sinks into widespread bewilderment, dulled brooding. No-one knows what to do next; they can only remain where they are, stick it out, wait, or send out quiet signals.

Night falls on the scene regularly; all becomes calm, and gentle medieval and Renaissance music sounds out, as well as Italian laments. Hardly anything happens for minutes at a time. A woman arrives, sits at the front, rubs a bar of soap to a powder; another winds a damp piece of string from a bucket into a ball. A bed is carried in and ironed warm; food is cooked in a large cauldron – everyday procedures and work which serve to pass the time.

An American Indian sits silently in the cactus forest like a relic of a bygone era. The silence is something else which must be endured; no-one is, as Pina Bausch put it during the rehearsals, "to be rescued by language". The programme notes quote a Sioux Indian: "Whenever we talk of holy things, we prepare ourselves through ritual. One of us fills his pipe and passes it to the person next to him who lights it and offers it to heaven and earth. We smoke together. Only then are we ready to speak." If words are to acquire any weight at all, then this must emerge out of silence. Mostly, however, words are witnesses to absurd conversations at cross purposes; three men bring armchairs to the front, wrap themselves up in blankets and lie in a row next to each other as if in a sanatorium. The first, who has wide-open eyes glued to his eyelids, sings Carmen's aria quietly to himself. The second, a picture-book Frenchman with beret and obligatory cigarette in the corner of his mouth, translates the text ironically for the third man, who, dressed as a Chinaman, sits nodding sagely, appearing not to understand a word behind his fixed expression. Time stands still; the only thing uniting the three disconnected figures is a song about love which has sunk to the status of hackneyed pop. But the passion it extols is as remote as any possible communication between the three.

As always the couples' relationships are characterised by alienation. While the woman walks in amazement through the desert a man follows her quietly with a gift, but she takes no notice of him. When the partners do meet it is in a friendly yet malicious duel. With smiling faces they demonstrate how to rip each other's arms out, strangle each other by pulling and twisting their tongues, how to twist their eyes out of their sockets and how to gag each other's mouths. When they behave thoughtfully to each other it is then only in the manner of a man who stuffs a woman as if fattening a goose.

Love is unpredictable, as Carmen's song says, and cannot be held on to. But suddenly, when we least suspect, it comes back. In two rows, one behind the other, everyone dances an intimate, calm couple's dance, slowly swaying forwards, while one performer plays piano and another saxophone. It is like the end of a party, relaxed and gentle: a time when

124

it is possible for people to comfort each other, like the men who rub a woman with bread. Time to dress the wounds lovingly, like the woman who sticks plasters over a man's gunshot wounds. However, the short, intimate moments are always undermined by a nameless, insurmountable sadness.

A demonstrably rich, lonely woman is led in repeatedly throughout the piece. Wearing sunglasses and a headscarf, she sits at the table, prepared for her by a butler, reading old letters in silence, dwelling on memories like loves lost. Depressed, she holds a revolver in her hand and toys with suicide. At one point she fires a shot into the air, as if she wanted to release a sign of her despair. At this everyone breaks off their intimate dances and flees. The butler straightens her up again, whispers gently in her ear and calms her down. Later she sits at the table again on her own and wraps roses in damp newspaper, which will never be given to anyone. In the background the butler irons the crumpled paper dry again: a pointless cycle of activity in an empty time filled only with waiting.

Sometimes the grief throws a dancer into a reeling daze. She has to be supported and led; she loses her grip. These are quiet signs pointing to wounds we cannot talk about, from which we cannot "take refuge in language". They lead a man to a silent self-burial: he lays himself in a large aquarium, pours water over himself until he sinks under the surface like a corpse – a dead man, or perhaps someone enjoying the pleasant feeling of weightlessness in the water.

*Ahnen* contains many images describing the desire to settle somewhere and rest. A man carefully prepares a bed of hay. A woman lies down to sleep in the desert and is walled in by another; protected from all possible danger. This is more than just stealing off for a quick rest from the struggle for happiness; it is the unspoken desire to finally arrive in the world, to be able to relax there; with a sense of security which has been lost, no-one knows exactly when.

Since then life has become an inhospitable place; we are washed up in a desert, chased by the wind like a scrap of paper in a western-film ghost town. The women sit at the front, speak into the void, fold their arms in a coquettish dance, till a large model helicopter drives them all away with its roaring, rotating blades.

Peace is uncertain and continually threatened. The mood can switch at any moment. To the sounds of guttural African singing the scene builds up into chaotic hysteria. A man carries a burning tray; two others attempt to keep their balance, one standing on the other's shoulders; another tries to jump up at the wall through a burning tyre. The dancers run in from all directions, mark out short, hectic dances on the spot, and run away again. Only one woman remains unmoved while the long train of her dress goes up in flames, until the moment of madness is over and everyone begins to wipe things up, to remove all traces of the outbreak.

The only thing which works against attacks of inner anguish is humour. A man at the front of the stage does various charming hat tricks. Later, accompanied by rousing music, he does a mincing, fan dance in a tight red dress and goes on to tell a cat and mouse story with a brutal punch line: running away from the cat, in a panic, the mouse allows a cow to drop a cowpat on him. Unfortunately his tail still sticks out. The cat sees him and eats him. The laconically-delivered moral is that not everyone who shits on you is your enemy, and not everyone who gets you out of the shit is your friend.

The humour does not provide a solution, just a brief moment of relief in which, together with the audience, the characters can smile about how hard it is to cope with their constant emotional ups and downs and not to give up the search for love.

Thus *Ahnen* ends darkly and chaotically, as it began. The world is out of kilter, and grief has not been eased. The mood once more heats up into hectic anxiety. The fire curtain falls. On the narrow edge at the front of the stage, the crazy punk does gymnastics on a bar. People push and shove to get by. Then the curtain releases the stage again. Deathly sad, the man lies in the aquarium and floats. The women sit down again to rub soap and roll up the ball of string: life goes on.

In the programme, Pina Bausch's dramaturge Raimund Hoghe describes an anecdote from the rehearsals: "In a magazine there is a photo of an aging dancer who washed up in Death Valley, where she realised her dream of opening a theatre of her own. She painted her audience on the white walls. In the photo she stands in a red ballet dress in the valley of death, dancing in front of a tumbledown house." Pina Bausch's reaction: "It really is impossible to outdo reality."

126

## Die Klage der Kaiserin
Film

A slow, slightly off-key funeral march conjures up a melancholy atmosphere. It is a cold, wet autumn. In a park full of tall trees, a woman fights with a leaf blower while holding a revolver. Cut. Two other women walk their dogs calmly through the undergrowth. Cut. A bunny girl totters on high heels as if lost, increasingly tired, across a moist, ploughed field. Cut. Another runs through a dusky forest like a little girl and calls desperately for her mother. The bunny girl staggers, falls, stands up again. Old men in thick winter overcoats trudge through heavy, broken clods of earth. Two women in bathing costumes wait, freezing, at the side of the street. A woman walks past a greenhouse smoking, wearing only her underwear and a jacket. Another woman, a curious farmer in a swimsuit and head-scarf, carries a sheep and leads an obstinate goat along behind her. In an attractive, blue evening dress, one arm apparently amputated, a woman wanders through the forest, looking for someone or something. The smoking woman sits in the middle of heavy traffic, stoic and unshakeable. The old men carry crying babies through the forest. Gasping for breath, a man in a black suit digs up the field as if he had to hide something. All this is accompanied by the funeral march, like an endless lament.

It is late autumn or early winter. Pina Bausch's film, which she created instead of a new dance piece in 1988, develops its characters in a long exposition, establishing a plethora of individual stories. A dark mood lies over the piece, desperate searching movements, loaded with psychological tension, persistent brooding, self-absorbed expectation – waiting for something, we don't know exactly what. A theatre company has been washed up in the countryside, away from the city. Interior and exterior have been swapped. Where the charm of poetic displacement normally consists of bringing an element of nature into the opera or playhouse, this time the theatre troupe with its colourful costumes is displaced into an alien environment. In their mostly summery costumes they come across as vulnerable and lost or misplaced in the cold inhospitable landscape. Nothing fits together; locations and times have been swapped, have changed places. No-one maintains their original identity any more. But in perforated breaking-points at the collisions of convention, in the sharp

cuts and switches between moods, space and time is created for an inkling of what this expedition seeks to bring to light: the reverie for that lost
time when we could still be at one with ourselves and with the world.

The title *Die Klage der Kaiserin* (*The Empress' Lament*) is taken from a
piece of ancient Chinese music, *Zheng Yingsun* or *The Empress' Lament*.
The film is structured in the same way as Bausch's stage pieces. There
is no plot guiding what happens on screen. The story is dissolved into
many small episodes. The shots, mostly extended, draw the eye in for an
extended gaze at things, people and their search for happiness: a story of
fragments in contrasting cuts, which nevertheless deploys the expressive
means particular to film. Exterior and interior are juxtaposed in a free
composition; an intensely intimate close-up shows a crying face for several minutes, cutting to a full shot of a tired, laughing woman in a ballet
hall. Full shots of landscapes are followed by images of rain in some dark
place, neither inside nor out.

But the film also sketches out a topography of the company's home-
town, the city of Wuppertal and the surrounding area, the Bergische
Land. The faces of the city and of the people are effortlessly interwoven
with the poetic, inner images of an excursion into present day landscapes
of the soul. Outer and inner landscapes mirror each other, sometimes
distorted, sometimes enlarged, sometimes calmly restful. As in Georg
Büchner's *Lenz*, the landscape reflects a panorama of shifting emotions,
between grief and hope, desperate protest and relaxed endurance.

This is the film's field of tension, in which Pina Bausch places the
results of her investigations; not providing solutions, simply the location,
the proximity and distance between people, all precisely measured. Layers of motif are uncovered very gradually, for instance the solitary smoking woman, naked from the waist up, sitting with a patch over her eyes,
as if not wanting to see the world or not wanting to be recognised. Later
she stands in the bathroom, dials a telephone number, makes splashing
sounds with water, rustles paper, flushes the toilet, saying nothing. She
stands with a man, soaking wet on a rainy night, asks the camera what she
should do, where she should look; no-one answers. For several minutes
the couple stands there in silence with no-one to relieve or release them.
She meets the man later for dinner. With Tutankhamen's jewellery on her
head she describes how the pyramids were built, quite incidentally taking
off her clothes as she speaks. The man shows no reaction. In her despair

128

she hams it up, playing the role of a drunkard in front of a theatre curtain, croaking out lines as if in a fairy tale: "I'll come once more now, then never again. I'm not surprised that someone dies in front of his lover's tent. I'm only surprised when someone loves and stays alive. I said: 'You are my life.' She said: 'I'll end it soon.'" The hurt, it seems, runs deep, and can only be tolerated with the help of drink. Lurching around with a swinging bottle, the unhappy alcoholic staggers through a herd of sheep with a black lamb in her arms. Then she lies as if dead in the meadow at the foot of the frame. An indifferent sky stretches above her, high and wide.

The film continually insists on the need to bring love into the world, to free ourselves from loneliness. Life is like a struggle with a heavy burden. Trembling, a man carries a heavy wardrobe balanced on his back across a meadow. He stumbles, puts it down, loads himself up again, refusing to give up. He ties a baby to a tree by a long swinging rope, as if he wanted to place it in safety. Later the lone wanderer sits in the gutter, shaving himself to the pleasant sounds of gypsy music. Passing cars splash him with water: a washed-up tramp.

Being thrown back on oneself, waiting, brooding and dreaming all take on multiple forms in *Die Klage der Kaiserin*. A man stands in the rain, soaking wet in a tulle dress, while a drum beats out a relentless pulse. He lies in water, in snow, already half covered as if dead, or wanders through the woods, wearing wings on his trench coat, as in *Renate wandert aus*. Or he stands wearing a long tutu, made up like an aging ballerina, pressed against a wall while a model helicopter circles around threateningly in front of him. The dress flaps in the wind of the helicopter's blades; he doesn't bat an eyelid.

Sometimes we are simply afforded an infinitely long gaze, encapsulating all possible bewilderment in a few minutes but also capturing the strength of persistence.

A man is repeatedly shown sitting in a florist's shop, his body smeared with mud. He waits, smokes, then stands up, attempts a belly dance to the accompaniment of Arabic music and sits down again. Another man walks thoughtfully through an imposing old ballet studio, runs his hand tenderly along the barres. Later he sits talking to himself in a kitschy cinema, as if dreaming of very different times. No-one comes. A woman runs across expanses of snow, singing and playing the accordion in a thin summer dress, defying the cold and the loneliness.

Life is also a game, in which we are mercilessly sent back to square one, like the man scrambling through a blizzard in the woods on his knees who is dragged back to his starting point by two others. He starts all over again. It is tempting to slip into solitary acts of megalomania when, standing alone in the rain in front of a table piled with crockery, someone conducts an opera to themselves with grand gestures. Or we feel like the child screaming again and again for her mother. In an extended tracking shot, the camera runs parallel to her while she runs crying across the fields into the woods. Billie Holiday sings *Strange Fruit*, a blues song about the horrors of racial violence, a lament of the profoundest desolation.

Time and again, the film examines, via couples, how much intimacy people can bear, and how much distance they need to maintain. Young lovers appear in changing roles. In one scene we see a woman's beautiful, immobile face in close-up, while a man's voice utters soft loving words, teases her, pinches her nose. When, both wearing tulle dresses, they begin to touch each other, she is concerned solely that her dress is in place properly and that her make-up remains spotless; she is, in a word, unapproachable.

There is also an older couple that persistently practises their ingrained rituals. He continually has to help her float through the room, standing on his shoulders. She wants to fly, to experience happiness but moans at him the whole time, never satisfied. As if making a silent complaint, she stands with two naked children who clasp her tight and cry; later she sits on a revolving chair and is measured and photographed as if for police records.

Faced with everyday constraints and blunt rebuffs, all light-heartedness is lost. A boy is instructed in classical dance by a teacher, subjected to pressure with cruel reproaches. He doesn't fare much better with his elocution teacher, who abuses him with strict articulation exercises and dismisses him as a hopeless case. Only when he gets together with his friend, both beaming, and they perform a heartfelt dance, is there a moment of wholly uninhibited happiness. Smiling shyly, they sit in front of a feast, smile and don't dare begin to eat.

Only for a few moments does Pina Bausch allow us a glimpse of carefree lightheartedness: the dancers circle round on roller skates, men and women in elegant evening dresses, filmed from outside through brightly lit bay windows: an unreal, hovering party, uninhibited fun like at a children's birthday party. In another long take, accompanied by tango music, we see only the legs of a couple; they swirl, court and play around each other.

Despite this, *Die Klage der Kaiserin* is not a tough film. The music – the funeral march, recurring like a leitmotif, Latin and Arabic music, drums, tango, boogie-woogie and early blues – does not just hold and bracket the changing scenes together. It also provides a familiar-sounding aural carpet, reaching out to the spectator like a memory and offering consolation. It is old music, often traditional singing, which rises up from the past, combining with the dreamy, fairy-tale scenes to create an agitating, disturbing but never hopeless experience. It is as if they wanted to say that even the direst need, the profoundest isolation, can be endured, because there has already been someone in the past who withstood it and forged it into something new. That is the consolation – no quick fix – provided by Pina Bausch's pieces and by this film: the certainty that life can be endured and shaped. We do not need solutions. We only need to look carefully and risk taking an honest look at how things really are. *Die Klage der Kaiserin* reaches from childhood to old age. It is all there, all the time.


## Palermo Palermo


After a break of nearly two years in which Pina Bausch shot her film *Die Klage der Kaiserin* and continued the reconstruction of her stage works with revivals of *1980* and *Keuschheitslegende*, this co-production with the Teatro Biondo Stabile in Palermo was the first new piece since *Ahnen*.

When the spectators enter the theatre three-quarters of the portal has been bricked up. With a thundering crash, the wall falls back onto the stage, freeing up the view to a field of rubble, the stage unadorned and open right back to the firewalls. Created in the year of German re-unification, some people understood this as a reference to current events in the two German states. However, *Palermo Palermo* is not a self-indulgent gaze at the German navel; it has fully absorbed the atmosphere of the Mediterranean. In a further stage of its research into the origins of grief and a possible end to suffering, dance theatre tells of the tensions between rich and poor in southern Italy, of the inner anguish lying beneath the superficial exterior. When the wall falls, it is like a long-overdue collapse, after which something new becomes possible. Something static, apparently unshakeable, falls and opens up our gaze to interior spaces of true feelings. The performers have to fight their way between the bricks, some broken apart, some lying in neat patterns on the ground, balancing on them and taking care not to hurt themselves: an obstacle course of love and the lack of it, of the desire for intimacy and its disappointment.

These are the subjects which have always interested Pina Bausch, and now they are transferred to an Italian environment. Red dust falls from the cyclorama, as if blown in by a Saharan wind. The oriental-sounding tones of Sicilian folk music, Jews' harps, African singing, interspersed with chiming bells and cicada cries, transport us into an archaic, rural world. Set against this come the gentle, 1930s blues voices of the US Women Independent Blues Group, soft Renaissance vocal sounds and lonely violin motifs by Niccolò Paganini. Only very rarely does the dance music of Ben Webster and Georges Boulanger allow us to enjoy a more relaxed, upbeat moment. *Palermo Palermo* describes the tough fight for survival in a barren, poverty-stricken landscape. The scorching southern sun seems to weigh down on the scene, and just as the intense backlight accentuates contrasts all the more sharply, the actions take on a precise sharpness.

As soon as the wall has fallen, a woman in a cheap summer dress totters up to the front on high heels, angrily paints a cross on the ground and across her face, sketches out selected revue poses. She calls two men over, who have to take her hand, to embrace her — yet nothing satisfies her. Finally she gets them to throw rotten tomatoes at her, shouts: "More! In my face!" A desperate desire for love bound up with self-hatred. The woman is one of the key figures leading us through the piece. A little later she lies on the ground; a man wraps her hands and feet with rags; she crawls on all fours, bestialised, a disabled beggar. Downstage she tells the story of the suicidal man on the roof, whom the sensation-hungry mob urges to jump. It sounds as if she is making a grumpy complaint; she does not lose her bad-tempered irritability at all during the piece. Sometimes she sits at the edge of the stage like a silent threat, wearing a stocking over her head and holding a revolver; sometimes she lets a whole dress full of plates clatter to the ground, like a helpless gesture born of loneliness. Only once, accompanied by a soft, tender song, does a man join her dance, gently letting her fall to the side, fall back: a protecting and loving presence surrounding her.

Her opposite is a small delicate-limbed dancer in an austere, black dress: a widow who needs to be led and supported in her grief. She is first brought in like a small cowering animal, later introduced to a man, carried by five others who wedge a water bottle between her legs; in a silent protest, she lets the water pour out. Numerous resuscitation techniques are demonstrated on her, including mouth-to-mouth and chest pumping as if after heart failure. Then she too experiences a moment of solitary happiness, begins a small gestural dance, as if she wanted to pluck something out of the air, runs through the field of rubble, turns blissfully around and about, the Paganini violin music opening up a wide, empty space for her to move in. The self-hating woman arrives, now dressed as a lady of leisure in white furs, takes the "poor little thing" under her wing, presents her proudly at the front of the stage and takes her magnanimously away.

Essentially they all dream of something beautiful: like the man who plays a concert on glasses of water, dressed in a shiny, red satin dinner jacket. But they cannot hold the beauty of the moment any more than they can hold water, which the man pours into the hands of his sorrowful, rejected lover.

Essentially they all dream of love: like the woman who wets her lips, dabs them with sugar, then calls a man in to kiss her. Superciliously, she drops a coin on the floor as a token gratuity. He tops her cool gesture by dropping a whole sack of money at her feet. She leaves, unmoved. Sober and thoroughly headstrong, a woman translates a gypsy song about pining for a lover. All trace of passion is banished from her voice, which serves to make what is missing all the more blatant. The fear of loneliness drives the characters into absurd forms of covetousness. In a sharp tone, the same woman declares the spaghetti in her hand to be hers and hers only, not to be shared or borrowed. She shows it off, piece by piece, verbally labelling each noodle with her name. Later she arranges a collection of court shoes on a table in front of her and begins to list the things she is afraid of: locusts, naked legs, stones, snakes, dry skin, kittens and so on. Shocked at herself she runs away, screaming, only to return straight away, taking up her stilted conversation with another dancer again. Keeping one's composure is often the only refuge.

Poverty does not guarantee "natural simplicity", and wealth cannot protect from loneliness. In the light of real desire the world is an absurd place; a festive picnic is laid out among the bricks – with a white table-cloth, crockery and cutlery – all for a dog apparently, who takes great delight in eating it all up. To the sounds of a funeral march the whole troupe strides ceremonially to the front of the stage, and in a selection of pathetic gestures scatter rubbish about.

If the women are prisoners of an unnamed grief or anguished rage, the men too are lost in their own world; staring doggedly one of them stands, his face painted black, smokes, bites smoke rings out of the air. In order to impress a woman he monkeys around and runs after her. She then does handstand against the back wall, but when he jumps upside-down he is rewarded simply with the blunt reproach not to make a fool of himself. Another sets himself up as a solitary bachelor with a paltry locker and a television, on which he watches a film about sharks. He dreams of being seriously scary, but all he extorts for the time being is a cigarette, from a man he throws to the ground. Alone at home, wearing a boxing champ's silk dressing gown, he fries meat on an ironing board, meat which he literally slices from his arms. A woman pours water onto the ground for him, and he practises swimming on dry land, to the sounds of Grieg's dramatic "King's Song" from his incidental music for *Sigurd Jorsalfar.* Then he sits alone again and burns a newspaper. Later, posing as a mafia godfather, he lets other men kiss his hands, but the most dangerous thing he manages to do is shoot a few tomatoes.

Essentially they all dream of love. They lie in the field of rubble and stick their outstretched index fingers in their trousers, under their pullovers and blouses as a gesture of horniness. Sometimes, in the quieter moments and in the dances, they gain an inkling of what it might be like to be truly relaxed. Accompanied by *The Empress' Lament*, a piece of meditative medieval Chinese music, the widow paints flowers on the floor. Another woman sits at a table with a cup of coffee, stirs it carefully before taking several sips, then swallows first her ring then her husband's in a calm, controlled mourning ritual. The music changes to ostinato Jew's harp rhythms, like an eternal pendulum beating time. Wearing a long evening dress, the distressed woman is lifted up by a man; she kicks her feet together lightly in the air. Another floats around horizontally, carried by a man, pushing herself off from the wall like a jumping frog.

134

All the men take the widow, let her run through the air and walk over their hands, which they lay on the ground forming a path; they cradle her on their feet: this weightless ease creates an image of grief and simultaneously one of peace, tranquillity.

This image, with its dynamic, earthy power, constitutes the end of the first half, which Pina Bausch brings to a close in a way similar to *Bandoneon*. A Sicilian fisherman's song is blasted out, raw and guttural. Stage hands have already begun clearing the stage, the bachelor dressed like a grotesque ring card girl announced the interval by holding up a sign, but the dance goes on. With stabbing, cutting gestures, first alone, then in pairs, the dancers maintain an apparently inexhaustible pleasure in movement. This looks like a series of duels, but it also represents shared affection, born of a primal energy.

As is often the case, the second part repeats and develops the motifs in a scherzo. It begins lightly, to the sound of blues, as a woman in a salmon-pink cocktail dress catches a ball in her dress, turns amusing contortions chasing after perfume she has sprayed in the air, finally rolls in a huge fridge and explains how as children they used to preserve snow right into the summer. Two smiling men in trench coats prepare to go out, rub lemon juice in their hair. Another tries lots of little tricks, blows a feather in the air and catches it with a pair of tweezers. Another lifts the entire table to his mouth in order to empty a glass: simply flirtation with the audience, little conspiratorial winks.

Suddenly the theatre mutates into a concert hall. Five old out-of-tune pianos are rolled in, on which the performers cheerfully bang out the first bars of Tchaikovsky's *Piano Concerto in B flat Minor No 1*. Then the women form themselves into a strict, rhythmic group dance, grasp their hips, run their hands through their hair. Gradually the mood dies down; an oppressively hot summer night sinks over the scene, and only the tense noise of cicadas is heard. A man paints his finger nails, goes to the back, takes his clothes off and washes. Another dips his shirt in cold water and puts it on, still soaking. Then he attaches several candles to his arm and plays *Stormy Weather* on the saxophone. The woman with the sugary lips lets herself be kissed again and pays; she washes her pearls, gets members of the audience to kiss her palms and gently dabs the sweat from the spectators' foreheads. The mood in the theatre becomes extremely intimate and straightforward, and the spectators are included in this cosy atmosphere. All pressure of expectation, all animosity, has subsided, and for a moment we can relax from the daily struggle.

Then the lights come up again. Arm in arm, and to the sound of a funeral march, the company walks to the front of the stage balancing apples on their heads, with a grief which remains contained and doesn't break out, in a mood of menacing seriousness. Then a festive bagpipe tune plays, and everyone hops along the front edge in a bent-over, broken posture. With hanging heads, they fold and unfold their arms and legs, and the triumphal music contrasts with their posture, which is utterly devoted to its grief. Workers come in and sort out the bricks; blossoming trees sway down from above the stage, their crowns inverted. This is how the piece appears to end. But just as the applause breaks out a dancer comes onto the stage and in an intimate, conversational tone tells a story about geese who could only rescue themselves from the fox by praying for mercy. He ends his story on a positive note: "And they are still praying today. Good night." We sit, united almost in complicity, in something "which we can smile about together," as Pina Bausch once put it.

Her pieces continually consist of attempts at love, not as the distant goal of all desire but as an omnipresent possibility. They describe the fear and the pleasure of being wholly in the world, with all our senses: awake. Those who can come to terms with themselves, they say, who can accept themselves as they are, have arrived at the source, the origin of all movement. This is not to be found at a point in time; its effect transcends time.

## Tanzabend II (Madrid)

A bare, snow-covered landscape, the space opened right to the firewalls again, ending in a black wall of steel. Only later does a forest descend from above the stage cyclorama, and slides – of blossom, mountains, desert and the sea – colour the pallid field of snow. Once again the Tanztheater Wuppertal is on a journey into inhospitable territory. And once again, what really matters is not the goal or the completion of the journey; this is an open-ended process. The important thing is to be travelling, to col-

136

lect finds and attempt to re-order them according to the laws of free composition.

The atmosphere of the piece, a co-production with the city of Madrid and its Festival de Otoño, is created in the contrast between the oriental, sensual sounds of Morocco and Egypt, a murmuring shaman's voice from central Africa, laments from Spain and Italy, soft Brazilian songs and medieval European music. The collage spans a wide range, making use of sharp visual and aural contrasts: between southern sounds and the icy northern landscape, between stylish self-absorption and outbursts of manic, at times self-torturing dance. The mood is calm, solemn. The landscape is like a topos of inner sensibility; stories of survival in the ice. Within this, the company explores the familiar subjects: poverty and loneliness, the fleeting happiness of intimacy and warmth, and the unbearably long moments of bewilderment, the absurd tangles of everyday life and painful moments of despair.

The piece begins with an explosion of short, splintered scenes. To the sounds of John Dowland, snow lightly trickles from the sky, individual performers enter the stage. A woman collects money from the audience in a piggy bank, another drops a stone, almost hitting her foot. In the middle of the snow a freezing man tries to sell a handful of personal effects, which no-one buys; another offers the audience a glass of champagne. Poverty and wealth, need and excess exist side by side. A woman dips her skirt in water and puts it back on, soaking wet. Two women in evening dresses suddenly lie face down on the ground as if dead, but a man comes over calmly, helps them stand up, and they leave. A fragile-looking dancer crawls on all fours through the snow till she hits the portal wall and tries to crawl on nonetheless. Here too a man comes along and carries her back to her starting point. All troubles, moments falling out of line, are silently rectified. The woman starts again from the beginning, undeterred, blind. At the front of the stage a story is told about a particular type of fly which lives in hippopotamus's eyes, feeding solely on their tears. In the same way, dance theatre's real basis, its fertile ground, is grief: an unquenched (and perhaps unquenchable) yearning to exist quite peacefully and in relaxed serenity in the world, without having to fight. But there is, at best, only a hint of this, an inkling, in the poetic symbols of dance theatre where unbelievable things occur as if they were a matter of course.

The mood switches. Accompanied by a reverberating roar of singing, the women squat down in a row, then fall over, curled up like little dying animals. Two men quickly drag a ladder to the front; a woman climbs up it as if she wanted to get over the imaginary fourth wall into the audience, to break out of the prison that is the stage.

Soon the scene calms down: in falling snow, to the sounds of gentle singing, a polar bear pads in, looks around for a moment, then turns back round. As so often with the animals in dance theatre, the bear appears like a dumb yardstick against which the hectic, sometimes hysterical human activity is measured. From the hippopotamus in *Arien* to the crocodiles in *Keuschheitslegende*, the animals are always silent witnesses to human quests, fortunate or unfortunate, with which they have absolutely nothing to do. Unlike the humans on the stage (and in the auditorium), they are able to simply exist. They do not question anything, and so they do not worry about anything. It may be that "nature opens her eyes through human beings" (Ernst Bloch); that nature becomes aware of itself and awakens into consciousness through the human race. However, the price for this is the expulsion from paradise, the loss of that sense of security which once allowed people to be at one with the world, undifferentiated from it. Ever since humans left their ancestral home, their natural roots, they have been at the mercy of a desire which originates in the past but can only be fulfilled in the future. They must first recreate the happiness of being wholly in the world and connected to it.

It seems as if the raging charges to the front of the stage, the hysterical outbursts and dumb, dogged struggles with ourselves all lead to one point: when the rage has been exhausted and despair has evaporated, peace and tranquillity will re-establish themselves. We can finally exist in the world without questions, without baggage.

Dance is an eloquent medium in both cases: for the struggle just as for awareness and oneness. It allows the pain to be experienced physically and intimately, and expresses its evocative power in the expansive, broad-ranging *tableaux*. More than simply being another example of dance theatre, *Tanzabend II* (*Dance Evening II*) is a piece about dance itself. Like an endless ostinato rhythm, dance weaves through the piece with solos, partner dances and calm ensemble moments full of tenderness. Accompanied by the soft murmur of Brazilian music, the men form a line and begin a small hand-gesture dance. The women insert themselves into the gaps, finally coming out in front of the men; they allow the gestures to play around their bodies, lie in front of the men; they climb on their shoulders, sit between their legs and let themselves be rocked and swung pleasurably in time to the music. For a moment all the sharpness gives way to a friendly, cheerful competitiveness. A delicate eroticism is introduced, for instance in a woman's solo where, to Arabic belly-dance music, her arms gently winding around herself, she examines her body in the midst of a projection of enormous flowers, filling the floor and back wall. In a further scene two dancers decide on the moves for a duet like a pair of schoolgirls, dressed in short, shiny, satin petticoats; they let their hands run down their bodies in delight and, to the sounds of swing music, walk towards the front making revue gestures, then leave again giggling.

The dances of loneliness on the other hand are hard, fast and angular. Accompanied by the smoky whisper of an African shaman, a man bends forward and lets his hands circle his knees, ventures a little way out into the room, turns his legs inwards. Another man's crouching dance continues where he leaves off. He experiments with large, outstretched strides, sinks into the splits, gets up again, as if he wanted to measure the room with his body, setting out to try different directions, making frequent starts but never really getting anywhere.

The woman on all fours repeatedly begins her crawling walks until a man sets her down in the middle of the room. In silent anguish she dances out her rage and self-hatred. To the sounds of an Italian lament, its tune played by a lone violin, her hands turn into slow-motion claws, pulling at her face as if she wanted to remove a mask. Other women are brought in; they crouch, run their hands round their stomachs and hearts, point to their mouths with their fingers, their chests, and are taken out again. Gradually this develops into one of the longest sequences in dance theatre. Snow falls again. The music changes to gentle Spanish Renaissance strings. The women come and go, stand on the spot, wind their arms around their bodies again as before, swing their hips with a gentle sway, jump a few steps forward, fall backwards, are caught: many solitary dancers in a pallid half-light, defending their territory in the middle of the snow. It is like a danced meditation that finds no end. Time seems to have stopped, nothing can deter the women.

A man lugs a stove in, cooks and clatters with pots and pans. He drags a bathtub in and then straight out again. Another woman places her leg between two halves of a baguette and tells a story, but the dancing women calmly follow their own rhythm. It is as if we are in a fairy-tale time which has withdrawn from all the noise outside and retreated inwards. This is where wishes are kept – in a safe place. This is where dance stands its ground.

Before time finally seems to stop for good, the ensemble forms one more group image. The men carry the women rapidly across the stage, letting them run through the air. Then all we hear are the isolated chimes of a bell, with long pauses in between. Two women sit at the front and wait, letting time go by. Another comes and rolls herself up in a plastic sheet as if to sleep. Another removes lice from her hair, has a makeshift wash over a bucket, puts on men's clothes, court shoes and walks around with her breasts exposed, holding a hat against them. The entire ensemble calmly enters the snowy landscape; they sit on the ground and mark out a sparse dance using only their arms, joggling towards the front. Very slowly the bodies sink down to the ground in a dying dance, till nothing more moves, and only the rhythmic pulse of time can be heard. The woman with the sheet rolls around among the lifeless bodies, solitary, as if in a body bag. Projections light up the ground and the bodies: a cloudy sky, a snowy landscape, a desert, snow-topped mountains, a field of corn, flowers, wind-fluted sand, a southern landscape by the sea. Slowly everyone stands up and leaves for the interval.

*Tanzabend II*, influenced by the 1991 Gulf War, takes the time to create a long *memento mori*, holding up an image of all possible catastrophes, in a forceful but quiet, unspectacular way.

The second half delivers contrast, creating an upbeat counterpoint to the first. In a thick forest the men dance closely together, while one of them sings Cole Porter's *Night and Day* with piano accompaniment. Slowly they retreat, bent slightly forwards, take up their formal dancing positions again and hold their balance in a tight group. When they are not dancing intimately with each other, they act like suburban Casanovas in front of the women: posing in bright orange suits with two bunny girls, adopt heroes' poses to drink beer, loiter enticingly in their pyjamas with two champagne glasses. They carry out grotesque suicide rituals, such as hitting themselves with a dumbbell and theatrically falling onto cushions, or passing a greased bottle around between each other's hands. Only one remains silent and lost, continually wandering through the woods with a lit candle looking for something. At one point he stands at the front like a bewildered clown, wriggles around, speaks mutely and disappears again.

The women are even quieter than the men, painting their legs and faces black, like symbols of mourning or to mark certain points on the body. In a "moment of truth" one of them pulls shoulder pads and breast padding out of her dress, removes her false eyelashes and wig and wipes the make-up from her face: she wishes to be seen as she is, without a mask.

The dancers are all under the thumb of a surly older woman and her assiduous assistant: a parody of the choreographic profession. In the first part she was draped in an armchair like a grotesque corpse, her head fixed to a stick with a string attached to her mouth. Now her assistant has to translate her brusquely delivered corrections to the zealous dancers. One of them always has to perform in front of the others, but none of them pleases her; they are all replaced. The critical old lady is never satisfied. Theatre too simply represents pressure: to be meaningful, to entertain, to demonstrate skills. And there is always, it appears, someone moving the goal posts and pointing out inadequacies.

With this image, the piece ends, almost incidentally. The belly dancer makes a final appearance, is constantly interrupted by a man, corrected, never allowed to stop, forced to repeat her dance, till it has lost all poetry. Finally the ensemble comes onto the stage for the curtain call, ending the scene.

The images and dances stay with us for a long time, describing the yearning for a very particular freedom: in the women's endless solos, they wind their arms around themselves as if they wanted to be certain of their bodies, their breasts, their legs, torsos, heads. However, it is as if they never emerge from this silent experience of themselves into the freedom which the arms clearly seem to want to grasp. When they seek to widen the circle, they only return to themselves and punish themselves with crude decapitation gestures. The rage is as great as the yearning to break free. The timeless rondo is a dialogue on the spot with the individual bodies, not yet concluded, and which cannot move out into the surrounding space.

First comes the return to ourselves, then the journey into freedom.

## Das Stück mit dem Schiff

A stranded group of individuals, run aground somewhere on a sandy, rocky beach which rises as it extends back to the depths of the stage: atop it sits the ship which presumably brought the travellers here. Once again the aftermath of a catastrophe is evoked on stage. And again the voyagers of dance theatre find themselves in a foreign country in which they have to get their bearings.

Pina Bausch continually pulls the secure, familiar ground from under her figures' feet, placing them in fascinatingly beautiful or wasted and abandoned landscapes. Here they must first get back on their feet, as the perspectives have been reversed. Just as the stage is occupied by nature, the outside moving inside, the performers must follow suit, turning their feelings inside out. An upheaval has occurred, leaving them on the edge of an abyss. They are faced with stark alternatives: downfall or survival. This is what makes for the excitement and power of dance theatre. Not only does it free dance from the shackles of superficial beauty, it reaches the existential questions beneath the apparently harmless surface. Dance theatre's barefoot expeditions are not embarked on out of choice; they are emergency undertakings in the aftermath of a recently survived crisis. This leaves the travellers stranded in places no-one has yet set foot on, in fantastic, inner locations, as frightening as they are enchanting.

In a foreign land we behave more cautiously and are more alert. Uprooted from the familiar rituals of a safe everyday life, we notice things, are sensitive to nuances and shifting moods. We see and hear, smell and taste and touch an unfamiliar world, experiencing things the way only children do: everything becomes new again, as if never seen before. Our impressions are stronger and have a longer lasting effect. The performers explore the new land with carefree charm and, confrontational though they are, a great deal of vulnerability. Because they do not claim to know more or to be better than anyone else, they invite the audience to follow them into the magical space and, perhaps, to discover themselves along the way.

*Das Stück mit dem Schiff* (*The Piece with the Ship*) spirits us away to a steamy tropical region such as the Amazon Basin, the origin of the sounds we hear: animal cries, birdsong, the swishing and dripping of rain, interspersed with smoother and rougher music from Latin America, India and Africa. Like foghorns sounding in the rain forest, the sad, still moments are accompanied by arias of Georg Friedrich Händel and Christoph Willibald Gluck, by music from the Renaissance and the Middle Ages.

A few extended accordion chords are the only thing heard at first. The piece begins with various solos and duets, each carrying another need, another yearning, within them. A man arrives with a woman hanging round his neck, who slowly slips off. He restrains her as she starts to crawl forwards on all fours; they move together, a curious tandem of man and beast. He continually appears with her and with other female partners, supporting them, attempting to console them, but the women are inconsolable. Another pair crouches close together on the ground in a swaying dance. A man goes nonchalantly past, throws a banana skin away, then slips on it himself. Accompanied by an aria from Gluck's *Alceste* a woman dances on the spot wearing black, makes backwards rowing movements, holds her head in her hands, spreads her arms out like wings, but has to hold her heavy head again. Her attempts to fly are doomed to failure. Another follows her in a colourful summer dress, hides her head, flings her arms out into space, encircles her breast tenderly with her hands. Then she stands there for a moment, we hear and see her breath; she has stood her ground.

When they are not weighed and drawn down to the ground by grief, the women act as if imprisoned in a beautiful sleep. One of them sits on the sand in a lavish evening dress, stands up and draws small hand signals in the air, creeps forwards like a lurking, clawed animal – all to the sounds of soft Renaissance music which creates a somnambulistic sense of safety.

Sleep resembles the desire to finally arrive, to unwind. A man prepares a meticulous bed made of blankets and rolls himself up neatly in it. Much later he is given a pendant figure when a shelter is made for the sitting dancer out of branches, and she lies down for a long sleep, as if she felt wholly safe in nature, at one with it. The image is like the premonition or the memory of a sense of security which has not yet been found. In the meantime a man practises survival by putting his head in a bucket of water and holding his breath for an interminable length of time.

In contrast to the grief, open arms are raised to the sky in longing – in a woman's solo or a man spiralling downwards and shooting upwards. In this volatile situation the mood is one of irritation. A woman brusquely demands a light for her cigarette from the audience. Two men fight a short duel in which they repeatedly place an arm on the other's shoulder and knock it off again. Another man pushes a dancing woman back with a matter-of-fact expression, bit by bit, till he finally succeeds in banishing her completely from the stage.

Occasionally, and only for short moments, the desire for intimacy is fulfilled. A woman collapses in the arms of a man whom she has called over, applies make-up, places a cloth over her face and walks to the wall, blind, leaning against it as if for protection while a soft Italian lament plays. He kisses her from her hands right up to her mouth, draws her into a passionate kissing dance, then he leaves. Another man comes in, lifts her up, turns her round, follows her every move and lies down under her to break her fall, but their individual movements somehow fail to fit together. She hesitates, he shouts at her to carry on. Her original partner tries to cheer her up with a stupid party joke, but she remains unmoved. The brief dream and the homely security are over. Furious, he takes a seat among the audience.

Later we see how shaky the ground is on which the performers must tread in their expedition: in an anguished solo a man continually falls, waves a wobbly arm, raises his heavy head, but then falls backwards into the void again. Soon after, in contrast, another man stands motionless on two bottles placed on a table: a triumphant, solitary balancing act. Then the dancer leads the other men in the piece's first ensemble dance. In a line, one behind the other, they raise their arms in a *port de bras*, letting their heads fall into their necks; the women step into the gaps and the very unsteady line moves slowly forwards. They would love to fly, to release themselves from the weight of the ground, from their grief, like the woman whom four men lift up off a man, lying prone like a human launching pad. But attacks of weakness continually push them back down to earth, where after a further solo the dancer wakes up, goes over to a sleeping woman and licks her neck like an animal. She sways and dances while he coats her in a refreshing mist, spraying moisture from his mouth. The sound mingles with the lovely, forlorn Gluck aria, but all efforts lead to nothing. Equally lost, another dancer wraps her legs and abdomen tightly in a plastic sheet and practises various ballet exercises.

Suddenly, however, all the suppressed pleasure in dancing is condensed into a powerful poetic metaphor. Latin American pop mixes with the

144

◁ *Le Sacre du printemps* (Malou Airaudo)  |  *Blaubart* (Aida Vainieri, Mariko Aoyama, Ruth Amarante, Cristiana Morganti, Julie Anne Stanzak, Barbara Hampel)  |  *Blaubart* (Hans Beenhakker)

*Bandoneon* (Dominique Mercy) | *Bandoneon*

*Nelken* | *Der Fensterputzer* (Beatrice Libonati)

◁ *Arien* | *Rough Cut* (Silvia Farias) | *Rough Cut* (Ruth Amarante, Pascal Merighi, Michael Strecker)

*Auf dem Gebirge hat man ein Geschrei gehört* (Helena Pikon, Pascal Merighi)

*Renate wandert aus*

*Viktor* (Anne Martin, Ed Kortlandt)  |  *Le Sacre du printemps*

*Le Sacre du printemps* | *O Dido* (Fernando Suels, Jorge Puerta Armenta, Azusa Seyama, Cristiana Morganti)

*Bamboo Blues* (Pablo Aran Gimeno)  |  *Vollmond* (Julie Anne Stanzak, Rainer Behr, Jorge Puerta Armenta, Michael Strecker, Fernando Suels)

*Nefés* (Na Young Kim, Nazareth Panadero, Ditta Miranda Jasjfi, Melanie Maurin)

*O Dido* (Julie Shanahan) | *Palermo Palermo* (Andrey Berezin)

*1980* (Meryl Tankard) | *Arien* (Josephine Ann Endicott, Christian Trouillas)

*Er nimmt sie an der Hand und führt sie in das Schloß, die anderen folgen* (Lutz Förster,
Mariko Aoyama) | *Für die Kinder von gestern, heute und morgen* (Helena Pikon)

◁ *1980* (Anne Martin, Jean–Laurent Sasportes)  |  *Masurca Fogo*

*Keuschheitslegende* (Gary Austin Crocker, Anne Martin, Jan Minarik, Beatrice Libonati)

*Ahnen* | *Walzer* | *Ten Chi* (Kenji Takagi) ▷

*Walzer* | *Nur Du* (Nazareth Panadero)

*Le Sacre du printemps* (Ditta Miranda Jasjfi, Andrey Berezin) |
*Die sieben Todsünden der Kleinbürger*

◁ *Palermo Palermo* | *Die sieben Todsünden der Kleinbürger* | *Café Müller* (Pina Bausch)

*Two Cigarettes in the Dark* (Josephine Ann Endicott, Jan Minarik) | *Kontakthof*
(Anne Martin, Kyomi Ichida, Dominique Duszynski, Anne Marie Benati, Nazareth Panadero)

*Kontakthof* (Jean-Laurent Sasportes, Nazareth Panadero) | *1980* (Hans Dieter Knebel, Vivienne Newport) | *Komm tanz mit mir* ▷

*Komm tanz mit mir* | *Die sieben Todsünden der Kleinbürger*

Stück 2008 (Helena Pikon)  |  Stück 2008 (Julie Anne Stanzak, Daphnis Kokkinos)

*Tanzabend II (Madrid)* (Nazareth Panadero, Julie Shanahan) | *Palermo Palermo*
(Azusa Seyama) | *Ein Trauerspiel* (Barbara Hampel) ▷

sound of surging waves. The company stands high up at the ship's railings and rehearses *ports de bras* and *cambrés*. Like staggering passengers in a raging storm they wave their arms in rhythm. Piercing animal cries are added to the mix. A transparent sheet with water running down it shuts off the stage, blurs the picture as if we are travelling through a monumental storm. For a moment, ballet is not only a drill; it becomes something to hold onto at a time of direst need.

Then the picture fades. To the sounds of soft hurdy-gurdy music the man wanders around carrying the crawling woman, unsure where to deposit her, how to console her. A solitary woman on the railings is shaken by an hysterical fit of laughter. A man's vest is filled with sand till he stands with a fat, pregnant stomach while the sand trickles out again. He drags a small boat on stage and lies in it in order to dream. The muffled sound of didgeridoos blares out like foghorns in a sea of disorientation. The men arrive, take each other by the hands and dance a polonaise in a rocking step. The women join them and for a long time they circle each other, their paths crossing. Then a man's voice intones a Lithuanian prayer, and it is time for the interval.

The second half begins with a storm, flickers of lightning and booming thunder. During the stormy noises the shipwrecked people lie on the beach, apparently sleeping. The storm soon passes, and a brighter atmosphere takes hold. We hear a woman's voice singing a gypsy song, and a man dances, increasingly energetic, stepping back and forth, till three men help him dance up the wall in a brief flight. With much *joie de vivre* a woman circles her head with her hand in a solo dance, while the last rumbles of thunder die away in the background. More and more dancers appear, running in circles, spurring each other on. The scene builds into a boisterous beach game. The men lie at the front of the stage, push themselves back away from the audience with a jump, and are thrown back like frogs by the women. People drag each other and throw each other back, as if into the sea. Scottish pipes sound darkly, and suddenly the scene changes again to a sorrowful moment in which, as in the beginning, the woman hangs round the man's neck, spun around by him in speedy swirls, while she runs helplessly through the air.

The uproar soon calms down. Birds' mating calls are mixed with the sound of dripping rain, and the company playfully tries out ways to regain the happiness of childhood. A man swings a woman round on a

145

stick as if on a wild carousel ride, and she cheers jubilantly, cannot stop laughing. Five men throw a woman back and forth like an upright pendulum; later two others swing another woman between them, and the lucky lady leaves, smiling radiantly. In the general tranquillity it is even possible to reveal little secrets. Dressed only in knickers and a bra, a woman frantically kisses a table-top, explaining that this was how her father always used to kiss her. She explains her body, every gesture she makes, and demonstrates how the Tanztheater Wuppertal dances are created from very simple translated stories. A man paints hearts on his chest, forearm and stomach, flirts with the audience and continues to undress. A bare-breasted woman, her hands over her breasts, tells us how much she likes potatoes cooked in their skins. A gentle, alternating weave of African music creates a calm aural tapestry in the background.

The audience are offered food and drink. A man climbs up the ship's mast to shave himself, awkwardly positioned, then reveals himself to be the captain. A little later he appears out of uniform, washes a mirror against which an exhausted woman is leaning, whom he ignores. He carelessly throws a bucket of water over her. Something like a mysterious rainforest night settles over the scene. The sounds of invisible animals mingle with the music. An absurd conversation about the correct use of a watering can takes place. A man in swimming trunks practises cartwheels; another cups himself with wineglasses, attaching them to his chest. A woman furtively shows us her naked bottom under her evening dress; another carries out a night watch on the boat with a tiny dog on a lead. Roles are presented and then immediately retracted, like scenic splinters, like shards of memory.

A woman begins a solo to music which sounds like a nocturnal gamelan orchestra. She points in various directions in the air with her finger, which the men follow, but then they dig their fingers into the sand. Along with the music, interspersed with gurgles and plops, this looks like an incomprehensible, alien ritual, and yet it is an attempt at orientation, at finding a path, based on the body and following its outlines.

Lianas swing from above the stage, and men calmly climb up and down them, swinging gently back and forth. Individual motifs are suggested again, to the sounds of soft flute music: the woman takes off from the human launching pad into the air; the man dunks his head in

146

the bucket and holds his breath; the man with the four-legged woman appears, attempts to cheer everyone up. Then they stand, mute and serious, lined up at the railings for a group photo. Someone takes a shot; first of the performers, then of the audience.

The journey has ended. Now it can begin.

## Ein Trauerspiel

This piece, created in 1994, takes its name from a genre, the German word for tragedy. In the press, the piece was seen as the ultimate definition of Pina Bausch's oeuvre to date. Yet the Tanztheater Wuppertal's *Trauerspiel* is not a tragedy. It dispenses with despondent drama as well as with any continuous, climactic narrative. A dramaturgy of desires directs the action, with no interest in reaching consummation; instead the piece more closely resembles a process of tireless testing for happiness: a process of trial and error. Every error inspires a new trial, because even though no-one knows the solution, at least it is clear which mistakes can be avoided in the future. In a precisely calculated interplay between density and vacuum, the pieces seek out the fissures which the spectators' imaginations can enter and fill with memories, dreams and desires. They take advantage of the freedom provided by drawing on life, on personal biographies: that of the dancers and actors as well as the spectators. In the free-form collage of fragmentary scenes we are not given a narrative thread to guide us, nor the context of a cast-iron world view. The cinematic montage corresponds to a merely fragmentary perception, which selects, accentuates and intensifies, whilst avoiding any excessive pressure and abandoning itself to a relaxed cheerfulness. It is a tragic and comic play on the various shades and tones of experience. Anything may become important – concentrating the gaze onto a detail, a nuance – as long as it tells us something. The hierarchies of significance and value have been abolished. This is a theatre refreshingly free of morality, but which still insists on a humanness which is ready and able to take everyone seriously. Unspectacularly but unswervingly, it demands the human right of respect and love.

In the face of all the dramatic expectations its title might arouse, *Ein Trauerspiel* begins gently and almost incidentally with an exposition of its subjects. The stage is black and void, its floor covered with a layer of earth; in the middle a large, severed slice of the ground floats in a pool of water like an ice floe or an island. Play commences on solid and on shaky ground: experiments in togetherness and solitude, encountering and withdrawing. A woman in a translucent black dress walks steadily through the waste land, playing an African string instrument with a bow, as if taking a calm, self-assured journey. We hear a tarantella, and a man in a tracksuit dances in with wide swings of his arms, crossing the island; another man joins him, circling his hands around his navel and his nipples. Another woman steps into the expansive arena; they run to various spots, cautiously taking possession of the space, touching the earth. Two men help a woman run through the air as if in a dream. Another woman cools a dancing man down, spraying water at him from her mouth. A tabletop is set on fire and immediately extinguished again; then all is quiet.

A woman in large, bright yellow shoes stands and does her hair – a grotesque clown who tries a few clumpy steps before waddling Chaplinesque into the stalls, kissing a member of the audience and vanishing. Soft Sephardic music begins, and another woman starts to dance, lamenting loudly, with serviettes clamped under her arm to combat moisture. She sinks to the floor in a *grand plié* and opens her arms out wide to the skies. She continually interrupts herself, curses and commands her body to adopt the correct posture. Dance is not a given; it must be practised and reinvented, but we already know where it is not to be found: in the acquired, traditional forms instilled through drilling.

*Ein Trauerspiel* begins entirely casually: a company, abandoned in a vast, arid landscape, in search of its dance amongst forms that have become damaged and useless. Only the elements are there: earth and fire, water and wind, rising to a raging storm. There is nothing they can hold onto; they are alone with themselves and their bodies in the wide expanse, left to find an elemental movement which can stand up to the power of nature.

Their search is undertaken almost entirely to the soft sounds of Sephardic and gypsy music. The space is repeatedly given over to silence and to the sounds made by the performers. Gentle harmonies from Italy and Portugal are introduced, as well as from the German Romantic period (Schubert chamber music). Underlying the mood of melancholy solitude,

148

in the second half the music increasingly consists of excerpts from Schubert's *Winterreise*. Only seldom are we free to enjoy a more relaxed atmosphere, with pop and dance music from Russia, Argentina and Poland, jazz by Louis Armstrong, Duke Ellington or Django Reinhardt. On this journey through the continents of the mind, gentle, traditional folk singing predominates; only once or twice are the dream-searchers startled by the martial horns of a St Hubert's Mass (traditionally played on hunts) or thrown into energetic panic by the hammering staccato of Siberian shamanic music. *Ein Trauerspiel* remains rooted in an inner place, out of which dance is born.

Visiting this place means playing with fire; the constant risk of failure. Shouting for joy, a woman takes a long run-up and jumps up several times onto the back of a chair, blissfully allowing herself to tip over into the void. Another vaults into the arms of a man and lands upside down in a bucket of water. Wearing a pinafore, another tears at her hair like a child, dancing, following the lines of her body her finger traces out into the open space. Another woman, in a glamorous evening dress, follows her, pauses in various poses, crouches on the ground, tries to open her arms up to the sky, yet constantly returns to her own bodily centre.

The gentle gypsy music is replaced by heavy, prayer-wheel-like dervish singing, and the atmosphere sinks into grim desperation. In a fragmentary solo a man falls repeatedly to the ground, tries to pull himself up again, and is finally run into and bowled over. The women jump aggressively at the men and knock them down. Equally uncouthly, one of the women is placed on a table and tipped off into the water. After these actions, executed mechanically to the rhythm of the music, four dancers remain for a moment, lying on the ground as if dead. In the middle of the resulting calm someone falls over with a loud cry, along with a clothes stand. Wearing a long, pink evening dress one woman sings a song while another releases her frustration by screaming, boxing angrily into the air. Then she bathes her feet and licks the flame of a cigarette lighter. The fallen man attempts another dance, to Schubert's *Piano Trio*, reaches his arms out, opening himself up, repeatedly looks for somewhere else to be, but it is no longer possible to fit a harmonious sequence together from this fractured material.

Because no-one knows what to do next, the dancers walk into the auditorium, sew the spectators together with fine thread and shoot themselves like arrows off the front of the stage. A dancer in a tight yellow mini skirt calls a friend in to show her a revue dance she has been practising, but the friend is unimpressed. Self-affirmation is continually sought through dance, and sometimes it seems to be found; a woman stands in profile, spreads her arms out and tenderly strokes her curves as if in front of a mirror, measures out her body with her hands, talking softly to herself or to her body. Someone asks the audience laconically: "What do you think this is about then? Nothing!"

This sounds like a key statement on dance theatre, which tells its story through moving images with a poetry formulated in the pure language of metaphor. There is nothing to be interpreted, no hidden meaning to be dug out. Everything is exactly what we see and hear: a disturbing, fascinating excursion into the labyrinth of the passions, as familiar as it is foreign.

When a woman rushes along behind a man, talking constantly at him and offering him panaceas against pain, she represents someone desperately seeking contact, extolling her own virtues. For a long time she stands there smiling expectantly, but the man doesn't react. Her smile dies; disappointed, she begins to sweep the floor. When a tall, thin dancer enters, her breasts padded out with water-filled balloons, then punctures the balloons with a needle and stands there, sad and wet, she breaks the spell of an empty dream, of her inability to accept who she is. Nothing else need be read into this. The little hysterical attacks, the attempted outbreaks show how hard it is to get really close to each other. The isolated tricks and comic self-drilling testify to the unrelinquishable desire to be loved.

The end of the first half shows how close these things are to each other. Accompanied by the infernal hunting horns of St Hubert's Mass, two couples appear, the women squatting on the men's backs. They slip off; the partners cannot reach each other any more, and the women are carried out, kicking around like helpless beetles. Then a dancer calls everyone in. She instructs them to undress, and for a moment uninhibited, pleasurable contact seems to be developing. Suddenly, however, the director changes her mind and puts an end to the fun. Buckets are carried in, and everyone runs busily back and forth as if they have to collect water. To the sounds of anarchic shamanic music some of the men throw themselves to the ground, crawl and turn over, fall back down, exhausting themselves in the increasingly excesses of their dance. Suddenly the frantic activity ends. A couple lies on the ground, the woman over the man, on his legs. Accompanied by a Louis Armstrong swing tune he slowly lets her swoop down for a kiss. Then the men stand sorrowfully at the front. One of them wipes away tears which another squeezes from his hands.

As is so often the case, the second half consists of scherzo variations on the same themes. The greater their anguish, the harder the performers try to get through it with cheap and cheerful jokes. First of all the affectionate motif from the end of the first half is picked up again. Several couples meet on the shifting island for a silent, intimate dance which breaks up again peacefully. The performers play for the audience's attention, but the quotations from the *Winterreise* underpin everything with a romantic, wistful sorrow. A woman quotes a famous line, attributed to Queen Victoria: "Lie back, spread your legs and think of England." She says it and does it, but no-one comes. A man poses effeminately in a green petticoat and does a somersault: "Well, what was that? A spring roll!" Later there are similar puns where words and expressions are enacted physically: a woman in an evening dress gathers up her skirts and places strips of *Speck* ("bacon fat" but also "flab", "lard", "blubber" etc) on her thighs and says: "Plenty of fat." Another responds by pulling an apple out of her bag, making a pun on *Apfeltasche*, a German apple pastry translated literally as an "apple bag". The game develops into a showdown. When one of them drips lemon juice onto a stick (*stocksauer* – "sour as a stick"), the other answers by holding a cigarette lighter under a dog: "Hot dog!"

Despite the emphatic cheeriness the situation deteriorates. The elements conspire against the performers. A woman is hit by a waterfall which suddenly rushes down from above the stage into the gap between the island and the mainland. Another blocks her ears and says: "You can all shout now." She sits down and sings to the roaring waterfall, then walks off through the audience. Two men wildly fan air at a woman; she stands swaying in the breeze and admits the bird she was given died – just like that. A man in women's clothes tells the story of his mother's vow that she would walk to church on her knees as long as his brother came back from the war alive. Dietrich Fischer-Dieskau sings Schubert's song *Am Brunnen vor dem Tore*.

Even dancing must be wrested from the dancers. A man drags a woman onto the island; as soon as she dances over to the mainland he brings her back, and makes her do it again. Even when she lies exhausted on the ground he forces her to dance again. When another woman arrives and poses on a chair, lustfully throwing herself in pin-up positions, he just laughs at her, sends her away and sits on the chair himself, unable to understand her self-rape.

Constraints cause open confessions to be made. A woman dances a few classical steps, breaks off and declares that she never cleans her shoes or irons her clothes. Another gives a dancer ballet lessons at the barre in a harsh, bossy tone. As he fails to press his buttocks together properly she sticks a pencil in between them, then a piece of paper. Both fall immediately. Nothing helps, certainly not training yourself or letting yourself be drilled by others to perform attractive tricks.

In the general bewilderment one of the women bluntly states that she feels insulted and is going home. Another summons the accompanist, demanding: "Play something; I want to cry. It's my turn." She spreads imaginary slices of bread and passes it out into the auditorium while making desperately cheerful small talk with the audience. The general decline cannot be halted, however. A couple goes for a silent walk round the edge of the water; they follow their path undeterred even when the man vanishes without a word into the pool, until only his head is visible. With great difficulty he climbs out, then goes for a solitary walk. As the waterfall comes rushing down again, he makes a few pointless attempts at flying, like a silly bird.

During a sudden storm everyone runs hurriedly across the barren field, stumbling, falling and trying to rescue their worldly goods. Only one of them stands alone in her high heels, balancing on one leg and holding her dress: standing her ground. A man comes, sets the water on fire, and then the scene calms down again. To the soft sounds of Sephardic music a woman in a pink evening dress sits on the ground and dances: the picture resembles an abandoned wasteland, yet also contains a floating dreaminess. There is fire, someone sings, the man stands and smokes, someone dances just for themselves. A woman fills lily flowers with honey and asks questions, anxiously at first, then hysterically, asking the air, as if expecting an answer from the sky. Accompanied by another song from the *Winterreise* a man begins a slow solo. A woman joins him; in swooping, swinging movements she touches her own body, tenderly and inquisitively.

152

Then the circle is completed, and the piece returns to its starting point. The dancer in the tracksuit comes back, followed by another man and woman. They mark out sites, try out possible places to dance, which have first to be found. In the middle of the music they stop. While the tarantella continues, the ensemble enters and bows to the audience.

Their journey is still far from over.


## Danzón


The Spanish title of the piece refers to a dancing fury, an obsession; in Mexico it is used to describe a steadily accelerating dance, similar to a bolero. Yet ecstatic dance mania is the last thing driving Pina Bausch's dance performance of the 1994/95 season, created using only eleven dancers and comparatively short at an hour and three-quarters. This exploration into what dance can be at its most honest is again careful and precise. In the search for clues, only fragments, isolated solos and short group motions can be found, overwhelming the performers all the more intensely: attacks and outbreaks of dance at moments when language, gesture and facial expression are no longer adequate. The *danzón* – the dance-devil – overcomes those it possesses by distress more often than by joy.

At the beginning the stage is barren, black and bare, open right up to the firewalls. To soft jazz from Ben Webster two women in long white dresses come in, lie on their backs and flap their arms and legs in the air like stranded beetles, as if dreaming, as if still unborn. A monster baby crawls in on all fours from one side, pushing heavy stones in front of himself, sucking his thumb and staring. He weighs down the two dreaming women with the stones, as if he wants to bring even the slightest movement to a standstill.

A dancer enters and offers the audience a terse assertion: "So you are here and I'm there." She walks into the stalls, fetches one of the dancers, dressed as an old woman, and asks him to do something nice. Embarrassed, the "lady" performs a fragile curtsey and leaves.

We hear Mexican pop music. One of the white-clothed women slips into a black dress, suddenly coming to life, and measures out her loca-

153

tion in a rapid foot dance while the baby drags the other, lifeless woman roughly off stage. Two women cross their arms to form a bridge and let two men relish the game of pulling a breezy summer dress from one body to another.

The scene has imperceptibly brightened to a relaxed cheeriness. A haystack is brought on stage, into which happily frolicking, kissing couples throw themselves, while a blindfolded butler stands in the midst of the romantic goings-on, the personification of composure and respectability.

The mood shifts yet again. To a rock 'n' roll song by Johnny Hodges, the men shuffle across the floor in sudden panic, sitting with legs spread-eagled. A gauze curtain descends for the first time from above the stage. An image is projected, showing branches of pink cherry blossom across the full width of the stage. Accompanied by soft easy-listening Japanese music, bathtubs are rolled in, and the women take baths, relaxing and forgetting themselves. When the gauze is unexpectedly raised again they duck under the water in fear. The butler discreetly rolls each of them out again in their baths.

An actress comes in and, in a calm, intimate voice, reads a letter announcing the dispatch of tea leaves to a friend as a sign of respect, including precise instructions for the correct infusion. The piece continually swings between the desire to let oneself go, to discover our own bodies, discover love and the strict forms of convention. But unlike in many previous pieces, this time the formality also carries a delicate, soft intimacy within it which does not impinge on the opposite partner, instead allowing them space to be themselves.

*Danzón* is set out like a travel report. The projections on the rising, falling gauze screens divide the empty stage at varying depths and show landscapes which might come from holiday photo albums: mountains, woods, icy expanses, surf, women in old-fashioned bathing costumes, a whole picture full of white swans. The reportage presents the finds from another reconnaissance mission to find happiness, searching amongst proximity and distance, alienation and contact, private and public. And as so often, dance theatre remains aware that it is carrying out its intimate research into desires and yearnings in public. Theatre, with the mute demands and expectations of the audience, is continually attacked.

The actress shouts angrily: "I have to do everything, everything!" She kicks one man and tries to strangle another. Later she delivers a sober commentary on a dancer in a pink dress who minces through the room on *pointe* shoes: "Dancers: first they dance to the right, then to the left, then in the middle." As if to prove that dance theatre is not about superficial beauty and edifying entertainment, rattling the doors to the auditorium she says: "The doors are locked. I'd like to be able to work with you in peace." Then, with only bright feather boas wrapped around her, she places herself in the "fifth position", shows of her physical assets and demonstrates tricks dancers use to make the body look longer. With irony at her own expense, she announces: "I am Auntie Mechthild. I really am very pretty. Well, you know what I mean."

The exploration of genuine desires can only begin outside the conventions of theatre, and it helps to remind ourselves what it was like at the beginning. Even learning to kiss was a thrilling experience, as a woman at the front of the stage demonstrates. She splits an orange and practises the correct lip positions, sensuous sucking techniques and tongue play. But what happened to make a woman later bandage her thighs with sticky tape to protect herself from attacks? The next man who reaches under her dress gets stuck; deeply embarrassed, he is eventually forced to carry the entire woman out with him. This can also be read in a different way; he has fallen for her trick and been captured.

The constant ambivalences and the uncertainty of every situation also lend this piece to its rhythm. Every cheerful outburst is countered by a darker image. As if on the beach, everyone darts around the stage naked between two screens on which crashing waves are projected. Suddenly they all fall on their backs, gliding in slow-motion as if paralysed or blissed out. The men drool over the women, who sit politely on chairs. Their admirers lie at their feet, their chins resting on the women's knees in admiration, but their pleas are ignored. To the sounds of a *danzón*, the women climb through the men's outstretched arms and let themselves be caught. Suddenly thrown off balance, the men fall on their backs. The dance becomes ever wilder and faster. Everyone falls down, tries to reach each other and embrace in vain, as if the ground and any secure footing had been taken from under them. The world is out of kilter; the search for intimacy has slipped into fathomless oblivion. Memories of childhood happiness are not left unsullied either. When a couple at the front see-saws on a narrow metal rod with no seats, flirting with the audience at the same time, it becomes a painful effort, hidden behind smiles.

Only occasionally is there a glimpse of a wholly intact intimacy. A camp is unexpectedly pitched at the very back of the stage. The dancers lie cosily next to each other and tell each other stories and jokes by the light of a torch, giggling like happy teenagers. Only occasionally is one of them so uninhibited and carefree that he poses proudly, opens his jacket to bare his chest and practises dramatic poses in various spots. But then a dance forces him to the ground, he flips up and down as if pulled both by gravity and the desire to be upright and attractive. Just once a woman skips across the stage in childlike innocence, pulling at her pinafore which reveals her breasts.

Mostly such pleasurable exploration of the body is punished forthwith. When the women sit on chairs at the front, smirking at the audience and holding lit cigarette lighters under their bottoms in order, with a smile, to "sit them out", the butler comes straight over and shoos them indignantly away. Such moments give us a hint of when and how intimacy might be allowed to get a foothold, despite all the social rules.

As in every piece, individual, consistent characters appear in *Danzón* too. The baby returns throughout the piece like the expression of a monstrous infantility, an element of anarchy, disturbance and destruction. He throws books and paper from up above the stage, suddenly appears as a muscle man letting a woman swing from his outstretched arm, and sits with a dumb look on his face: a constant irritation.

There is the solitary man, repeatedly breaking into angry, anguished dances. He stands, stigmatised, wearing out-sized cardboard ears which he wiggles sadly. Alone in the huge, gaping space he waves mutely as if in farewell, then leaves. In another scene he suddenly appears on stage in lurid drag, wearing the actress's boa, sits in the corner of the proscenium trying to listen to an aria, crossly removing the women's clothes. Wearing his own clothes he dances a solo, tumbling about and swinging his arms to a dramatic Purcell overture, drawing himself up, breaking off and starting again from scratch. He is driven by an unidentified unease. While the actress is massaged on a table he waits impatiently, pulling at her feet. The masseur pulls the actress back again, and another man comes and takes the solitary man's place till the actress is pulled comically backwards and forwards on the table in time with the music, while the solitary man nervously tears at his hair and complains loudly.

156

There is the chubby, padded-out woman with the holdall, a wayward time-traveller who continually experiments with crooked, truncated dance poses. Right at the beginning she appears, clicks her fingers, twists her mouth manually into a smile, outlines the suggestion of a pirouette and applauds herself softly. She will never achieve the dream of ethereal lightness and beauty symbolised in the image of the swan, but later she appears again and sketches out steps and moves. A man joins her and dances with her, lifts her up ever so slightly, and a very individual dance is created, highly tender and delicate. It is accompanied by Camille Saint-Saëns' "Swan" from *The Carnival of the Animals*.

The dances in *Danzón* are seldom this calm and at one with themselves. Right at the beginning the men mark out wild zig-zags on the stage with a sudden uproar. Their scattered solos are angular and sharply accentuated. The men throw themselves on the ground as if into a grave. They clap their hands, try to stand up and fall down again. They punch the air with their arms, shake themselves, force themselves into empty embraces, leading their hands to their mouths in bewilderment. When the women dance to Portuguese fado music there is no release either. Spinning rapidly they try to open their bodies but turn back inwards immediately and carry their own arms like long, elegant swans' necks – across the water.

Again, as in earlier pieces, earth has a role to play. In a long sequence accompanied by sad but beautiful fado the solitary man scatters it carefully in particular places round the bare room, like a gravedigger's *memento mori*. A woman dances a crouching, twisting floor solo while another attempts to bury her in shovelfuls of soil. Dietrich Fischer-Dieskau sings from Gustav Mahler's *Lieder eines fahrenden Gesellen*.

The underlying sentiment of fado music is encapsulated in the word *saudade*: a gentle, melancholy sense of loss which is wholly surrendered to and does not fight against anything. Pina Bausch's own solo, her first since *Café Müller* in 1978, is also accompanied by three fados, evoking a sense of solitude and resignation. She stands in the midst of a video projection showing brightly coloured fish, in a lively, colourful underwater world which fills the entire stage. Her arms reach out into the space, return to her body, touch her cheek and initiate the next movement, letting it flow lithely through her entire body. With relaxed precision Pina Bausch creates a character who, although alone, is entirely at one with herself, holding her ground in the face of all vicissitudes. She does not have to do anything; just be there, awake, alert and present in the world with every sense. With a wave she leaves the stage, as if in final farewell or as if waving from a great distance.

The piece ends with a similar gentle message. The actress describes how, as an old man, Goethe returned to the hunting lodge where fifty years earlier he wrote one of his most famous poems on the wall next to the window with a pencil: *Über allen Gipfeln ist Ruh'*. "Well," he said after a moment of silence, taking measure of his own long lifetime, "now we can go again." As the light slowly fades, the words reverberate on.


## Nur Du


Like *Danzón*, *Nur Du* is a piece about love. Once again, Pina Bausch whisks her audience away to that carefree childhood world where wishing and dreaming were effective. No-one has ever actually been there; it is a place sustained by desires of the past but searched for in the future; a place where feelings might perhaps be reinstated, neither falsified nor mediated. As this is only possible in a fairy tale, *Nur Du*, which takes its title from the song *Only You*, is set in a veritably enchanted forest.

The back of the stage is filled with broad tree trunks, amongst which the twenty-two performers seem like lost children. They are thoroughly grown-up, however, as one of the dancers succinctly demonstrates: unlike Little Red Riding Hood, she coolly announces: "I'm off to see Grandma, in other words I'm going vodka shopping." The problems the performers have with each other and with love are also of an entirely adult nature. However upbeat the familiar 1950s songs – the nostalgic blues and rock 'n' roll – might sound to the audience, the atmosphere of solitude and the misunderstandings inherent in each encounter are all the same as ever. In *Nur Du* Pina Bausch once again asks: when can we really engage with each other, when can we be free from artificial posturing and the extortionate desire to be loved? When will we be capable of just being there, emotionally naked, vulnerable and insecure, ready for genuine intimacy?

Up to this point, everyone, dancers as well as spectators, is running a tragicomic obstacle course of entanglement and exaggeration, full of mas-

158

querades and anguished, lonely attacks of rage, because seldom are we wholly at one with ourselves or certain that we can be loved just as we are, without pretence and without fear. Dance theatre allows itself the freedom to scrutinise everything (all tension, every mistake), and it judges nothing. It doesn't expose its characters to shallow laughter; rather it maintains a fundamental love and understanding for all human behaviour, as long as it is honest. Everything is allowed, including – for instance – exaggerated self-dramatisation, because only then can we discover charm and vulnerability. Only those who disclose themselves with a child-like lack of self-consciousness and venture wholly into the world can be recognised and loved. Thus, radical as it is, this tireless exploration of an age-old subject is also very careful and affectionate. Dance theatre goes to the roots of emotion, but at the same time protects, respecting anyone with the courage to reveal themselves as they are. In the space thus created the longed-for, apparently impossible, can happen; the hoped-for intimacy can succeed, and the power reconnecting everyone to the *élan vital* is unleashed.

*Nur Du* begins softly, feeling its way. A dancer sits on a chair at the front, lifts up her dress to show some leg and sings a pretty, sad blues song, alone in the enchanted forest. The mood swiftly changes. Three men hurriedly help a fourth crawl up one of the tree trunks. Then the spell of hysteria is over. A smiling woman comes on stage, lies across several willing men's backs, as if on a chaise-longue, and observes coquettishly that under her dress she is entirely naked. Giggling, she wonders what it would be like if everyone in the building were naked too. As if to bring her frivolous idea closer to home, she repeats the whole procedure again in the auditorium. During all of this a man sits, silent and lost in the forest, next to a tiny tree (a real one this time). Throughout the piece he acts as a discreet overseer and silent witness. Sometimes he simply casts a mute glance from the fringes to see what convoluted activities are currently going on, observing the constant emotional ups and downs from a calm distance. He has long ceased to have anything to do with the others' inner conflicts. Like a detached director he watches everything, only intervening in cases of emergency. He is taking a different path, which, in its silent musing, already leads to the future. He builds himself steps up to a high fork in a tree-trunk with planks of wood, brushes old leaves and feathers out and settles in, smoking a cigarette, as if beginning a new life.

The others conversely take a journey into their own past. Wearing a glittery corsage and laddered stockings, a woman rushes in, excited, to announce that "he" is coming. She runs out again to look for him, and then, thoroughly frustrated, cancels the long-awaited arrival. She continually scurries in and out. As with adolescents, anticipation and disappointment lie side by side, oscillating uncertainly across the apex of agitation.

Everyone in *Nur Du* gets the chance to be young once more, as they were at the start of their life's journey, when hope flourished and emotions paved the way with unrestrained élan. A woman is carried away on a wave of her own enthusiasm, till the distant director plucks her from the edge of the stage and cools her hot head down with ice cubes. Everyone diligently attempts to impress each other, to win the love and affection of a partner. A man repeatedly jumps over the back of a chair from standing. Another plays the infamous joker, making origami glasses for himself and his adored one and filling them with champagne. They toast each other in style, but then he suddenly responds to the whole incident with hysterical laughter. Giggling inanely, he cuts up an apple in such a way that what he finally passes her is only the core. Proudly and skilfully, a dancer swings her body around a ballet barre she has brought in. A man gets someone to fill a plastic bag tied around his head with water, in order to then hold his breath for a heroic length of time. A woman sticks a pair of cigarette packets to the soles of her shoes to make heels and totters away smiling.

In the struggle for attention and affection no trick is too absurd to be tried. A woman at the front of the stage delivers a whole litany of rallying cries from her former college days, till she is silenced by exhaustion, and then leaves, alone. Everyone wants to be a winner, because they have been taught that only winners are loved. A woman indulges in a virtuoso verbal aria on the subject of a colleague's name, taking delight in letting the Spanish pronunciation of "r" roll off her tongue. "I can do it," she concludes with satisfaction, "he can't." Unfortunately, however, "he" isn't there; the impressive act slips smoothly into the void. Later she stands alone in the forest and sings a Spanish love song. She repeatedly holds a note for a long time, checking the time, bored. No-one comes to admire her virtuosity.

*Nur Du* is a piece about love and about the dreams attached to it, assertively loud or quiet and reticent. Wearing an evening dress and a glitzy necklace, a man stands in front of a projection of a tear-jerking film and describes how he has always wanted to be a star, to be famous. Later he builds little houses cut out of paper bags, spreads gravel and sets out a neat little garden. Smiling with satisfaction he enjoys his simple good fortune, builds larger and larger houses: the dream of a success story. Two women join him and realise their childhood dreams: one quietly hatching out her future, the other noisily trumpeting her success. Together they make a strangely lost, abandoned still life: many lonely dreamers, with no-one there to share their good fortune.

Often the problem lies in the individual's uncertainty, as a man demonstrates in a later sequence. He continually tries new experiments to produce happiness: fans a breeze at himself, listens dreamily to watery noises in a bottle before finally establishing himself as a fountain statue, spraying water from his mouth. Glances in the mirror to see how he looks alternately provoke happy smiles and bitter disappointment in his face. Nothing can banish his dissatisfaction. Happiness, it seems, begins with the art of accepting ourselves.

Or perhaps it begins with the cautious shyness in which a man, partly obscured by a rubbish bin, slowly crosses the stage and removes his clothes piece by piece, his gaze remaining fixed on the audience. Perhaps it begins with the exuberance with which a woman skips through the forest and removes one pair of knickers after another, laughing. Perhaps the next rendezvous will immediately fulfil all desires; reinforced by several older gentlemen, the ensemble of men come in with irons and cardboard boxes and zealously iron their shirts, then later clean their shoes. What drives them on is always the hope that next time the yearned-for embrace, the deep intimacy, will succeed. Thus they throw themselves into their ensemble dances with continual delight – into precise tangos or crazy rock 'n' roll, sometimes spurred on by a leading dancer, sometimes meeting in intimate encounters. Yet these outbreaks of festive momentum never last long, as is always the case in dance theatre. Soon they break off: for instance when a man enters, orders them to remove their clothes and march. Then he forces everyone to the ground, where they have to continue moving like helpless animals. "Why do they fall in love?" asks the song.

And why *do* they fall in love, when so much of what they do backfires? When she crouches anxiously at the foot of a tree and he talks relentlessly at her, it brings her little comfort. When the woman orders the man in so she can see him cry, he is barely able to produce genuine emotion on demand. When another woman slides in with hunched up shoulders and announces "breast hidden: woman hidden", no-one can reach her, let alone touch her, behind this defensive armour.

So why do they fall in love? Probably because the loneliness is unbearable, because they have to find a way to reach each other to avoid the anguish of being alone in the world. To this end a man hits his face with a woman's hands, with her hair, her legs, checking each time to see if she will eventually show some reaction after all. To this end the performers repeatedly inflict pain on each other and seem to end up despairing of themselves, unable to believe that there will be no emotional boost to lift them up into a carefree *joie de vivre*, releasing them from the torture of solitude.

Pina Bausch incorporates this *élan vital* and this grief into the many solos interspersed more frequently throughout *Nur Du* than in most other recent pieces. When anguish is at its greatest and all words and self-orchestration cease to be adequate, when no powers of disguise can halt the revelation of our true nature any longer, it is dance which gives form to these extreme outer limits of self-expression. There is anger and rebellion, which refuses to give up till happiness has been reached, till the searching hand grasps an opposite in the empty space. Solitary dancers desperately put their ears to the ground, comfort themselves in the crook of their own arms or scrabble in a pit like trapped animals. However, at these moments they are always entirely at one with themselves; the moments bear witness to an intimacy and candour which is otherwise not shown on a stage. In elegant self-absorption the dancers explore their bodies, make intimate indications of the true condition of their inner nature, are vulnerable and thus also approachable. All hope for a better outcome to the story lies here.

After three hours *Nur Du* ends with a dance. As at the beginning, a woman balances on several men's outstretched arms, high-up and insecure, as if life were a delicate tight-rope walk, right on the edge of the abyss. Accompanied by a melancholy Brazilian melody, a man throws himself frantically into a fidgety dance, as if his own limbs refused to follow him. His body seems to have gone off the rails, to have broken down and gone out of control. Increasingly exhausted, he constantly starts up again, as if at the outermost edge of desperation. But the fact that he cannot give up – his strength – endures.

162

# Der Fensterputzer

Life, said Pina Bausch in an interview once, is like a journey. A journey, it could be added, in which we undergo some very surprising experiences. Unwittingly, we suddenly rise to unexpected heights or find ourselves sunk in moments of profound distress. And in this respect, the supposedly foreign is not nearly as distant from our localised, individual experience as we tend to think.

There cannot be many companies for whom a journey into other cultures could be as significant as it has been to the Tanztheater Wuppertal. From the start, Pina Bausch, her dancers and her musical assistants have collected a wide range of music on their lengthy tours all over the world. The criteria for subsequent inclusion in a piece are genuineness and emotional power. And it often transpires that for all the cultural differences, the repertoire of basic human feelings creates a common ground on which we can meet. Oscillating between fear and security, love and hate, joy and sadness, the human journey through life follows its same path everywhere. Dance theatre is not concerned with superficial harmonisation but with its opposite: an accentuation of polarities. For only at the centre of the tensions, if they can be endured, are the incendiary sparks which drive the travellers onwards.

From these visited countries come other observations as well as the emotional content of powerful music, which feed into the Tanztheater Wuppertal pieces. The gaze does not, of course, simply rest on the surface: it seeks to get to the bottom of things with determined precision. The company's many co-productions always absorb particular cultural hues from each place, yet rise far above folkloric impressions. It is not the pared-down prose of guidebooks which determines the tenor; regional particularity is just one aspect of a world theatre of feelings and changing moods.

Thus *Der Fensterputzer* (*The Window Washer*), a co-production with the Hong Kong Arts Society and the Goethe Institute in Hong Kong, therefore also alludes to the particular idiosyncrasies of this Asian metropolis. The allusions are, however, integrated into a language of poetic signs which takes cultural idiosyncrasies simply as evidence of a more fundamental similarity. In Pina Bausch's own words: "You can make friends everywhere without denying your own individuality."

An enormous mobile mountain of flowers dominates the stage this time, which is otherwise bare, black and open to the firewalls. In the bare space the red flowers create a festive atmosphere of devotion to love and life. They rain down on the stage, are arranged by the dancers into labyrinthine paths on the floor or thrown into the air in a jubilant, firework frenzy. This already hints at one of the basic subjects of dance theatre: the marking out of individual territories and their wholesale destruction soon afterwards to free up space for new encounters.

In *Der Fensterputzer* – as in *Nur Du* previously – a cheery, genial atmosphere sets the basic tone of the piece. The mingling of mellow Chinese songs, melancholy Portuguese fado and rhythm 'n' blues underscore this overwhelmingly humorous exploration into love, in all its possibilities and impossibilities. This is both a journey to Hong Kong and to a place which is everywhere, where everyone can find themselves. Right at the beginning one of the dancers greets her fellow travellers in the audience with an enthusiastic "good morning, thank you". It seems a little exaggerated, but also demonstrates a child-like, effusive lack of inhibition. A man eagerly attempts to satisfy all the audience's needs for tea and snacks. Exuding charm, the ensemble invites the audience on a two-and-a-half hour excursion. Its intension is first and foremost to be a pleasant one.

The performers continually demonstrate how to do good deeds. Seeking protection, the women put their arms around a man and are placed softly on the ground. Some men lift a woman in the air and ask her if she has any particular wish right this minute, which they proceed to fulfil. Everyone pays great attention to their own bodies. They wash themselves, shave their legs and faces and oil their entire bodies, in order to emphasise their gleaming muscles. Unlike in *Nur Du*, these daily ablutions do not testify to the endless competition for attention and affection, they are carried out with utter composure. Even when a man lying face down over the edge of a table scoops water out of a bucket in order to train his stomach muscles, this is something we can smile about. And when another man lovingly blows a woman's hair dry, letting the warm breeze blow under her dress, the action is free of all intrusiveness.

Yet along with happiness comes danger. We suspect this right from the start when a man with a long stick cautiously fishes snakes out of the sea of flowers. Later, a swaying suspension bridge is lowered from the stage ceiling, and he carries a woman across the uncertain abyss. Even the flower-mountain itself can become a threat: it is rolled along in pursuit of a dancer and forces him to dance his solo closer and closer to the front edge of the stage, till he finally escapes, stumbling through the flowers; nevertheless he does not easily give up. A woman buries herself under the flowers, and only a neon light confirms her continued existence.

Such quiet moments continually occur, which – in their succinct way – display a strangely ambiguous allegiance to both life and death. A women enters silently with a chair and a cushion, sits down and lets herself tip back for a soft landing. Screaming, another lets herself topple backwards and is carried out, floating, by a group of men. The recurring longing for sleep seems to be like the overriding desire finally to arrive, even if it is in the ultimate sleep of death. The one thing not encountered in this piece is resignation, self-defeat; even when a man, as lonely as a dis-orientated travelling salesman, eats his meal at a table before lying down quietly to sleep. Everything seems to be endurable, more than endurable; it is like feeling around our individual boundaries or like the anticipation of a new experience. Even death retains a certain glamour: in one scene (following an Asian custom), a bright yellow cardboard model of a limou-sine is carried in, the deceased's favourite object used in a final tribute.

Nonetheless, *Der Fensterputzer* is predominately humorous. In an absurd moment of de-familiarisation, the flower-mountain is adapted into a ski-slope for "flower skiing". Two women act as living metal detectors forc-ing a man to take off his clothes, piece by piece. They play their power game, perfidious yet cheerful, with the utmost charm. Such moments are characterised by the same laconic presentation as the serious moments. This gives the scenes a strong presence while ridding them of any over-stated acerbity. The scenes are only intended to serve as pointers or sug-gestions; they carefully guard themselves from any kind of patronising attempt at definition. These delicate ambivalences serve to indicate that things cannot often be taken so lightly.

The structuring device which holds *Der Fensterputzer* together is not only – as in every piece – Pina Bausch's extraordinary feeling for suspense and timing, it is also the recurring scenic complexes, circling around the core theme. The actress first holds forth on the subject of efficient seduc-tion techniques. Then she explains in detail how to deal with a lover's chronic bad breath if necessary. She details every last unbearable nuance of its aroma, and, in conjuring it up, actually works herself up into an ecstatic desire to kiss him. Finally she appears as a strict ticket attendant, checking the spectators' tickets and sending them to the seats she deems correct. She recites a poem sullenly, saying – immediately afterwards – that absolutely no-one in her family has any interest whatsoever in poetry. Obviously this is an inverted hint of what dance theatre is really about: the pure power of poetry. What someone says and what they actually mean is not always the same thing.

Along with the recurrence of particular motifs, travel photos from Hong Kong serve as another thread running through the piece. At first the city is shown in street scenes via large slide projections. Then the eponymous window cleaner descends like a forgotten angel behind a transparent sheet of plastic, going about his business unmoved. Finally a woman sings along to a Chinese pop song, with much excitement and delight, while three others sit smoking under her skirt. A dancer is crossed by cyclists during her solo, but even in the hectic city bustle she is unflappable. These are various impressions which, divorced from their original environment, have long since begun to describe other things.

In *Der Fensterputzer*, as in most other recent works, the many dances are ambivalent and demand a great deal of space. The solos and group dances are sharp and fast, sometimes posing a threat – as in a man's solo where he throws himself at the feet of the women's ensemble in desperation – and often reaching the limits of exhaustion. Dancing returns a form of personal overexertion, in order to cross personal boundaries, take risks and finally find oneself, even in this very light and loving piece. Sometimes it is stubborn or heated, sometimes extremely measured, as in the sitting dance in which the entire ensemble rotate in tiny quarter turns on the spot, flapping their arms and clapping their hands – full of *joie de vivre* and charm. After the ensemble has left, a lone dancer remains, unable to stem the pleasure in his own movements.

*Der Fensterputzer* is a deliberate response to our increasingly hard times. While the pieces from the 1970s and '80s (when Germany was more affluent) confront us with a harsh rollercoaster of emotions, towards the end of the '90s Pina Bausch turns this around; humour becomes more important than ever before. *Der Fensterputzer* collects impressions and lovingly observed travel pictures and joins them to form a gentle, smiling continuum. The piece ends with an image of eternity: the company forms a long procession up and down the mountain. Projections show landscapes, a harbour at night, the neon lights of adverts. It is as if life's journey doesn't want to end. The transparent plastic sheet falls one more time; on it hangs the high-rise window cleaner who gets on with his work. Anything is bearable; you just have to believe in it.


## Masurca Fogo


It almost seems as if it love and lust were more a burden than a joy. At the very beginning a dancer runs on stage, twists and turns at high speed, crouches down and leaps up. Sizzling saxophone music drives him through his dynamic solo, then he is gone. A woman comes on stage and starts moaning into a microphone. Accompanied by soft blues music the men lie in a row on the floor and let the woman glide through the air across their hands. She climbs onto one man's shoulders and lets herself fall backwards into the others' arms. Then she is spun around on a chair as if on a merry-go-round; her moans become more and more fervent. As is so often the case in Pina Bausch's dance theatre, we don't know exactly whether these are sighs of pleasure or if she is suffering from an excess of some kind. The one certain thing is that she trusts the men implicitly and is enjoying the child-like pleasure of flying.

Another dancer enters and, as if in response to this surrender, dances an intimate solo in which he circles alternate arms around his head before swiftly reaching out into the surrounding space with his hands. A projection comes on, showing musicians on the Cape Verde islands, and the succession of dance solos continues, with constantly changing atmospheres, underscored by diverse kinds of music. The sources feeding these dances seem never to run dry. However defined Pina Bausch's dance style might be, the endless range of variations remains enormously rich; it allows new atmospheric nuances to be caught again and again, then shown to the audience in all their tremendous wealth. Five men interrupt this immersion in the stream of emotions, throw themselves to the ground screaming and turn somersaults as if, in this tropically charged atmosphere where feelings are approaching boiling point, a harsh incision were necessary to bring everyone back to consciousness.

The Tanztheater Wuppertal has set out on another quest for the sources of life. This time the stage is framed by a large, white box, trapezoid-shaped to evoke perspective, through which solidified lava has poured. Various associations are possible here: a frozen stream of emotion, a narrowly escaped danger. At any rate the mountain of lava narrows the dancers' field of action, generates a visual antithesis to their free dancing movement – something for them to work against. The lava slope takes on many functions in *Masurca Fogo*: acting as a mountain to be run up, a sea shore for a group of mermaids to wave their tails and sun themselves on, a beach where various intimacies can take place between couples.

This co-production between Lisbon's EXPO '98 and the city's Goethe Institute does not so much present a dangerous balancing act, as a generous homage to life. This is achieved alone through the countless fados (by Amália Rodrigues and Alfredo Marceneiro), tangos (by Gidon Kremer), and a Brazilian waltz (by Radamés Gnattali). A few energetic pieces of music succeed in balancing the web of inner suspense in *Masurca Fogo* thus preventing the piece from slipping into a flat, saccharine aesthetic. They emphasise all the more clearly what *Masuca Fogo* is about: an affirmation of beauty, intimacy, warmth and affection. These things may not be easy to find, but the soft, seductive impression left behind by *Masurca Fogo* is that they are – in principle – possible, that we are allowed to dream; indeed, that we must dream if we are to sustain our ability to live. August von Platen's romantic dictum applies here, with one important modification: he who has seen beauty with his own eyes is prey not to *death*, but to *life*. Dance theatre thus quite incidentally severs an age-old false connection made in the German philosophical tradition, no longer banishing beauty to the underworld.

Such intimacy must first be established with the audience so that it doesn't remain a claim made by the action on stage. The protagonists of *Masurca Fogo* continually tell very personal stories: memories of significant dreams and aspirations or memorable relatives; the grandmother, for instance, who was so beautiful all the men looked at her and idolised her. Sometimes the longed-for intimacy must first be demanded. In stentorian tones the granddaughter of the much-admired grandmother summons men to her, from the stage as well as from the audience, and plants a heartfelt kiss on their foreheads. A woman forces a reluctant man to look at her over and over again. And sometimes the attention-seeking escalates into a bitter, silent duel, in which couples fling glass after glass of water in each other's faces.

One thing which can help deal with such tension is humour, for instance when a woman lustfully rubs skin cream into a man's knee; yet when he tries to kiss her, he proves far too short for her. Another man comes to the rescue and lifts him up so he can kiss her patronisingly from above. Conventional hierarchy is thus simultaneously restored and smirked at. The joke as weapon is also a means to banish unpleasant memories. A dancer appears in a bikini covered with balloons and describes a terrible teacher who was nevertheless thoroughly admired by all her pupils. The men standing around her pop the balloons with the glowing tips of their cigarettes: the oppressive past bursts like a bubble.

The dancers continually return to their acts of tenderness: to solos where they caress their stomachs or to happy runs across the stage. It is mostly the men who form the contrasting element. They hold their own heads during their solos, manipulate their arms and legs as if their bodies were threatening to fall apart or as if the inner excitement were too great to bear. Yet everyone is overcome by a child-like abandon when a large plastic sheet is held up at the sides and filled with water so they can take pleasure diving in and slithering through the water. A man pushes a beautiful bathing lady into a bathtub onstage. She passes him freshly washed crockery out of the foaming bathwater, which he carefully dries. A large walrus creeps across the stage at an unhurried pace. From this relaxed atmosphere the piece releases its audience for the interval.

As is so often the case, the second, longer part of this two-and-a-half hour piece constitutes a series of variations on the themes established previously. Travel images are increasingly projected, beamed across the entire stage, submerging it in colours sometimes lively, sometimes alien. They show people on journeys, travelling in buses, watching the landscape. We see rare birds, flocks of flamingos, a tropical wealth of colour.

There are further attempts at intimacy, which by no means all succeed. A pretty woman dances, taking self-absorbed pleasure in her own body, but when a man joins her and admits he has taken a shine to her, her initial reaction is to run off. The two slowly and hesitantly come closer, but in the end it still doesn't really work out. The excitement is in the game, in the mutual caution and respect. In another scene, a man in a long evening dress acts as a dance instructor: leads couples in, observing them silently and precisely. Then he takes on the woman's role himself and explains to the men how gentle they must be when leading in a dance. In a lengthy sequence later on the projections show a dancing competition from the Cape Verde islands.

From the very beginning, Pina Bausch saw ballroom dancing as a form in which the much-sought intimacy between couples can be allowed to blossom in safety. It appears in her pieces in a diverse range of variations: as legless sitting dances, tangos lifted into the air, or in group processions meandering through the space. A similar leitmotif runs through *Masurca Fogo*: a closely-danced rumba procession, in which the men remove some of their clothes. It is very clear that an intimacy is possible here, one which would otherwise only be possible in private. The audience is always included and – with a smile – challenged to try it themselves some time, perhaps at home.

The pleasures do not just include our own bodies and those of others; good food is also an essential pleasure, even when the well-meaning mother thoroughly over-feeds her son from an enormous cauldron. Life can also be a party, such as when the ensemble builds a small hut at lightning speed in which they hold a crazy, loud party. Space can be found, quite literally, in the smallest of huts, and poverty does not necessarily inhibit *joie de vivre*. This is not to devalue the essential role of social criticism. It simply allows moments to be experienced, without prejudice, which helps us remember what life could be about. Such moments appear like a flash of light and vanish just as quickly. Dance theatre limits itself, despite all its scenic clarity, to hints, to little pointers. It could be a small waking dream, yet is actually wholly real. The important thing is not the ultimate fulfilment of the dream, however great the desire for this may be. As in childhood, the important thing is to keep the dream alive and not to give up.

Alternating between outbreaks of chaos and tender intimacy, between hasty, angular solos and sensuous self-indulgence, Pina Bausch allows the second half of *Masurca Fogo* to spill out into ever longer scenic sequences. Jokes are told, such as the corny gag about the three levels of orgasm; beginning with a delirious, affirmative "yes" it rises through a restraining "no" before culminating with "oh my God!" The men play bowls or darts. Two women challenge each other to a hairdressing duel, in which they painstakingly back-comb their hair, only to be completely

170

outstripped when a woman with a veritable lion's mane enters. Striding majestically in, she dons her finery and leaves her defeated competitors standing around helplessly.

Towards the end a moving projection of frothy waves dominates the entire stage and submerges the performers in an evocative underwater world. Very gradually the piece begins to calm down. A dancer holds her ground in the midst of the elements, accompanied by soft fado music, while the walrus creeps past once again. Three mermaids are given a lesson in dry-land swimming. The moaning woman we saw at the beginning reappears, with her burden of happiness, and the long line of couples enters the room to peaceful guitar sounds. Without interrupting their dance, the men let their shirts slip down onto their hips. Then they lie down on the beach, closely entwined with their partners as if on a warm summer's night. The loving couples are covered by projections of flowers covering the whole of the stage. In a series of time-lapse images, buds burst and bloom. This homage to the sheer energy of life and of renewal is sustained for several minutes. We hear the song *All I Need is the Air that I Breathe.* Then one of the women slowly stands up. Life can go on.

## O Dido

An exclamation with no exclamation mark, this piece's title could be taken as reference to the Purcell opera, from which Pina Bausch used arias over twenty years earlier in her melancholy, solitary *Café Müller.* Although the mythical figures of Dido and Aeneas do not appear in person her, *O Dido* nevertheless deals with love, but with its potential more than with the difficulties obstructing it.

The upbeat beginning sets the pace. We hear loud tango music, individual dancers run in, dance brief solos and disappear: racing shadows which come and go, fuelled by hasty agility. They are illuminated by projections of flowers, covering the entire space of the stage. *O Dido*, a co-production with the Teatro Argentino in Rome, almost seems to be a continuation of *Masurca Fogo*, which ends with time-lapse images of opening flowers: an optimistic tribute to life and new beginnings of all

171

kinds. In *O Dido* this message seems to have reached the body. It clearly arouses an overwhelming desire in the performers to dance. In the course of the rapid changeovers it gradually transpires that a party is in preparation here: a festival of love, of intimacy between couples dancing closely together and holding each other.

Like a meteor which has fallen out of the sky, a steep, grey rock soars up to the ceiling, covered with tropical vegetation: an impressive, towering island of the blessed, although unlikely to ever be ascended. The performers circumnavigate the rock, as if it were the embodiment of all their desires, as if they had all suddenly been smitten with love. They keep fit, ready for the long-awaited encounter with "the one", "the only one", training at a ballet barre they have swiftly carried in, showing off their muscles. A man is hurriedly supplied with braces and wineglasses, and a bottle is thrust into his hands. He must look good for the rendezvous.

In stark contrast to the previous pieces, the extended solos now seem less like self-absorbed, moving meditations and more like vital exercises in desire, fired by an overwhelming lust for life. A woman takes pleasure in swinging her hips, coquettish but with a refined eroticism; another dances endless spirals, as if caught up a whirl of happiness. A man uses the heel of his lover's shoe to test her reflexes, kissing the foot each time it automatically shoots up. Later his lady love manages to conjure up a necklace and rings out of bread, as if any kind of miracle were possible in the euphoria of love. Or had she simply hidden the jewellery?

Women unceremoniously paint unripe, green bananas yellow; anything not yet mature can at least be made up to seem so. Hand in hand, women stand at the front of the stage and fall happily back into the arms of waiting men. Shouts of joy are breathed into handkerchiefs, and hurriedly passed to and fro by each couple, as if to make visible the breath of life and love, which is always also the breath of desire. It is as if the company is enjoying a relaxed summer holiday. They wriggle pleasurably in hammocks slung from the ceiling and explain the subtle sign language of turban knots to the audience: an interested admirer can easily identify whether their adored one is already engaged, married or still available according to the kind of knot tied in the turban.

The flirting and attention-seeking sometimes escalates into childish games of catch, the dancers literally climbing over tables and chairs to outwit each other, soon reaching a mood of heated exuberance. While a group of men turns the table she is standing on, a woman calmly continues walking. Nothing will put her off; the power of love seems to allow her to overcome all barriers. Anyone who cannot keep up in the competition for affection is helped along by the others. They teach each other various love-marks, such as the imprint of red kissing lips on an arm; the spot is then sealed with a bandage so that it isn't lost.

Lasting just under two hours, *O Dido*, like the two previous pieces, is buoyed up by a "realistic optimism". Pina Bausch allies herself squarely with life, not in blind over-enthusiasm but in the certainty that difficult times must be countered with a glimmer of hope. If contrast was previously engendered through the hard edges between the main scenic blocks, now it is seen in the opposing movements within the individual dances themselves. With much sophistication, they demonstrate that each individual holds within them a wealth of conflicting hopes, fears and desires, which will not necessarily ever be pacified, but which together provide a strength with which life can be shaped, perhaps helping it turn out better in the end.

When the party finally happens, it seems more like a pleasant, happy dream. Wearing roller skates and elegant black suits, the men bring in chairs and tables with white table cloths and proceed to wait on the women in their fine evening dresses. All chivalry, they invite the ladies for a roller dance around the rocky island. The sound of wind is heard, and suddenly the love-feast vanishes, as if it were a scene in a Federico Fellini film.

To the sounds of Italian rap music, the men then show off excessively to the women, start up their motorbikes (in pantomime style) or lie stoically between two tables like a plank: hard men, softened by nothing. As always, dance theatre scrutinises the behaviour surrounding love in all its forms – without value judgement, simply with a wry smile.

Then the subject of love changes to the virtual world of film. Projections show train journeys on Wuppertal's monorail suspended railway. Loving couples stand undeterred in the midst of films showing busy traffic, serve each other coffee and kiss; nothing can disturb them.

With childish delight the company falls into a series of water games, as if the heat of love must be urgently cooled. Boots are filled with water, buckets swung around; dancers sit in a puddle on a chair as if this were perfectly normal; a man drenches a sitting woman with bucketfuls of cooling water. A tarpaulin is swiftly draped around the rock, and the stage mutates into a sauna. A man produces dry-ice mist; another is massaged thoroughly by two women, and even a rubbish bin comes in useful as a steaming sauna tub. The men usher in the interval with a hearty Bavarian thigh-slapping dance – wearing rubber boots, smirking and flirting with the audience.

Throughout the hour-long first half Pina Bausch sustains the tension of the underscoring rhythm. Using proven techniques of alternation, a mixture of tango, blues and vocal tunes, as well as murmuring African music, is contrasted with contemporary music such as hip hop to accompany the sometimes excited, sometimes calm atmospheric images. The costumes again position the piece somewhere between summery breeziness and opulent elegance. And as is often the case in Pina Bausch's wide-ranging excursions, the fifty-minute second half presents itself as a variation on the central theme of love. However, in *O Dido*, for the first time, Pina Bausch repeats whole scenes exactly as they were before but interspersed here and there with new motifs.

Despite this, the atmosphere of the second half presents a strong contrast to that of the carefree first. The energy slowly sinks away in a large rondo. Some moments resemble the exhaustion after a party. The men crawl awkwardly and cumbersomely across the floor and finish up stranded at the edges like beached seals. A man hacks at a tree trunk and is immersed in a projection of elephants. He lugs a huge table in and lies down under it. Three men stand on top of it, and then he carries the table out again. Even the blissful backward falls take on a peculiar seriousness.

It is as if, after all the chirpy bustle and nonchalance, the ensemble has to get a grip on itself again. Everyone sits silently on a semi-circle of chairs on the rock. When individual women step forward, risking a dance, it seems lost and lonely. Even the driving rhythm of a loud tango fails to animate them to erotic intimacy: everyone runs hectically around holding chairs, unable to find a place for themselves. Good behaviour is strictly rehearsed: a woman marks out a line on the ground, and each man has to perform a bow at this "line of good conduct" before being allowed to enter the space. Even during the meal a piqued lady uses her fork to spike two men's elbows, which are resting improperly on the table till they are removed.

All this cannot banish love and affection, but it casts the love-seekers in another light. The rediscovered childhood *élan* and the playful lovingness of the first half are countered strongly in the second. While at the beginning the dance solos conquered the space dynamically, in the second half of the evening they appear very isolated. A conspicuous feature in *O Dido*, for which Pina Bausch used only fifteen members of her company, is the presence of an Indian guest dancer. This is not only testimony to her deep respect for the ancient, elevated art of Indian dance, it also reveals a fundamental kinship. Pina Bausch effortlessly marries her own particular style of movement to the traditional steps and graceful arm gestures of India. An entirely unique beauty emerges, proving that the language of dance, at a high level, really is universal. In a precise and moving way, it allows all the nuances and shades of human inner life to resound and requires no interpretation in order to be understood.

At the end of *O Dido* a crowd of extras comes on stage; they stand kissing in pairs. They are given coffee as sustenance, then carry on kissing, *ad infinitum*. This plea for love demands eternity too.

## Wiesenland

This production, too, begins with a race of images, as if someone had cut up not just one but several films and spliced them together in a colourful sequence: a wild and expansive patchwork of sensual impressions. Despite this the momentary shots, in their pop-video montage, all seem to address the same subject: the search for love in hectic times.

A woman comes onstage with an inviting tea-tray and a candle and, as if to cool her desire for intimacy, is rewarded with a bucket of water tipped over her by a man. Wet and smiling, undeterred, she steps to the front of the stage, making a silent offer to the audience. Another woman hurriedly brings a ladder in and sniffs enthusiastically at an imaginary hay loft. Hers is above all a sensual desire. A man knocks himself and his partner out, with a blow to the head using a paper roll, as if this were the only way to engineer a cosy twosomeness. When she tries to slip away from him he quickly pulls her back to his side. Sleep, alone or in twos, is a recurring motif in this piece. A literal "sleeping car" is rolled in: a large box with bunk beds in which two elegantly dressed women loll around smoking. One dancer uses another as a living mattress, and someone continually tosses and turns between two pillows.

But sleep – in the sense of *arriving* and resting – is an illusion which never becomes reality in *Wiesenland (Meadow Land)*. Life seems too short to allow time for a rest. A wildly fighting couple storms into the scene and gets a third man to photograph their hectic passion. An "Indian" is swiftly drawn across the stage on a "flying carpet". The solos are danced at breakneck speed, taking up more and more space in this two-hour piece. It is as if the men and women wanted to protect themselves in these arm-twining dances and at the same time wanted to break away. They fall to the ground, gather themselves up again and open themselves longingly to the sky. An absolute desire lies behind this, turning dance into a dramatic tightrope walk, a game of life and death. The performers seem driven by tremendous pressure: internal or external. "Dance, dance, otherwise we are lost," a gypsy girl once said to Pina Bausch, making a lasting impression on the choreographer. The existential urgency of dance in the Tanztheater Wuppertal's work could hardly be expressed more clearly. At the point where all words fail, movement begins and lends inner distress an even greater insistence.

Yet the stage sets for *Wiesenland* evoke a place more of calm and safety. A huge cliff rises up in the background, overgrown with moss and ferns, water splashing softly down it. It is reminiscent of a secluded, protected spot in a forest, a meeting place for romance or quiet self-discovery. Although this is an element of *Wiesenland*, the piece is dominated by moments of unbridled passion. In this picture-book on love, Pina Bausch does not illustrate happiness which has been achieved or is at least within reach; she describes an insatiable longing. This is what drives the men and women through constant emotional ups and downs; but for all its drama, it remains breezy and light. Like carefree children the players take each other by the hand and spin each other round in circles over the ground. They cheerfully lift each other up in the air for little glides and back down again for soft landings. The little burst of happiness, the kindergarten rush of excitement, has grown up but been kept alive. The men throw themselves close together on the ground and let a woman walk over their heads. The amorous services they offer each other are diverse and imaginative. The audience is also questioned on matters of the heart: whether they love anyone, have children, are married. These questions are not intru-

176

sive but arise from the simple wish to remind the spectator that love still exists, that perhaps we just need to look for it again, very close to home, for the misery of living without love, without security, is simply too great.

That things are not always easy when it comes to love is hardly a secret to the protagonists of dance theatre, when, for instance, a couple weaves through an ever taller tower of chairs, in continual danger of crashing down. And sometimes they feel so thoroughly worthless they beg a much admired colleague for just one dance so that they can feel better. Intimacy can be dangerous, as when a man bashes two saucepan lids together and a woman runs quickly into his arms between bashes: playing with the gravity of love.

Everyone – men just as women – takes risks, because they neither will nor can give up the dream of love, even if this sometimes means dreaming all by yourself, like a woman who paints big colourful blossoms on a long strip of paper to the sounds of dark, raw singing. Perhaps it is just necessary to hold out long enough till the big moment finally arrives, like the dancer who measures the room alone in long strides before the women gradually all join him, in fine, long evening dresses; he has become the unchallenged, brilliant cock of the roost – a festive, glamorous image, which corresponds to another group image in this first part of *Wiesenland*. Here again the women stand in their elegant evening dresses, which they fan out with their hands, swaying on the spot, as if they have finally caught up with the heartbeat of time. They place men in various locations: a curiously moving moment; stiff as dolls they also evoke a primal image of all desire.

As in almost all of her works, Pina Bausch ensures that this piece's perceived meaning remains up in the air. This is the only way to approach the multi-layered, multi-nuanced subject. And this is the way the seventy-five-minute first part ends. The men pour water back and forth between two buckets while the women kneel on the ground smoking, sticking their heads under the resulting waterfall, blowing smoke into the water. It could almost be said that the relationship between the sexes is like that between fire and water – incompatible. However, such an interpretation is immediately refuted again by scene's smiling charm.

The sixty-minute second part initially seems to wish to pursue the subject in a more individual way. The cliff has now been tipped to form a hill which can be walked up, as if offering wider prospects and free-dom. Between the solos – again numerous – more individual scenes are interspersed. Two men tenderly blow smoke into a woman's hair, which slowly rises up it as if she were on fire. Another woman reads out a love letter and exuberantly kisses every object within reach. A further woman stands shaking her head around, as if unable to sleep, gets a man to kiss her and implores her idol to rescue her. Jealousy also demands its dues: a woman provocatively sets up a table in front of her lover; another man appears and lays his head in her hands. She becomes literally weak with laughter.

The intimate exploration of the highs and lows of love unexpectedly mutates into an outing to the countryside. The façade of a small house is built out of cardboard, and washing is hung on a line. A man in a bright red suit with a fat cigar in his mouth, like a suburban dandy or a gypsy baron, releases chickens into an enclosure; then the country life is cleared away again. Everyone stands on the hill once more and watches like amazed children as a balloon disappears into the air, only then throwing themselves back into their energetic dance. The men throw themselves violently to the ground; *Wiesenland* gradually speeds up again and heads towards the party, a scene familiar from many other pieces.

The first harbinger is a waiter dressed in white, who carefully sets up tables and chairs, yet no-one comes to be served by him. Later the entire company leaps for joy and throws food into the audience in delight. How-ever lovelorn we may be, it is still important to celebrate abundance and let rip. Everyone sits down at a large table to eat. However, the peaceful meal is continually interrupted by acrobatic interludes. Dancers play catch like badly brought-up children, pull chairs out from under each other or stand on the table and let the table-cloth be whipped out from under them as they jump. When the party is over everyone comes back in and stretches out comfortably on the floor. Now they can dance, to a musical pot-pourri. Like many of Pina Bausch's pieces, *Wiesenland* moves towards a relaxed ending.

The influence of the host country – Hungary – is less conspicuous than in previous co-productions. It is primarily in the music where along-side the familiar mixture of memory-laden tunes and harder, contempo-rary beats we hear the raw tones of the Balkans, and Pina Bausch's interest in gypsy culture becomes apparent. It can also be felt in the moods evoked

178

in *Wiesenland*. "Dance, dance, otherwise we are lost," seems to insistantly determine the fundamental tenor of *Wiesenland*. And yet at the end peace and a sense of arrival return. Like the first part, the second ends with amusing water games, the sound of moving water testifying once more to the endlessness of desire. However, at the heart of longing it is always virtually silent already.

## Água

If *Masurca Fogo*, created in 1998, is a testimony to the self-renewing power of life, the production created for the 2000/01 season could be read as a plea for beauty and pleasure.

The set design is unusual: the open stage presents a view over a white dance floor towards a plain, white semi-circle divided into three parts. No plants, earth, grass or trees occupy the space. This lack of natural elements purposefully alienates the dancers' actions. From the first moment, an absence of sophisticated interplay between inside and outside opens new horizons. The minimal stage retains its secret for almost half an hour. Nature appears only in the form of films projected on the floor and walls; palms wave continually in the breeze, exactly as if the spectators were lying on the beach, abandoning themselves to daydreams, lost in thought. A gentle holiday atmosphere prevails, relaxed and happy: a place almost too pretty to be true. In this Brazilian co-production, it seems as though Pina Bausch and her company have taken an extended holiday in a South American garden of Eden and are determined to whisk the spectator away on the trip too.

It does indeed all begin with pleasure: a dancer enters the bare room, peels an orange and eats it very noisily; a colleague holds the microphone for her, to amplify the sounds. Between moans of pleasure she tells a story of how she woke painfully from a dream and then saw a wonderful starry night sky above her: an unusual angle on things, suggesting we look at the world in different way. Because – who knows – what we take for reality might be a bad dream from which we simply have to wake, in order to see the world anew in all its beauty.

Another dancer enters the palm grove, circles her head, tosses her hair around, loses and finds herself in one of the powerful, arm-twining dances typical of Pina Bausch. Two men take over from her, get down onto the floor, freeze in a press-up position, put their heads down, roll sideways and open out into precise leg poses. Other men join the duo, till the dance makes it back onto its feet; all this is accompanied by a heavy, grinding rhythm. Wearing stunning evening dresses, the women enter, extending the scene into a furious group dance in which everyone opens their arms and quickly folds them behind their backs. The palm tree projections fade into a film of Brazilian drummers; a remarkable dialogue suddenly takes place between Pina Bausch's arm-circling dances and the accurately co-ordinated movements of the musicians: two superimposed dances, two energies forming an ideal alliance to fuel each other's incendiary rhythms.

Every so often one of the dancers steps out, performs a solo and runs away. The scene accelerates imperceptibly. A couple runs after each other and rolls swiftly to the ground. A lone man follows them like an echo. The ensemble returns; the men hold the women up and let them fly at a rate of knots through the air. A hotheaded mood takes over, finely balanced between tense urgency and explosive energy. As so often in dance theatre, this sequence of scenes refuses to be unambiguous. Then suddenly it is all over. All that remains is a woman in a bright red evening dress who dances into her own outstretched arms, moves her hips sensuously, draws her finger down the length of her arm and circles her head, as if there were nothing finer than to "lose one's head". The dance is fast and precise, like most of the solos in this piece, with constantly changing arm directions: an expression of powerful vitality which feeds on itself.

Only later, after this long choreographic opening, does the scene calm down, and Pina Bausch counterpoises the furious dances with contrary movement. A dancer comes on stage and declares that she hadn't really wanted to perform at all. She would much rather have turned red, sawn the leg off a table, burnt it and unleashed a terrible fire, before extinguishing it. She had wanted to pour water on the floor and sink down into it, wearing a wonderful dress. She wanted to smash glass to bits with a stone, to dress up very nicely, then throw all her clothes in the bin. Although she speaks in the subjunctive, she in fact acts out almost everything she describes. Possibility is reality; the apparent rejection of the theatre is itself a theatrical moment. In other words: it is perfectly reasonable to doubt reality, and the possibilities – dreamed perhaps, or feared – sometimes take form faster than we imagine.

Thus the courage to dream, in which this piece emboldens the spectator to trust, is in no sense banal or one-dimensional. It includes a delicate hint that we should not immediately think that everything which broadens the boundaries we ourselves have tightly drawn is impossible. Happiness, tranquillity and pleasure are all possible too, if we only allow them to be. For the delight in letting oneself go and the perception of beauty are no less real than sadness, abandonment and loneliness. In this piece Pina Bausch yet again bucks the general trend and rumbles an established taboo: that "serious" art is born only out of difficulty, drama and confrontation. Here she turns her back on aspects of her own work which have long since become conventions, and grants herself – and her audience – a glimpse of primal pleasure in movement. New times demand new means; this can be seen throughout all of her recent productions. While the 1970s and '80s were a time for breaking routines and taking a painful as well as sanguine look at human relationships, now is the time for encouragement and remembering our individual creative potential. It can be glamorous, it can be a party, and no-one need lose their sense of reality at all.

This piece does not seek to be read as a document of classic dance theatre but as a piece of pure choreography, obeying solely the laws of contracting and expanding energies. More seamlessly than ever, traditional and contemporary music weaves together into a dense emotional carpet, over which time may stretch or suddenly contract. At times forceful, then tranquilly expansive, it allows a mildly melancholy gaze at human nature, but what the dreamy spectator sees is not all sweetness and light.

For they are still there, the moments of danger: two men throw a stick through the air, and a woman who wanders into the risky game is pulled to the ground by another man for her own protection. Such moments fit swiftly and easily into the quick-fire sequence of images without confrontational drama. They appear more like short eruptions of passion which then settle back into the gentle flow of time. There is space here for tender, timid approaches. He and she appear in a flashing suit and a dress covered in fairy lights, risking only a very cautious, flirtatious glance at each other, from a long distance. Alternatively, he presents himself as a power-dressed macho, and she forces him to remove his clothes layer by layer, with disapproving looks and grumpy gestures. Only when he is half naked does she consider her lover suitably dressed to go out. Another man sinks to the feet of the woman he adores and tickles her arm with his eyelashes. Imagination seems to know no limits when it comes to such amorous favours. And when someone does actually sit around, hung-over and depressed, he is immediately comforted by the rest of the group, given a drink and rocked in a bath towel as if it were a hammock.

For Pina Bausch, conventions have long ceased to be a target to be attacked with rage. They are addressed with playful ease: two men in press-up poses politely shake hands, or two finely dressed ladies hold forth with amusement on the various masculine and feminine forms of greeting. The tropical heat has clearly mellowed everyone. When the walls are raised, luscious rainforest vegetation seems to want to sprawl into the room and soften the hectic bustle. Only the loud animal cries – faked by the ensemble from within the forest – rob a restless, slumbering woman of her night-time peace. Aside from this, the illustrious company meets between fleshy green bushes for a standing party and take sips of shining liquid from illuminated glasses. Later they loll about on white sofas arranged in varying formations and parade around, laughing, at the front of the stage holding bath towels with pictures of pin-up in front of their bodies.

The European antagonism has abated in this moist, hot climate: all is quiet on the sex-war front. Everyone cheerfully goes with the flow of beach life. After sunbathing, for which everyone applies suntan lotion, they hold a beach party with unrestrained whoops and cries, while two men on long ladders keep a sceptical eye on the sea. One isolated outcast meanders through the scene from time to time, attempts a swaying dance full of air-beating gestures, crouches and rocks himself. At the end of the first part, after an hour and a quarter, everyone rolls lethargically around on the sofas; only one couple still dances, closely entwined and finding no end. Slides are projected over the dozy end of the party: static images for party people who have settled down to rest, images of a coastal landscape, deep green forests, flying birds.

The films and slides are finely tuned to correspond to the action: a shaky image of a ship at sea appears, and a woman dances with chirpy little jumps along with the moving waters. Inner and outer movement

182

become one. Two men in swimming trunks then enter the room, lie down under thick plastic sheets and practise dry swimming while a film shows bathing children. Under the sheet the dancers look as though they are submerged in water. In between, the scene returns us to the austere, white room or sinks into an atmosphere of nocturnal dimness. Seldom can we guess what turn the piece will take next.

As unusual as the sets is the second half, where the principle of variation is usually followed: this time, Pina Bausch does not repeat whole complexes of scenes, placing them in new contexts. Instead, she takes only particular dramatic elements and mixes them with new elements so that the piece seems almost to continue infinitely. The second half begins very quietly and calmly. A woman lolls on the sofa, repeats excerpts of the solo she danced earlier, but now interrupts it with fits of giggles, till a man drags her out, drunk with happiness. Another woman comes on stage and shows us a white hair she has discovered, which leads into a whole scenic parade on the subject of hair, running like a thread through the opening of the second part: a woman sits wearing curlers and fans herself; another has her hair brushed softly by a man, who brushes her shoulder-strap off at the same time. She shyly pulls it up again. The sequence climaxes in an hysterical lament by a beauty with a mighty mane of hair, whinging that her hair is too dry; all attempts by her partner to calm her down lead to even greater distress. Beauty brings problems; happiness does too, sometimes.

For once things seems to go right, when he carries her in his arms and throws tiny parachutes in the air for her, which float gently to the ground. But another man is much less successful; when he presents his loved one with a superbly well wrapped car tyre for her birthday, an object she really has no interest in whatsoever. Sometimes excessive love becomes unbearable, as when a man persistently pursues his lover with continuous diminutives, till she slaps him back onto the sofa with her long hair.

For a short while nature dominates the action in this second part. The performers bring several large palm-tree crowns in, which they lie between on the ground, painting signs on each other's bodies. They seem to have melted there, as if dissolved into the rainforest. But soon the familiar rhythm of life takes over again, with an accentuated male solo. Like a whirling dervish he dances in a bouncing crinoline dress, introducing another accelerated sequence of images with impressions following each other helter-skelter, as if they were a series of flashbacks. Fragments of memory, barely able to grasp life in all its richness: a man pushes a woman around in a wheelbarrow; a couple glides in swift turns around each other, holding hands; a woman climbs a held-up pole and slides down again, while in parallel a man climbs hand over hand up a plank; the men throw the women over their shoulders and whirl them round at break-neck speed; a man paddles in an enormous palm leaf. A woman entices a man, waving her skirt, but shyly pulls it down over her knees to protect herself from his curiosity. Finally all the women surround him, waving their skirts, and the chaste coquettishness turns into a genuine attack.

Towards the end, in a parade of solos rapidly succeeding each other, the tension once more builds up a powerful energy, before releasing itself in wild, enjoyable water games. The projections now show the endless flowing and falling of the Iguaçu waterfalls. In their dances, the perform-ers coat each other with the cooling water, squirt each other with hand-held water bottles and construct an improvised water pipe to widespread jubilation: so many simple excesses, all within reach; a childish party providing unlimited fun. They hurriedly carry tables in, on which they revolve, still sitting: an image of happy, swaying, turning children. It is freshly rediscovered joy, sheer pleasure in being alive. Then the stage is suddenly empty. The game could begin all over again.

Time is endless in Pina Bausch's dance theatre, and it is a plea to enjoy life, here and now, without reservations. Sometimes theatre can do this too: can give an impression of what could be – and clearly always has been.


## Für die Kinder von gestern, heute und morgen


Pina Bausch chose a dedication as the title for the piece she produced in spring 2002: *Für die Kinder von gestern, heute und morgen* (*For the children of yesterday, today and tomorrow*). It is not a "children's piece", although it does appeal to the child in every adult, to the hope that the memory of that time of primal energy and carefree ease could bring us a little closer to our much-desired goal of love.

How would it be if we could let ourselves be lifted up once more for a short blissful flight? If we could imagine ourselves as birds, free and unfet-

184

tered? If we were still standing at the start with all the doors open? These could well have been the questions Pina Bausch asked in the search for her new piece. Again, this is not about nostalgia or the glorification of childhood but a reminder of our own powers of imagination.

The scenery alone reminds us that nothing need stay as it is, that there are no unshakeable certainties. As so often in past works, the stage set consists of a variation on the larger-than-life, austere white room of an old residential building, this time with an enormous window in the far wall and two doorways in each of the side walls. Later we realise that the space, which seemed so clearly defined, has a life of its own. As if by magic, the walls begin to move, gliding backwards and forwards, narrowing or widening the room. The scenic changes accelerate throughout the piece, together with the moods created by the lighting and the performers' emotions. The world is out of kilter. At times nothing is certain any more, spreading a benign and occasionally pleasurable disconcertion.

Pina Bausch approaches the subject of her nearly two-and-a-half-hour excursion with extreme caution. Accompanied by gentle music, two dancers bring in a table and sit on its edge. One of them lowers himself very, very slowly to the side. Only at the last moment does his colleague grab his leg, preventing his fall. They switch roles: the catcher lies on the ground in a sitting position, the other brings him a chair so that he can sit and lie down at the same time – an image of beautiful contradiction.

For a moment this scene of gentle solicitude is harshly contrasted by two men running repeatedly at each other; they collide and fall to the ground as if driven by an excessive need for intimacy. Then a man carries in a sitting woman, shakes her gently, places her on the ground, lets her glide through the air as if she were weightless. In response she cautiously lifts his leg and his head, testing their weight. Finally he leaves her alone for a dreamily slow solo, in which she runs her hands over her body, suddenly stretches out her arms, then crouches again like an animal, protecting herself. Her dance-partner lets her float once more, and then both are replaced by three men lifting a fourth, who tries out various sleeping positions. Wholly trusting, he lets everything be done to him, so great is his apparent desire for sleep and sheltered dreaming.

Then this mood vanishes too, like a beautiful vision. A dancer runs backwards and forwards with hasty steps, grasps himself in solitary embraces, pauses in bewilderment, manipulates his own limbs and shakes his fists, not knowing whether he is coming or going. Accompanied by rapid percussion the scenery opens up. When a pedestal is removed through the large window, it is the cue for a swift sequence of solos, a moment of release from the self: two men chase each other on an office chair and a skateboard, and dancers run in and out; soon it calms down again. A woman lies down on the ground; a man pulls her towards him as if on an invisible thread, stands her up, marks steps on the ground for her and initiates her dance. For a moment she remains alone, beating her "wings" in self-absorption, then he returns, takes her on his back and lets her flutter and fly. The joy of flying seems contagious. Ever more women come in, beating their wings and running circles around a man who dances a solo in the middle like the cock of the roost.

In Pina Bausch's dance theatre it is always this imperceptible heightening and extending of a subject (once it has been found) which seduces the spectator into dreaming, in a highly organic way. An image may be multiplied or condensed, or sharp contrasts and unexpected confrontations made, before room is suddenly there for us to catch our breath. *Für die Kinder von gestern, heute und morgen* circles around its subject in apparently endless spirals without marking time, even for a moment. Along with the solos and duos of the introduction, Bausch gradually introduces paired actions which are carried out by the whole group. The women sit jiggling up and down on the men's laps in cheerful impatience. Later they are drawn back by a rope and shot like an arrow at their dancing partners so that everyone can then perform an intimate, interwoven partner dance.

This piece, underscored largely by Brazilian music, again deals with love but also with the hurdles which must be overcome on the way to intimacy. When a woman paints a heart with a romantic arrow through it on the window, a colleague immediately responds with an anatomically correct representation of the organ. Happiness must be out there, somewhere between romantic dreaminess and dry realism. Endurance is certainly called for, as with the man who tries, laboriously, to persuade his partner she should start with the basics when it comes to matters of the heart, and should first try a little cuddle. The couple runs through this piece like a leitmotif. Even when she deliberately misunderstands every compliment he pays her, he never gives up.

186

Sometimes couples want to literally gobble each other up: he sniffs at the freshly cooked food that lies on her body. Then a woman takes the initiative again, kissing and cuddling two men one after the other, literally taking them to her breast. Relations between the sexes remain tense and ambivalent in this piece too, oscillating between willingness and sudden disinclination: longing for each other yet also shying away. Sometimes they lay into each other in a restrained fight, kicking each other in the rear or trying to hit outstretched hands with their pointed heels. They use dares as a measure of their strength, holding the flame of a cigarette lighter under their fingers to see who can stand it the longest. They angrily brush their own hair with a broom and, with much bellowing and delight, burn holes in their own pullovers: a fine balance between self-hatred and the desire to break out. The ensemble begins a close, swaying partner dance and then, in an abrupt shift, sinks to the floor to a banging fairground rhythm, manipulating their own limbs as they joggle with difficulty to the front of the stage.

Pina Bausch has often used such sitting dances in her pieces. They seem to put the players under a sudden spell, to rob them of the dignity of their upright gait and throw them into an animal state, making them helpless on the one hand and, on the other, placing them on a level with the audience. Normally dominant from up on the stage, the dancers suddenly find themselves at eye level with the audience, as equals. It almost seems as if it were necessary to hit the hard ground of fact from time to time in order to make possible all the other light, floating moments. At the end of the first part a dancer appears as a curious kind of gardener, dressed in a tulle dress. Another man joins him, moving him solely with the force of his breath. He glides back and forth like a gust of wind. A carpet with an enormous sandcastle is dragged in, and the entire troupe diligently joins in building this transient work, wholly dedicated to the task.

If the (roughly) one-and-a-half-hour first half consists mostly of long, gentle passages, in the hour-long second half things gradually speed up as if, unnoticed, the conflicts had sharpened. The couple with their slow attempts towards intimacy now talk busily at cross purposes. In a swift solo the woman reels off clichéd phrases from arguments: "Over my dead body! Oh no! You can't have it both ways! That's the last straw!" As a precaution, he says that should he ever be nasty to her, she is allowed to hit him. Then he moves into an oblivious solo, making signs in the air, measuring out his body with his fingers, giving himself the impulses to move his body. Dance – an action – is much stronger than words, and it seems as if the players can reach genuine feeling only through movement, in a state of wordlessness.

Such moments are soon swept aside by a sudden hustle and bustle. Large black boxes are rolled in and rolled out. A man tries to lie on one, without success. The mobile walls move forwards and backwards. A man repeatedly attempts to blow up a balloon through a hollow ballet barre, but the distance is too great, and he fails. The hair-brushing with brooms accelerates into a ruthless demonstration of self-hatred. Gallows humour is evoked when the men line up in a barber's scene at the front of the stage and a loudmouth among them tells the story of how his father could, allegedly, bite mice in half and fart in rhythm. The performers' tone towards each other sharpens; their actions become wilder. Increasingly, black becomes the dominant colour of the costumes. In moments when things do calm down again, the woman who dances a solo partnered by various men seems hypnotised, unaware of herself.

Another man has to hold his own head throughout his dance, letting his arms and torso swing heavily as he spins in wild, twirling jumps, somewhere between depression and anger. When one of the dancers tries an Elvis Presley number in a glittery stage shirt, the music suddenly cuts out. Percussion sounds drive him to make wild falls to the ground, and then he runs away. In his place the other men run into the room to the sounds of frenzied rock music, deliver short, swift solos and then vanish. In pairs, the ensemble of fourteen dancers rolls to the ground, and the men lift the women in an open-legged half turn. When a man continually introduces his wife with the phrase "by the way", the effect is one of distance rather than togetherness. While he makes her up, she combs his hair and holds his head, which continually falls, as if it were too heavy. Something curiously furtive underlies their relationship. Two men hug each other so firmly it hurts, and they push each other away again. Even the demanding woman from the first half, who takes the men to her bosom once more, seems much less amusing in this atmosphere than she did before.

The scene calms down again. With a steady coming-and-going happening in the background, one of the dancers tells an old Native American tale. It is about a squirrel who finds the sun lost in a tree, and in rescuing it narrowly escapes being blinded and burnt. As a gesture of thanks the sun gives him the ability to see at night and to fly. The squirrel becomes a bat. The story leaves us with strangely mixed feelings.

After this moment of calm Pina Bausch sends her ensemble into a parade of solos once more, full of swiftly tumbling bodies, leaving us unsure whether they are driven by pure pleasure or sheer panic. The scene falls into sudden darkness; the piece ends with a sharp incision and leaves all questions open.

## Nefés

The 2003 production is unusual in many ways. The scenery alone diverges from the usual parameters. It offers neither a variation on the spacious, white interior space – mostly enlargements of rooms in old houses – which have often set the stage for pieces dealing with the possibilities and impossibilities of love, nor does it bring a slice of nature to the stage in a deliberate process of poetic alienation. Echoing the piece's main theme of the *hammam*, or Turkish bath, there is an expansive, dark cedar wood floor, its edges lost in the darkness, which dips into a large hollow in the middle. Later on in the piece the shallow pit begins, imperceptibly, to fill with water from beneath till a small lake has formed; by the end of the two-and-a-half-hour performance it has emptied again, just as imperceptibly. The process resembles the soft ebb and flow of the tide; equally minimal are the increases and decreases in the emotional temperature of *Nefés* (which simply means "breath" in Turkish). In the year of the war against Iraq, Pina Bausch responds to the tense global situation with an almost seamless sequence of images depicting love almost entirely eschewing hard contrasts and contrary movements. The endless succession of music – mostly Turkish – is scarcely interrupted. This co-production with the international Istanbul Theatre Festival seems like an endless Sufi meditation, like dancing dervishes turning on their own axis in ecstatic spiritual yearning.

First used in the "Madrid" piece, Pina Bausch's technique of lining her dances up like pearls on a rosary has the effect of allowing time to come to an apparent standstill – as if it were possible to overcome the temporal bondage of physical existence through dance and extend it into eternity. The rondo recurs frequently in her work as a choreographic principle of composition. It eases the usual tight focus of events on stage, playing around the subject in a spiralling motion of increasing and decreasing circles. Behind this lies an attitude of pure observation, which abstains from any value judgements and does not pretend to know everything. In *Nefés* Pina Bausch uses this compositional principle without a counterpoint for the first time and allows her gentle sequence of images to overflow expansively.

"Me in the hammam," says a dancer, coming on stage to soft music, who demonstrates on a colleague how hard a massage can be at a Turkish bath. He immediately becomes the victim, enjoying the manhandling with a wide grin on his face. Then he comes in with a wet cushion cover from which he drips fine foam onto a man lying on the ground. The bodily pleasures and labours of love – which Pina Bausch has examined in all her previous works – play a decisive role in *Nefés* too. However, the women's love favours seem almost to contain self-hatred, like when they brush their wet hair out over the men, wetting them with a fine spray. And when they later get down on all fours in front of the men, who are sitting formally on chairs in their suits, and let themselves be stroked like dogs, this image of animal trust leaves us with somewhat mixed feelings. They wear their hair combed over their faces like veils and stand in a row next to each other. The men cautiously approach them, part their veils of hair and kiss them softly. But they also kneel down in front of the women and use the hems of their skirts to fan cool air up towards them.

The battle of the sexes has, as in all of the recent pieces, receded far into the distance, and the protagonists render each other tender favours of love instead. As so often, Pina Bausch initially introduces such scenes as individual actions and then expands them for a moment into group motifs in order to take them beyond the individuality of the intimate moment into the wider arena.

In the realm of tentative rapprochements only light irritations surface when, for instance, a woman walks across the men's shoulders as if she needed urgently to cross a chasm. When she later lets herself be lifted like a plank of wood, we don't know whether we should be shocked by the sudden *rigor mortis* in her body or full of admiration for her muscular control. In another scene, a dancer walks the same fine line between danger and artistry when he fixes a large table to his stomach and whirls it around in circles at breathtaking speed.

The protagonists are otherwise mostly in a party mood, like the laughing couple: they empty their champagne glasses and throw them over their shoulders from offstage, to the sound of exploding fireworks. Squealing with pleasure, the woman stands up and does a swaying dance for her partner, declaring with amusement: "I'm much too fat for you." In another scene she stands and washes up in a bucket. Suddenly she breaks off this everyday work, flings herself round her partner's neck, kissing him wildly, before returning, just as suddenly, to her housework. These two figures recur like a leitmotif through the hour-long first half. In stentorian tones, she proudly states: "All the good things I have come from grandma!" Then she holds up a suspender belt and says: "Why shouldn't I show something like this off? It's very sensual after all!" Her grandmother brought ten children into the world, she says, and to illustrate this several bodies roll out from under the long dress of a fellow dancer at the side of the stage.

The advocation for sensuality and pleasure seems to be the omnipresent credo. Whether two women sit down for a picnic, giggling and fishing honey out of a pot with pieces of bread, or a man helps a woman reach a little box hidden high up in the arch of the proscenium so she can treat herself to its delicacies, *Nefés* is first and foremost a celebration of physical sensuality. We get the impression the performers are already standing at the gates of paradise, ready and able to enter.

The dancers describe their organic movements in the expansive space with airy ease. Towards the end of this first half a woman dances with various partners one after the other, letting herself be dropped and lifted, moved by gentle touches. One man gazes at her admiringly, clearly entranced by so much carefree grace and beauty.

The one-and-a-half hour second part picks up the relaxed, cheerful atmosphere again. A dancer enters the initially silent space and measures her body with the span of her fingers. Then Turkish music begins, the dancer sinks into low *pliés*, flutters her hands and swiftly swings her hips. Another dancer takes over, stands on the spot and sings a Spanish song in falsetto, his eyes closed. Then, lying on the ground, he begins a sleepwalking dance, pausing repeatedly, listening inwards. Finally he stands up and turns in a wide radius on his own axis. The space has been freed up.

A couple enters it for a short, close dance. Another man takes their place, and the woman jumps into his arms; she lets herself be carried and then washes herself with filtered water from a bowl in which she has spread her dress. She changes to a new partner who rolls her right down to the ground; then the other man returns. He dutifully accompanies her in her solo dance, continually passing her a glass of water, taking it away again just before it falls. Short pauses and light syncopation are thus created, joined by a tender cord of mutual restraint and consideration. At the end he dances for her, smiling and flirting.

Out of this gradual crescendo Pina Bausch produces a profusion of courtship strategies; the men attempt to impress the women in every conceivable manner. One of them carries in a large table, takes a run-up and slides down it, finally landing on a chair; he and the chair topple over together in an acrobatic performance. Another man, sitting on the ground, kicks a cushion into the air and catches it with his feet, before taking similar leg-twining turns with his partner through the stalls, treating her much as he treated the cushion. In the background someone demonstrates that he can drink out of the large pool in the middle of the stage even while doing a handstand. A couple is separated by the entire width of the stage, standing one on either side of the proscenium arch, and they flirt with each other across the space. Finally she goes over to him, but brings a chaperone along with her. He looks annoyed but then cheerfully accepts the third party.

Gradually, interspersed with duets and solos, the subject of twosomeness is expanded into a group motif. Men and women enter the room, arm in arm, then the men twist out of the embrace for a moment. The motif is repeated in a man's solo when he is accompanied by the entire group of women who hold and protect him. The calm, caring embrace, which stands isolated in the room for a moment, seems like a dreamy image of desire. It is possible to come and go while remaining protected.

Even when something goes slightly wrong, a guardian angel soon comes to the rescue. In the midst of her solemn dance, a lady's flowery dress suddenly bursts at the seams. A gentleman holding a halo above his head rushes over and stands behind the unfortunate lady to obscure the split, accompanying her safely out.

This scene is directly counteracted. A white gauze curtain is pulled across to serve as a screen for a projection of water. In no time at all a restaurant with chairs and tables is set up behind it. Scurrying waiters vie for a woman's attention by bringing in more and more ghetto-blasters, resulting in a veritable cacophony. To cap it all, the waiters turn out to be manic bazaar merchants, keen to flog all manner of goods. Then suddenly it is all over.

*Nefés* pauses briefly for a calm, male solo, but the mood heats up again with the next dance, a floor solo. The curtain is drawn once more for a projection of heavy city traffic, from which a woman on stage tries to flee. Then the outburst of hectic daily bustle is over, and the piece returns once more to its theme of love with soft solos and encounters between couples. Very gradually, however, a new stringency is introduced. The men enter the room, slide to the floor on their stomachs, lean up and shake each other's hands formally. While a woman dances alone in the background, the men hold hands to form a diagonal across the space. The women copy them but edge shyly away from the stage and out through the auditorium. For a moment night falls on the scene. Women with torches walk through the water looking for something. One of them washes her jewellery with only a toothbrush. The men push each other slowly and calmly into sitting poses on the ground, each laying a leg on the other's shoulder; it is a curiously ambivalent image, of almost affectionate dominance. On the floor they shake each other's hands again. One of them sips from a blue, shimmering drink, which inspires him to do a short, virtuoso techno dance. Another dancer follows him with a solo of flying hands and expansive leaps. The curtain is drawn again, and the woman tries again to flee, screaming, from the surging traffic. Separated into groups of men and women, the dancers hold hands and form silent lines of steadfast solidarity.

Amongst all this, a picnic scene involving the entire, united ensemble seems like a dream, forming a brief group image. An oriental princess glides in on a rolling armchair like a mirage. No desires or yearnings are abandoned; all we need is a different kind of strength and community so that our dreams can withstand reality. Thus the women join to form a close group and stride backwards and forwards in a circle, accompanied by a light which draws all kinds of letters on the ground.

Meanwhile, amongst all this, the mutual teasing and courtship seems likely to carry on forever. The performers offer each other drinks and float them across the pool on a tray. A woman flirts happily with two men and finally stuffs her hair in one of their mouths. A woman eases a man to the ground and lies down demonstratively next to him. The eternal game of near and far will never stop, but it is being played during a time in which group solidarity is apparently needed more than ever.

Pina Bausch ends her piece with an ambivalent image: a row of sitting men slide on stage from the left, one leg on the ground, carefully placing one foot in front of the other, then pausing. The women echo their poses in the background, smiling and waiting. It is as if, across this great gulf, each sex wanted to impress the other with their poses. There is something dubious yet enormously charming about this.

In the auditorium the lights slowly come up. On stage the water has sunk away, unnoticed. Perhaps it was all a dream.


## Ten Chi


In an interview, Pina Bausch once observed that she sees life as a journey. A journey, it might be added, during which we collect very diverse experiences, in which foreign places allow us to see clearly both the differences and the similarities between them and our own cultures. The main subject of Pina Bausch's work, the longing for love, is a fundamental constant which connects across all cultural differences. In *Ten Chi*, a 2004 co-production with several Japanese institutions, this longing again provides the link which connects diverse impressions from a very different cultural arena.

On the stage, which is draped in black, the tail of an enormous whale sticks up from the similarly black-covered floor, like a photo capturing the moment of diving: a movement frozen in time. The ascetic stage set is thus divided into two worlds: above and below the implied sea-level. That which is visible on the surface is only a tiny fraction of what is actually happening in the depths of the emotional world. Pina Bausch lets her Japanese theme unfold with great peace and tranquillity, underscored with western and Japanese music which develops, for just a few moments, a driving rhythm. *Ten Chi* resembles a quiet meditation on the theme of love, like listening into one's own body and its emotions.

194

To soft string music, a petite dancer comes on stage, sinks into a *plié* and begins a long, calm solo during which a man joins her, lifts her gently under the sheltering roof of the enormous whale tail and carefully lets her float there. Compared to the dimensions of nature, humans seem small and vulnerable. Later the difference in scale is expanded even more when a woman tells the story of a newly-discovered star and how it doesn't make it any brighter on earth because the earth is very far away and very small. From the cosmic perspective, the earth itself is a pinprick; how much smaller, then, are humans? But humans assert themselves through their desire. A woman in black prances on stage and calls a man to her. They both take delight in shredding her tulle dress while she emits tiny, sharp screams. Then she restrains him, but he carries on again just as eagerly as before.

It is love which allows people to grow and to cope with their own futility. The piece dreams of love in ever new ways: a couple sits on chairs holding fans and flirts discreetly with each other; a woman comes in with two little dishes, as if she wanted to feed birds; a man on a stool draws her to him in a gentle embrace and puts her down again. Another coolly ties the hem of a woman's skirt to his clothes like a napkin in what appears to be a ritual accepted by both of them. Love literally makes people flighty: a woman, alone with a man in the cinema, talks of how excited she is and mutates into a fluttering butterfly with the aid of two sticks held under her long dress. For a moment the dream of love expands into a group image: many closely-entwined couples press against each other, then move slowly apart. In another scene the men carry the women in on their backs, and one single woman dances as if under water, weightless. The others quietly leave the room, as if they don't want to disturb the dancer's intimate moment alone.

As is so often the case, it is in the solo dances that the protagonists of dance theatre can really be at one with themselves. These solos may be coquettish and full of *joie de vivre* or dances of self-absorption. A man in a long, black dress and a train comes on stage, takes careful steps, circles his hands around his head and supports it as if it were heavy: melancholically musing on his own body. Danced in drag, this solo is a reference to the Japanese tradition in which female roles were originally played by men. But the man, who cannot be at one with himself or anyone else, hides away in his own loneliness; he pulls at the transparent dress, leaving himself unprotected and exposed right up to his shoulders, and crouches, taciturn, while a man does press-ups on the ground. The woman doesn't even notice him.

The underlying mood of the piece is juxtaposed with contrasting images. The actress brings everyone down to earth and back to reality when she soberly assesses the modest contents of the fridge for the weekend ahead, tersely noting that her dearest is himself like a fridge: closed and full of white wine at the top, frozen solid down below. As if in response to an unspecified emergency, panic breaks out. In a furious solo a man tips out of his axis, almost falling to the ground; two other men engineer their own movements and shake their heads. A woman is dragged around, hanging between two men, dances a short solo with clawed hands – as if her animal nature demanded expression – and is then carried out.

The action calms down again towards the end of the first part. Snow falls lightly down onto the stage, and an absurdly everyday atmosphere takes over. As if sleeping or resigned, a woman sits immobile with a cushion; another does her hair and another presents her face in the form of an elaborate mask, posing with a pair of fans. A man is given first a kimono, tied with several belts, then a dustpan and a brush and is photographed. But he is not going to sweep the snow away; he is only posing for a souvenir photo. With a calm female solo Bausch closes this first half.

The second half introduces variations on the same theme, but makes sharp contrasts and deliberately forces the humour. Initially the piece seems to return to its starting point. The little dancer enters the increasingly snowy space again, looks around her at the enchanted landscape in amazement and begins a joyful, waving dance. A woman joins her, bowing with dignity and then teaches her the proper way to bow. Sitting on chairs, she has to practise good posture with chastely closed legs and then she is allowed to return to her joyful solo. She is banished by a tour guide who, becoming increasingly agitated, tries to encourage imaginary tourists to move on. Despite apparently being under extreme time pressure, she still attempts to remain polite.

Bausch follows this with an array of solos and duets interrupted by theatrical scenes. Sometimes swaying hips permit a flash of eroticism, but hands immediately shoot up to the mouth, as if the dancer had said something naughty. A man in a long skirt whirls across the stage like a dervish,

196

crouches on the ground for a moment and whirls out. A woman playfully throws a cushion into the air, flings herself to the ground, turning at the last moment to avoid it as it falls. At this point the atmosphere still seems relaxed. A man performs a labour of love for an immobile, seated woman, moving her lifeless hand with fans and blowing air at her hair. An air-walking woman is carried in. There is teasing, dancers hitting each other with a rose or watching in fascination how others smoke. With mutual lifts and soft interweaving, two men and a woman dance with and around each other as if playing a gleeful game. The actress fervently extols her lover's kissing skills.

But slowly the mood darkens. A man's initial attempt to lean on a woman seems far too abrupt: he brusquely lets himself fall against her, and she carries him out like a heavy weight attached to her body. Two men stand opposite each other ready for a fight. A woman interrupts the incipient rivalry by inserting a neat handkerchief into one of the men's jackets and leading him out. With an exaggerated Elvis hairdo and wearing a glitzy, spotted suit, a man dances in front of a woman, trying hard to impress her. He too suddenly leaps onto her back. They stare at each other, perplexed, and then, to pounding drum music, he dances to the point of exhaustion. Suddenly his courtship takes an aggressive turn. At the end he stands exhausted while she seems to be frozen stiff on her chair. Even the actress, who has styled herself with the dramatic costume of a *grande dame*, seems unable to win over the passing men with her story about the newly discovered star. She becomes increasingly timid and subdued till she finally gives up.

In a comic interlude with excessively loud Godzilla noises a woman beats up a cushion, poking out imaginary eyes and behaving like a deranged fighter. Yet instead of impressing the man sitting at the table, she succeeds only in frightening him. Acting as if nothing had happened, she approaches him and pulls him towards her with the tablecloth. The man can only manage comic contortions as he attempts to impress her with a plastic snake wrapped around his head. The more the communication between the sexes goes wrong, the greater the need to find a way of coming together. A man removes layers of bathrobes, worn one on top of the other like protective skins, and dances a fast, staggered solo. He runs with dangling simian arms, groping his own body as if he has to check whether he is still in one piece, but he's already long gone.

For a moment the situation calms once more: a male and a female solo appear dreamy and lost amongst the now wholly snow-covered landscape which resembles an enchanted garden above a frozen sea. Then the finale is ushered in, with a series of disturbing images. A man folds a woman's arms across her breast; another makes up a disinterested, sitting woman; a third puts a woman to bed who, apparently drained of life, is leaning against a chair. Men and women carry each other in and out, as if they were a burden. Two men lean their heads against each other in bafflement. Accompanied by hard, accentuated string music, a man makes sharp hand signs; a woman desperately plunges her head in a cushion; two men move each other as if their heads were too heavy to respond to their own impulses; a woman dances, shaking her head, seeming to fight something off, unable to find calm. The men fill the winter landscape with countless ties while the music speeds up. The women scream and cover their ears and are carried out by the men, wriggling helplessly. In the panic, no-one knows where to go. To the intensifying sounds of drumming, a racing parade of short solo extracts from the piece begins, while the lights slowly dim.

In *Ten Chi* the *Tanztheater* performers have – yet again – gone unsaved.


## Rough Cut


The year 2005 brought a further co-production with an Asian country, this time South Korea. References to the country and culture are much less conspicuous than in *Ten Chi*. It is mostly in the music, consisting primarily of contemporary pop, that the atmosphere of the host country is felt.

*Rough Cut* is set in front of a white, craggy wall of ice which towers imposingly: a landscape image of dangerous, icy beauty. It is ideal as a surface for projections and as a cliff to be climbed by dancers as well as mountain climbers – members of a Wuppertal branch of the German Alpine Climbing Association. Pina Bausch has often recruited people from her chosen home, Wuppertal, for her work: members of an amateur music club, elderly athletes and a group of energetic senior citizens with whom she restaged her piece *Kontakthof* in 2000. In this way she connects parts of the world on her doorstep with the wider world of other cultures, both of which have their own importance.

*Rough Cut* begins with playful levity. Two men enter the stage and look into the audience, smiling. One of them whistles a tune which the other immediately copies as if plucking it straight from his lips, and the song springs forth from the two of them in turns till a couple enters. The man takes the woman by her arms and turns her very calmly into a deep squat, as if this were an exercise in trust, a labour of love. Even when two men throw a heavy wooden block at each other, falling over as they catch it, there is no aggression involved. A woman joins them and stretches herself out on the floor, her hair spread out around her. The wooden block is placed on her hair, but when she stands up it rolls easily away. One man hacks at the block while another, sitting on a chair, rapidly throws paper tissues up into the air, making it snow on himself. It is the approach to the material which alone determines what is light and what is heavy, and in *Rough Cut* it seems as if Pina Bausch wants to point out that everything which is heavy also has a light side.

When a woman is passed from one man to another, the dancers' attitude is affectionate. A courting dance develops with cheerful charm as she is moved, led to the ground, pulled to her feet by a man, swung through the air. At the end she stands next to a man in a suit. With an ambiguous smile she rubs his tie and pulls him out with her. Another couple also clearly likes the look of one another: the bare-breasted beauty appears in a long, tight skirt; the coffee-drinking gentleman ties it up to show off her long, slender legs, and she leaves proudly. Another woman grazes at some "kitty grass" she has brought in, behaving like a surreally alienated nibbler, and then dances a hip-swinging, accentuated solo ending with a sharp glance at the audience. A woman in a long green dress puts on gauntlets and sets down a wooden block. Another woman sits on it, while a man lies at her feet, smoking and talking about a battle – upcoming or long since fought. The red-skirted woman walks by, whipping her own leg; two men catch each other's dropped glass of water at the last moment. Following a long female solo in which the dancer appears alternately as a busy little animal and a whirling dervish, a woman calmly sets fire to one paper flower after another, putting them out in a bucket of water: a tranquil image of transience.

Screeching music accompanying a staggering, plummeting male solo introduces a typical Bausch moment of panic. Swinging her arms and hopping forwards, a woman dances a lament; she hangs from the head of a man, is dragged rapidly round in a circle, lifted up in the air and thrown back and forth between two men. She throws chairs around, runs for her life, and no-one can stop her. The general distress is interrupted for a moment by a calm female solo in which the dancer attempts to pick herself up by her own hair. Then the woman is on the run again, to the hard sounds of percussion music; she is rolled to the ground, straightened up again by her partner using his feet, dragged in a circle hanging from a man's head and finally carried out, running through the air, by two men. Two others turn a woman upside down like a windmill; the fleeing woman returns and climbs frantically up and down a man. Then the turbulent atmosphere settles with a short floor solo.

As if he needed to hurry her along, a man holds a lit cigarette lighter to a woman's heels; another woman cheerfully throws a plate in the air and catches it at the last moment; another dances sexily to a grinding, sensual rhythm. Then a man lies down on the ground, and the women cover him with cabbage leaves till he is invisible. The women walk around in long, pretty summer dresses, fanning themselves with cabbage leaves. The men – also fanning themselves – join them, take their clothes off and, bent over benches, get their backs scrubbed. For a moment the area in front of the wall of ice mutates into a peaceful bathhouse. Then drumming starts up. Climbers abseil down, and the dancers hastily clear up. One man runs back and forth between the proscenium walls, greeting and seeing off imaginary guests, and introduces a real colleague, who he says has a girlfriend who is a good cook. The famed girlfriend makes a brief appearance wearing an apron and waves shyly. As the climbers leave, the scene vanishes like a mirage.

A man ardently lists everything he finds attractive about a woman who's wearing a smart black evening dress. Quietly but persistently, she asks him to continue repeating his hymns of praise. In delight, the man makes tissues snow on him again, building up to a twisting, running solo till he is carried out. The women appear, with the hems of their dresses over their heads like veils. Meanwhile two men on benches demonstrate how casually they can fall over. But the Madonna-like women merely smile and leave via the auditorium. While a projection transforms the ice cliff into a blossoming alpine pasture, a couple climbs onto a ledge and gazes lovingly at each other. A woman's voice sings "I wanna fall in love with you". The mountain climbers ascend again, and the veiled ladies return to the stage. Then it is time for the interval.

In the second half *Rough Cut* returns to the subject of love and its associations with nature. With the projection of a tree in the background, a woman walks calmly across the stage. A man carries a branch which her hair has been tied up onto: her hair literally stands on end. Another, assisted by two men, climbs up a tiny tree as if she were entirely weightless. A man who is dragged in against his will kneads a large eiderdown and describes a nightmare in which he had to knead a huge amount of dough, with the constant feeling he had forgotten something: the yeast. Carried by two others, he sails through the air and lands softly in the eiderdown. A woman does the same to him again – whatever seems difficult can also be taken lightly.

Pina Bausch continues to investigate the possibilities of a genuine encounter, somewhere between dream and reality, and continually intersperses the theatrical scenes with various solos and duets. Very politely and gallantly, a couple kisses each other's hand in front of a projection of waves. Another couple clings to a man like little animals. Love itself is animal-like which we see when a couple, assisted by colleagues, runs around like a pair of playful dogs. Air-walking women cross the scene; a man turns a woman in circles, holding her ankles. She enjoys the brief flight, dancing afterwards like a whirling dervish, rushing at a man whom she cuddles furiously before vanishing. Two women wearing divers' goggles are carried as if weightless as they look around. The woman is turned again into her low squat. A man demonstrates a trick, which no-one pays attention to, lying across three chairs and tipping the outer two in a delicate balance. The nightmare-sufferer is dragged in again; this time, however, he dances in front of a landscape of lakes. But when the mysterious veiled ladies enter he is disturbed and feels watched. The projection changes to a continual cascade of neon-lit advertisements, while the mountain climbers work their way up the ice-cliff. A cosy sleeping place is prepared for a woman on the floor, and her lover is also neatly folded in. Another couple fails to come together. She totters around on the spot in excitement, desperate to sleep with him. He, on the other hand, is clearly self-conscious, removing his clothes awkwardly and carefully folding them. Finally she loses interest and seeks pleasure with another man, who runs a stimulating needle up and down her leg. In fake exuberance they slap each other on the thighs.

An explosive projection of fireworks interrupts the intimacy. The men form an infinite ballet diagonal. One of them describes how, when he told his father he wanted to become a priest, he advised him it would be better to be a ballet dancer. A screaming woman crosses the men's mechanical, unending lines. One of them dances with two sticks like an Asian martial arts fighter. The projections now show people gliding up and down escalators: another big city impression. Intense drumming pushes a dancer to the edge of exhaustion. The woman runs in circles again, as if her life were at stake. Stones are strewn on the ground and then immediately cleared from the path of a dreaming dancer. In distress, she hits her head against a man's chest. Another comes and consoles her, she is given a glass and then turned upside down so that she drinks automatically. A woman carefully balances two glasses between her toes and takes a measured walk across the stage. As so often after the atmosphere has reached boiling point, there is a moment of calm. A couple flirts silently with each other. A man is given a surprise present in the form of a curiously wrapped up woman, whom he cautiously leads out. Another man runs like a bull into a woman's held out dress. But the light-hearted mood, in which love is tried out like a playful experiment, soon fades.

The finale is introduced with a projection of forested mountains. Accompanied by percussive music and ocean sounds, several couples enter the stage, and each lets a hand fall powerlessly onto their heads. The fleeing woman rushes around among them, throws chairs around and cannot be calmed. The couples slide heavily to the ground. With a firm grasp a man rolls them together into embracing positions. Together they crawl across the floor, accelerate into a roll, gradually get up and fall again: a helpless attempt to raise themselves against gravity and come together. The music changes to fast strings. Once more a man and a woman sail into the awaiting eiderdown, and then a parade of solo fragments takes over with unending runs, in and out, extending into the auditorium, gradually fading away with the light and music.

Pina Bausch once more ends her piece with a hint that the desire for love is existential and should not be denied.

# Vollmond

After several years of foreign co-productions, *Vollmond* (*Full Moon*) was premiered in Wuppertal in 2006; having a cast of only twelve dancers, the piece has an intensity like chamber music. Like *Ten Chi* it is a "black" piece, and like *Arien* or the *Macbeth* work *Er nimmt sie an der Hand und führt sie in das Schloß, die anderen folgen* a "water" piece. The stage is covered and draped with black material, and a ditch of ankle-deep water crosses it towards the back; above this, on the right-hand side, sits an immense rock, like a bridge, a refuge, or a comet fallen from the sky. Lit from behind, this harsh, ascetic landscape glimmers silvery grey, as if it were a full moon. Rain falls repeatedly in *Vollmond*: soft drizzle and heavy, persistent rain. In their wet clothes, the players seem sensual and defenceless in equal measure. *Vollmond* shows people in the search for love and exposed to the elements – in both pain and pleasure. In this piece Pina Bausch again indulges her preference for the fast string rhythms of the Balanescu Quartet, juxtaposing them with the dark, rough voice of Tom Waits or the bright sounds of René Aubry.

*Vollmond*'s tone is sharp from the start. Two men draw empty bottles swiftly through the air to produce a muted sound. A third man whips the air with a stick to create a cutting sound and then dances a stumbling, half-falling solo. A man joins him, and they interlock in a rapid fighting duet, at the end of which they run hand-in-hand in circles, as if it were a matter of life and death. A woman is captured by two men and thrown into the air, then kisses another man who tries to evade her, extremely irritated. His solo, full of classical arm-swings and self-embraces, forces him to the ground in exhaustion. Joined by his partner they continue their fighting duet till they separate for individual solos. The woman flies through the air again, and the man is kissed aggressively off the stage. Another woman casually observes: "And now, and now – fasten your seatbelts. I think it's going to be a stormy night." Then she tightens her belt hard to give herself a wasp waist. The smiling man who watches her is turned into an armchair by another man. "That is wicked. Wicked," she observes, sitting, satisfied, on her human seat.

A whole series of competitions follows. Two men throw a stone in the air and move out of its way at the last moment. Two women compete to see who is better at turning her legs outwards and bending her hands back. Then one of them literally beats a laugh out of her belly, punching herself in the pit of the stomach and demonstrating how to make yourself laugh when you aren't really in the mood. Two men run and jump in a slalom between a row of glasses placed on the ground. A man runs his nose sensuously along a woman's arm. In response she suddenly jumps at him. The attack culminates in good-natured, childish teasing. This exuberance is taken up in a woman's solo while a prying man attempts to get under her skirt. Then in a flash he skilfully wraps her up in a bath towel. She dutifully plays the stretching, wriggling sleepyhead. One of the men goes to bathe naked, but suddenly feels caught in the act and quickly withdraws. The female announcer makes an interim statement: "Ghosts have to sit down sometimes too. It's full moon – you won't get drunk." Either in sheer clumsiness or perhaps deliberately, a man spills water on a woman while filling her glass; another unceremoniously throws water in the face of a woman enthusing about her dream man, as if he wanted to cool her down and bring her back down to earth and reality.

As rain sets in a woman dances alone on the stage, very cautious and tentative, apparently hesitant yet with great dedication. Two men spray mouthfuls of water all over each other. With great difficulty a woman pushes a glass under her dress into her cleavage and drinks. Then love-exercises are practised. He gnaws at her arm, letting it swing lifeless from his teeth. He places her hair on his breast like a chest wig, lets her caress him, sticks a necklace of shredded paper round her neck and blows it away again. She fans herself with his hand, suddenly pulls him into an embrace, and the pair twists and turns away and off. Two men, one after the other, have to learn how to undo a brassière at speed. While one of them is contemptuously dismissed from his loving duties for being too slow, the other has his back caressed. But the women's hands unexpectedly become claws. The announcer, perhaps playing a ghost who has "to sit down sometimes too", brusquely demands a chair and a jacket and asks the million-dollar question: "What is better – one big love or a little love every day?" She doesn't get an answer. As if in a trance, a woman lets herself fall from a chair into waiting male arms. A woman jumps suddenly at a man. Afterwards he tries to escape another woman's aggressive embrace, and a third – enthroned on a man's shoulders – hits out at him.

The attempts at intimacy in *Vollmond* are frequently miscalculated. They either simply fail or are discharged in extreme displacement activities, scaring the partner off. Everyone then attempts an abstruse drilling act. Seated on chairs, women wait for the men, who leap into the women's ready-prepared kissing and embracing positions. Then the situation is reversed: men wait for the women, but the women thrust their shoes aggressively at the men's chests. Together they jostle back and forth on the ground as if handicapped, unable to come together properly. A woman presents flowers with childlike naivety, and it seems that genuine happiness is possible only in childhood. But as the rain sets in again, the mood darkens. Interspersed with female solos, the men leap about the stage with poles and swim one after another like reptiles through the ditch. Like an aging fisherman by the shore, one of the men sits down on the rock in the rain and ponders the times and tides of life. When a dancer delightedly announces that she is young and pretty, she actually seems lost. Even a dancer who performs a *tour en l'air* from the water impresses no-one with his technical brilliance. A woman kisses the melancholy fisherman for a long time, but he is unmoved and leaves. Despite this she dances happily to herself, running in and out of the ditch, letting her wet hair fly around until finally she ends up on the ground. A man enters, draws a line around the shape of her body on the ground and leads her out. Then the women swim through the ditch too. The road to love is long and hard. It is with this image pointing to infinity that Pina Bausch releases the audience into the interval.

The second part begins with child-like playfulness. A man lies on the rock, hugs it and proudly announces that it belongs to him. He walks happily away. Another man places a woman by the rock and shoots a plastic cup off her head, as if playing William Tell. A woman strides with giant steps across the stage and paints enormous feet for herself, clearly wishing to be larger and more powerful than she actually is. Lying sideways on the ground, a man makes a piece of rope rise behind his back and, with a smirk, pretends to be a dog wagging its tail. A woman on all fours, covered with pink silk, is introduced as the Pink Panther; another drizzles herself with lemon juice and declares: "I'm a little bit sour." As she lets herself get carried away in an hysterical, desperate, spoken aria, saying all she ever does is wait and cry, another woman skilfully undresses a man and leaves with him. It starts to rain. The announcer tersely declares while dancing: "What doesn't kill you makes you strong." Then she gives orders to a colleague, instructing him in how to touch and lift her up properly, before devoting herself to her dreams, alone again.

A quiet desperation slowly spreads. A man mutely hits a woman, hurting himself in the process, but in a grotesque distortion of the facts it is she who apologises copiously and consoles him. Another man seems to want to shake emotion out of a woman. Suddenly she leaps at him, and the two men rushing by are unable to separate her from him. The solitary fisherman does a dance which expresses all the bewilderment of being thrust into existence: restlessly hitting his stomach, forehead and thighs, standing and swaying, not knowing where to go. A woman on the run is dragged by her coat into the water and lies there paddling helplessly, gradually losing strength and finally giving up. At no point do we know whether, in holding her, the man is performing an act of aggression or doing her a service by protecting her from danger. A man attempts, without success, to comfort a woman lying motionless on the ground; another man tries out formal embraces in the air. A further couple indulges in similarly futile exercises. For a while the atmosphere falls into mournful lamentation, but one which is unable, nonetheless, to abandon the desire to achieve genuine contact.

Two men run hurriedly through the water. One of them lowers a bucket from the rock, fills it with water and washes himself. As if led by an invisible hand a woman floats by on an airbed, on a deathly journey through the underworld, or perhaps simply sleeping and dreaming. In another woman's dance, she seems to want to wipe her own face off and forget her identity, while at the same time sending out highly affectionate signals addressed to no-one, or perhaps to anyone who is able to read them. Very slowly the atmosphere begins to soften again. A man plucks a dreamy sleepwalker from the rock and carries her carefully around and about; she dances in slow motion, alone with herself, like a little animal cowering cautiously in a hole. Another is pushed across the stage like a statue. A man turns cartwheels. All the women enter the room, hold their arms out at an angle and turn, searching, like birds with injured wings and then slowly leave. It is as if, in such moments of self-absorption, they all find new strength and courage to keep on living.

The atmosphere changes abruptly. A woman clinks a glass against her forehead and sits with it in her hand as if frozen. Four men bite her arms;

she seems to enjoy it. Various couples stroll along tenderly together; one of them steals another's woman, but this doesn't cause any outrage. A woman brings a man in who flaps his hands with his arms outstretched. Beaming, she stands underneath him and is automatically patted. For a moment everyone finds themselves in swimming costumes, dancing close together in a pool party. The lonely fisherman does a trick, balancing on two glasses. In a strange communal ritual everyone cleans the rock with water while two solos lead us gradually back to the familiar state of distress. A man and woman stand in front of each other, each jabbing their arms past the other's body into thin air. A woman in a diving suit congratulates an imaginary group on their tremendous achievement, but her praise seems forced and she seems helpless. Even when individual performances attempt a return to relaxed self-absorption, the mood shifts gradually back to bottomless insecurity. With an air of sad resignation, the fisherman burns matches and places them in another man's water-filled hands, as if he had to snuff out lives. One after another two men take control of the whole group, directing it in one of those sitting dances typical of Pina Bausch, joggling with full energy on the spot. The men fill the women's glasses as if for a formal reception then drench the women instead. Accelerating alongside the quickening rhythm of the music everyone rushes into a water fight. The men leap wildly into short solos and throw themselves into the ditch. Again the man hits the woman and she apologises. Another shakes his partner, who clings to him. Two men throw a woman in the air. All playfulness and levity has vanished. At the end of *Vollmond*, men and women run through the pouring rain till they are exhausted, dancing for their lives.

## Bamboo Blues

*Bamboo Blues*, created in 2007 in collaboration with the Goethe Institute in India, seems like an optimistic rejoinder to the existential distress and desperation of *Vollmond*. Pina Bausch stages her evocation of the subcontinent as a kind of Bollywood fairytale, with an ironic smile. From the beginning of the 1990s she had begun to move towards more dance-orientated work, and in *Bamboo Blues* – more than almost any previous piece – this emphasis is evident. This time, not only are there solos, but it is dances in twos and threes which are the primary feature, and in them all possible forms of intimacy and affection are tried out. The Indian tunes, with their contemporary production sound, often immerse us in a relaxed lounge atmosphere.

In the first half, the stage floor is covered with a black surface; in the second it is brilliant white. In the background, perpendicular to the front of the stage and attached to a broad bamboo construction, long white sheets of cloth hang from the ceiling, blown in the breeze like the curtains of a giant room on a mild summer night. Indian fabric appears here in minimal white, stripped of its typical splendid colours, returning later in diverse cloth dances. The cloth might also be seen as a reference to the former bastion of the weaving and dyeing trade: Wuppertal.

The piece begins with protective intimacy. A single, moving spotlight picks a dancing woman out of the gloom. Several women who sit and lie together, forming a group image, watch the audience intently and then leave. Two women hold lit cigarette lighters under a man's soles as if they wanted to make him "hot" for them. Two other women mime a human snake, lying on top of each other on a table and conjuring up an elasticity that neither of them possesses on her own. Women come and go, folding long white cloths as if engaged in tranquil work. Everything seems to be a dream, but sometimes the dream is just a trick. Rock music drives a man into a solo, extending far and wide into the space. Then we are suddenly at a fashion show. Men and woman go along the diagonals in pairs and skilfully tie up their lunghis – the traditional wrap-around skirt – in ever newer arrangements.

A series of encounters between couples follows. A woman moves a narrow hoop up and down; a man has to try and kiss her through the ring like a circus animal. A couple fills each other's glasses in celebration. A man traces his partner's body with hovering hands in order to experience her sensually. She bends down towards the audience and paints a red dot, the Indian caste symbol, on some of the spectators' foreheads. A bed is quickly made out of thick bamboo stems; a couple snuggles up in it and gently rocks to sleep on the loosely positioned poles. A woman rolls over a man lying on the floor, and they romp and roll around together. Another man catches his partner in a cloth and draws her to the floor with it. Two men carry a sitting woman, a third strokes her dress with his hands and twitches so violently he seems literally electrified by the contact. A woman walks calmly through the scene and sniffs at her wrists. A man frantically wriggles out of his clothes and throws a cushion onto the ground in front of him. He won't be sleeping. One couple remains alone on stage and gives the spectators in the front row a long, cardamom-scented ribbon. Slowly they pull the ribbon back again so that as it glides through the spectators' fingers it leaves its scent on their hands. The ensemble lays out a large circle of colourful cloth on the stage, like a symbol for the sun. A woman lets little paper ships tied to helium balloons float up into the sky. A couple opens coconuts and drinks them dry.

The situation gradually becomes more intense. A man carries a woman in his hands and throws her, turning, in the air. Another rolls his partner up from the ground into his arms. A woman turns in a man's arms and is drawn to the ground. The string music – by the Balanescu Quartet – becomes more sharply accentuated. Throwing her arms open explosively, a dancer seems to rear up against something. Then couples glide to the ground, tightly entwined. The rolling and falling theme extends into a group scene with several couples falling to the ground while rapid, sweeping spotlights scour the scene as if in a war. A man carries a screaming woman on his back. A trio runs for their lives. The woman is turned by various men and spun in changing directions. Alone and bent double she spirals out and dances a long solo with a gyrating upper body. A man comes back to join her and frantically transports her along. Another runs with her; using a chair as a springboard, she leaps into his arms. Two tightly entwined men run in circles; one spins the other out into for a solo full of turns and falls. He briefly joins in again and manipulates his partner before releasing him back to his solo, which is then followed by a further male solo. The situation is dire and cannot be saved. A man desperately attempts to put his clothes on as he is followed by two others; he runs and falls. Then suddenly the whole wartime scenario vanishes into thin air.

With unshakeable calm and concentration, a man walks diagonally across the stage, while ever more branches are placed on his shoulders and arms which he has to keep balanced. Another man glides a dreamy, sleeping woman to the ground and leaves. She fans herself with her hand and begins a long solo, turning blissfully: a nocturnal self-affirmation, observed by a moving spotlight. Then a man dances a short sword dance with a branch. A woman takes the stick off him and gives him harsh directions till he leaves. She dances on alone till three men join her, and the entire group fuses into a moving sculpture of tender interplay. Like an echo of the recently ended war, men swarm across the floor; only one of them dances upright, and he continues long after the rest of the group has withdrawn. A man unceremoniously dunks another's head in a bucket of water, till he can stand it no more. Alone, a woman sticks her head in a bucket of water, repeating the action undeterred. But this dumb aggression is soon subdued.

A long female solo combines steps from traditional Indian dance with typical Bausch arm movements, as homage to the sheer beauty of dance. As if sleeping in the air, the dancer is carried out. A man rubs cream onto his skin till he is completely white. Using a mist machine, another man creates a steam bath atmosphere in which several dancers refresh themselves. A woman lies on the ground and sleeps. With the sound of meditative music, time seems to stand still for a moment, and then it starts again with a woman's solo. A man spins a woman flat across the floor, holding her ankles; she draws circles with a piece of chalk as she flies along. Another man takes her over and wraps her briefly and tightly round his waist. Then she is lifted up in the air as if sleeping. The scene becomes increasingly filled with sleeping, dreaming women. A projection shows a peaceful film panning through a tropical rain forest. While a gauze curtain is drawn in and out from the left, dividing and doubling the projections, a woman dances in front of it and behind, alone in the tropical forest. The women form their lying group image again and gaze persistently. With this silent challenge Pina Bausch releases her audience, after an hour, for the interval.

In the second half the floor is now white, and the gentle breeze has eased off; in effect, the dancers will have to produce their own wind. A projection shows the classic Bollywood couple on an enormous film poster. In front of it stand two dancers, a man and a woman, looking just as blissfully into the distant future, while two assistants fan them with huge pieces of cardboard. The man leaves; the woman announces enthusiastically that she just went flying. A male solo follows, cooled by a human wind machine. The man rolls and spins, falls off balance, dancing out his solitary passion to a lavish, opulent film score. Then he leaves. Someone briefly crosses the stage on roller skates; two couples fall, wound around each other, to the ground. Supported by a man, a woman runs up a second man; he falls and she literally tramples on him. Further lengths of cloth drop from the ceiling like a forest, and the film music changes to raw recitative. Alone in the cloth woods, enlivened by reflected light and shade, a man writhes around on the ground like a reptile, comes up and continues with various slow-motion movements. A woman takes over from him and dances to soul music, simultaneously coquettish and childlike. Then the fabric forest disappears and makes space for a projection of shiny, golden, Indian deities. A man carried sitting across the stage mimes the Indian elephant god Ganesha using a plastic hose. A dancing woman is surrounded by roller skaters: a group of men bring in a rack of electric fans. In the cooling stream of air they wind white cloths around themselves before standing in a row in front of the women. Accompanied by jazz music and general jubilation they lasso the women with long cloths and then suddenly vanish. For a moment the women stand bewildered. When the men return, the women tie the cloths round the men's necks like giant ties and leave. The men walk upstage and then manoeuvre back down stage, rolling around on their backs; they stand up and dance, each for himself. Their ties whirl around while they gyrate like bent-over dervishes. Then the women interrupt the frenzy of the male dance with their austere recumbent image. The situation calms down along with the music.

A woman crosses the stage thoughtfully. Another dances impetuously in front of a man who shrinks away from her. Images of sleep follow again, an expression of the desire to finally arrive on life's journey. A small man stands between two sitting women. When they stand up, they simply take the man with them *en passant*. Then the scene darkens, illuminated solely by images of the curtains from the first half, when they were blowing in the wind. In the dusky half-light, a crouching group slowly pushes a table across the stage. A man, clearly working at a pizza takeaway, takes continual orders in a stereotypical manner. A woman attacks three men, throws herself at their feet, rolls across their backs and is finally rolled over the ground by them. A couple stands in the middle; she hangs from him, wriggling, and it is unclear whether they are arguing. A man attempts to catch a woman but fails. In the general running around which sets in again, three men send a woman spinning through the air. Then a man appears in a yellow dress with which he is clearly not happy. Another, also wearing a dress, dances a flamenco-like solo to grinding beats. This forms the prelude to a whole series of solos, between which a man and a woman sit next to each other on chairs. Unimpressed, she blows air into a plastic bag for him, which he lays into as if it were a punch bag. The woman is indifferent and lets him get it out of his system. A man sits on the ground and organises his legs with great difficulty, standing up very slowly. Elsewhere two men, spinning each other wildly, cross the path of a woman twisting up and down. A man continually directs a woman to perform backward rolls, before throwing himself into a floor solo with great *élan*. The scene is filled with women – lying and standing – being transported across the stage. A woman dances crouching poses; another lets the strap of her dress fall from her shoulder and is marked with swift strokes of paint.

The actions speed up once again. Everything which previously resembled a gentle embrace now seems like a fight. The woman runs over the chair again and is safely caught; a woman turns in the arms of a man and sinks to the ground; two closely entwined men run in a circle; two others spin around all over the place. It seems as if the piece is heading for the familiar panic-laden escalation, but in a flash all urgency evaporates. Assisted by a man, a dancer wraps herself in a sari; a tender duet follows. Points of light dance in the twilight atmosphere like glow-worms, then the image becomes clearer. Indian masked dancers appear in the projections, wearing splendid costumes and turning somersaults. The gauze curtain is drawn again, and behind it a line of dancers flows past in a sitting dance, like a caravan. Tender moments from the piece are echoed once more, interspersed by solos; the wheeled bed is built up, and a couple wraps themselves up in a long cloth. At the end a woman dances alone while the curtain is opened and closed, the tropical forest drawn in and out. The dance could continue for ever.

Unlike previous pieces, the Indian excursion does not end with the feeling of existential anguish: it drifts peacefully away. This time, a tranquil place seems to have been found in dance, where one can simply exist: a place which can be taken on all journeys, anywhere in the world.

## Sweet Mambo

One year after *Bamboo Blues,* Pina Bausch took an unusual step: using the same stage sets she addressed the same subject. The accompanying pro-gramme states: "*Bamboo Blues* and this piece together represent an attempt to see how two separate pieces can be created beginning at the same point of departure but with varying dancers." As in *Bamboo Blues,* translucent white sheets of cloth hang at the back of the stage evoking the atmosphere of a warm summer night. But the piece, using only nine dancers, three men and six women, has a soft and melancholy underlying mood. It is a piece which is about thoughtfulness and against forgetting. The dancers continually step to the front of the stage, say their names, explain the cor-rect pronunciation and beg not to be forgotten. Even the silent projection of an extract from the marital comedy *Der Blaufuchs* (*The Arctic Fox Stole,* 1938, by Viktor Tourjansky, with Zarah Leander, Willy Birgel and Paul Hörbiger) seems like a reminder of long-gone times. The extract cho-sen shows a conversation. That the talk is of love, jealousy and all manner of entanglement we can only surmise. We do not hear Zarah Leander's famous song *Kann denn Liebe Sünde sein* (*Can love really be a sin?*), which she sings in the film. Despite this, the piece is about Pina Bausch's lifelong subject: the longing for love.

The introduction is quiet and tender; a woman in a long, elegant summer dress creates a soft sound with a gong. A man joins her, cir-cles her with a fascinated gaze and kisses her tentatively on the shoul-der. She breaks off the action before taking it up again. Later she steps to the front of the stage, states her name and asks the audience not to forget it. Pina Bausch's working methods, based on individuality, are engraved in our memory once more. Then she removes her shoes, dances, spins through the space in the sheltering half-light, seems briefly to have sunk into sleep and then dances on. Another dancer takes over, strokes her hair, holds herself in her own arms, appearing to absorb energy with her hands, breaking into dance to counteract attacks of fatigue. Then the inti-mate atmosphere is interrupted. A woman wearing a silvery-black dress explains how to manufacture the perfect party smile, by softly murmur-ing the word "brush". Holding champagne glasses the rest of the ensem-ble enters and toasts each other, friendly but polite, all with perfect smiles.

213

The following duet resembles a good-natured courtship, a teasing game of catch and hold, interrupted by the appearance of an entertaining, talkative woman. Clapping her hands, she takes off her rubber gloves and laughs into a plastic bag with a comment: "For later." In a shrill voice she announces her words of wisdom: "Life is like riding a bicycle; you either ride or fall!" The duet is continued, more assertively; the woman defends herself from her admirer and sends him for a shower. In a rasping tone she informs the audience that she really is quite nasty. The talkative woman with her words of wisdom explains that it is better to save one's voice when competing with the neighbour's parrot. Then the series of tender duets is continued. A man cautiously initiates his partner's movements, in order to nestle in towards her while in the background his colleague seeks out the half-obscured women. It is as if they are not yet in the world, as if they must be enticed out of their dream with extreme caution. In a further duet the man grabs the woman's hair, tousling it as if in a soft summer breeze. Another shows himself in need of support, throwing his head unexpectedly at the woman's breast. She laughs out loud and they leave together. In a cutting tone the talkative woman pipes up again with a further commentary, this time with false teeth and a wonky blond wig. Things are going well – daft but well.

Following this strange number, the piece returns to calm self-discovery. A wind blows a long, white curtain like an amniotic sac onto the stage from the right. In front of it a dancer explores her senses, sucks her thumb, her gestures suggesting that she is dreaming of motherhood. Finally she explains which parts of her body take after which of her ancestors. We are all, this is to say, part of a wholly individual history, spanning generations. Then she states all their names, with the soft, emphatic request not to forget them. She asks a member of the audience to undo her dress; a man joins her and puts his hand inside. She gently pulls it out again. He looks in his wallet, takes a cigarette lighter and runs the flame around her body. As if passions have now been rekindled, a woman in a glittery mini-skirt holding opera glasses enters, while behind her an excerpt from *Der Blaufuchs* is projected. She gyrates, moaning, on the lap of a sitting man, builds to a delighted climax, greets imaginary guests and cries: "Brava!" We have no idea whether she is rating her lover or an invisible performance she has witnessed. She offers her services to the audience, available to scream for them in proxy when problems occur,

214

before leaving. The talkative woman laconically drops in another story from her life. Her grandmother was looking for her mother in the woods but got there too late. She had been born already. Circling her arms with enormous steps, she marks out her spot in a short solo, then a colleague tells her the story of an extremely tiresome admirer, who wanted to talk to her at all costs. She responds with a memory from on tour, of a fantastic canteen dinner, where she wanted to be the first in the queue. Suddenly they both run around in circles. A man joins them; while she is still talking about how she wanted to be the first when food was dished out, her colleague suddenly just wants to talk to the man. He, however, shows no interest whatsoever. She dances alone, for herself, exploring her hidden desires and passions.

Night falls on the stage, and a storm blows in. The talkative woman sharply orders a colleague in from the dark, but hard as she tries to follow the order, she is continually thwarted by two men who grab her midway and drag her back to her starting point. In the midst of rumbling thunder and flickering lighting her desperation and panic increase. Her cries of "let me go!" mingle with the curiously peaceful piano music. The circle motif is taken up once more, with a woman running incessantly, accompanied by changing partners who hold her hair and her dress aside, as if she were running in a gale. This moment lasts for ages, then a projection of forsythia branches takes over from it. A dancer comes on stage in a black dress with a long train, which a man arranges for her. During her dance she gradually finds her hands, holds the hem of her dress in solitude and turns dreamily. The motif is taken up by a couple which circles peacefully in, the woman panting as if in suppressed excitement, we cannot tell whether from pain or pleasure. With their hems in their hands, the rest of the women enters; they are spun by the men, remaining absorbed in themselves for a long moment. Finally the woman from the duet remains alone and cheerfully demonstrates how she turns cartwheels in all corners of the world. The talkative woman demonstrates melodramatically that she is able to whinge best in her own language. Another woman dreams of sleeping and lets herself fall softly into a sheet, held at the ready by two men. Assisted by a man who holds her clothes-stand, the talkative woman repeatedly carries out a classic routine, enacted using her flapping dress: "It's getting better." Another man comes, attributes wonderful qualities to her and two other women, one after the other, then the piece returns to its starting point. The woman from the beginning reminds us once more of her name and dances an upbeat solo. The sleeping woman revolves a bucket of water, is lifted out of her turns and soaks herself repeatedly, lying on the ground, in sheer delight. The experienced party-goer releases the audience after an hour's performance for the interval: "Don't forget: brush."

Also an hour long, the second part of this piece which is devoted largely to women, now allows the men some solo appearances, and explores its subject more often via group scenes. Its beginning is replete with tenderness. Three men and three women line up in a row, one behind the other. The men caress the women's naked backs with their chins. Assisted by two other men, the sleeping woman rises; she is lying sideways on a cushion which she cuddles, alone on the ground. In the background a row of sleek cats in masks slink by on all fours, enticed along by a woman. Wearing a wig and false teeth, the talkative woman delivers another pearl of wisdom: "The old can't do what they know how to; the young don't know how to do what they are able to." She leaves, laughing. This seems like a comment on the piece, largely featuring long-serving dancers. Through a curtain, which floats over her body, the sleeping woman is carried from the world of dreams to that of reality. Full of charm, she explains the significance of her movements using words, being handed the necessary props, or by pulling one of the men over to demonstrate on as required. It becomes clear that in dance theatre dances are never simple variations of movement; they are always based on little stories. A procession passes through the hanging fabric banners again: the men pass by first, half flying, half resting on their elbows, then the entire ensemble takes a turn at the movement, as full of sensual delight as it is difficult. The women writhe pleasurably on the men's laps, sitting half-obscured behind the curtains. The talkative woman tries with utmost strength to push a man along, but gives up. Driven by the increasingly alarming music he dances a powerful solo, falls to the ground, then carries on. The curtains are raised; a woman takes over from him, full of poise and clarity. He runs out and, helped by a colleague, drags a table into her path, which buries her in ever shorter intervals. She is called again and carried back to her starting point by the men; her desperation increases as she fails to reach her goal. Then the scene calms down. The woman in the black, long-trained dress appears and sings a song, her gaze skywards, then slowly leaves. The cur-

216

tain blows in from the right. A woman dances in on herself as if in the womb. Her hair and dress blow in the wind. Then the dream is gone.

The line-up reforms once more for a tender caress. The singing woman sits alone on the floor. A man attempts to stand her up using all the affectionate means he can. Another woman behaves coquettishly and self-confidently, letting two stones fall from her hands, which are then caught by two men; she attacks one of them violently and, held back by her, he runs ferociously on the spot. She lets him nowhere near her. A third woman leaps into a man's arms and knocks another over with her legs as she flies. Back on his feet, he dances a powerful solo as if trapped in an inner conflict, while a strong wind blows the hanging fabric. The piece's mood intensifies; the initial melancholy is joined by rage. Using bottles and buckets the talkative woman demonstrates how empty she feels. From the auditorium she shouts over the music: "I'm not short, I'm just a long way off!" She says her name, and back on stage she performs a violent duet, while the group in the forest of curtains, which has descended again, runs backwards and forwards frantically. The scene accelerates into chaos, from which individuals continually break out to sketch out a solo. Women are lifted up by the men, hidden behind the fabric banners, and tipped off kilter. Dressed as a blond oddball, the talkative woman screeches into a microphone and repeats her cycling allegory. A man in a tight, black, gauze dress runs breathless to the front of the stage and claims that the only amusing thing is that his shoes are four sizes too large. Using a taller colleague, whom he continually pushes down, he demonstrates that really he is the taller of the two and recalls his name, shouting. Then the curtains are raised again to make space for two men's limping circuit, followed by a series of parallel, falling and standing solos.

The turmoil which normally ushers in the end of a piece gradually settles, and Pina Bausch lets her piece die down as gently as it began. The dancer from the beginning returns to her solo, followed by the dreamy, sleepy woman who failed to answer the call to go out in the stormy night. Now she sits in mute conflict with her partner, refuses to go with him, tries to escape via the auditorium and can only reluctantly be persuaded to return to the stage. She dances alone while a strong wind blows the fabric, wraps herself in her own arms, goes to the ground, lies down, feline, and enjoys the breeze, entirely in her own world. Dancing and dreaming can continue like this forever.

## "Sometimes you stand there feeling pretty much naked"
How the Tanztheater Wuppertal works

Diversity is the order of the day at the Tanztheater Wuppertal. Although other world-famous ensembles may also be composed of dancers and actors of varying nationalities, mentalities and personalities, it is this which is Pina Bausch's starting point for work that seeks to discover something about human beings: their ability to understand and communicate with each other. At the Tanztheater Wuppertal everyone is visible, unmistakeable in their individuality and unique in their personality. The different nationalities provide the material and the various mentalities the timbre for a world theatre continually aiming to transcend boundaries: a theatre calm and composed enough to observe every individual and highlight their particular abilities.

This openness allows the company to be receptive in its work to other cultures and their attitudes to the world. They may collaborate or contradict, create understanding or talk at cross purposes. In this process, nothing is buried under superficial harmony. Conflicts are held out till, as if by themselves, they mutate to reveal new possibilities. Thus the work of the Tanztheater Wuppertal is a model for a potential way of relating to each other. Nothing has to be covered up or glossed over. There is always the possibility that a situation, however extreme or inextricable it might seem, will change. It may resolve itself in merriment, with a wink and a laugh or in the kind of humour which can smile at itself, or it may fall into unfathomable grief, at the rock bottom of which we find new access to the self. This continual change is not only one of dance's principles *per se*, it establishes a hope; not the hope which can only glimpse its goal in a distant utopia but one grounded in something real: an unshakeable perseverance, making its way calmly through all the essential experiences of life. Life – everyday life – is liveable, say the Wuppertal dancers, and happiness is nothing other than being wholly absorbed in it just as we are – but ready to change at any time.

This kind of work comes at a cost. "Sometimes," says dancer Heide Tegeder of her experience of rehearsals with Pina Bausch, "you stand there feeling pretty much naked." The capacity to expose oneself, in other

219

words to be open and vulnerable, was and is the greatest challenge facing the Tanztheater Wuppertal dancers. But whoever takes it up soon discovers a personal source of strength. Anyone who doggedly pursues this path reaches a truthfulness which strips away everything superficial and penetrates to the essential. A vitality is reached which is simultaneously protected the moment it reveals itself. And it becomes apparent that change occurs very naturally, if we only allow it.

Even in the earliest pieces it was clear that a new, different quality of dance was being sought. In the Gluck operas and particularly in *Le Sacre du printemps*, the choreography demanded a level of dedication from the performers which pushed them to their physical limits. This is what provides the pieces with an authenticity and dramatic force which transmit directly to the body of the spectator. Pain, suffering and despair are no longer hinted at nor encoded in fine gestures. They are discharged through the power of extreme physical and emotional presence. This requires dancers who are not afraid of themselves, who are prepared to uncover the elemental human urges within themselves and present them unmediated on stage.

At a certain point Pina Bausch began to alter her working methods. She started to ask her dancers questions, which marked the beginning of an ambitious research project into the limits and potential of communication. Where do we touch each other, and how do we separate ourselves from each other? Responses are sought to keywords, short sentences and suggestions; it is not vague improvisation but something very specific which is investigated: a moment of candour which is only given choreographic form when something has really been touched. This is the beginning of a journey of discovery, started anew in every piece, with the knowledge that in each of our bodies is stored a wealth of behavioural patterns: of hopes and fears, of lusts and loves and – not least of all – potential solutions.

An ensemble knows more than a single choreographer can ever know. This method uses the knowledge preserved in each human body and brings it to the light of day. It provides every dancer with the freedom to find and present his or her individual experience of the world. It testifies to a deep respect for every individual, each having the right to exist in uniqueness and distinctiveness.

It is this respect, coupled with an unerring precision and frankness, that has consistently emboldened the Tanztheater Wuppertal's dancers and performers to accompany Pina Bausch on this extraordinary journey. At the beginning it was not at all easy to step into these zones of freedom which gradually open wider and wider. It was necessary to part with all predetermined definitions of dance. No longer important to invest the skills they had acquired solely in learning and copying sophisticated sequences of steps, it was now necessary for the dancers to start right from the beginning, rediscovering dance entirely. It has always required joint investigations, targeted questioning, enduring one's own perplexity, cautious exploring of both unfamiliar associations and undreamt-of dimensions of movement. This demands courage and stamina. At the time it was extremely disturbing, because suddenly it was no longer a case of judging choreography but about something human, familiar to everyone. Dancers could thus no longer be judged according to the usual criteria. People had to learn that the Wuppertal dancers' bravura is not to be found in technical masterpieces, but that their virtuosity sometimes shines through when reciting a poem or singing a nursery rhyme; that natural, unaffected charm carries more weight than studied, standard smiles and that a particular truth and beauty lies in tiny, ostensibly insignificant events. All this requires unusual performers and exceptional dancers. For it is precisely the simple things which can only be shown by someone who has knowledge and mastery of their body.

The special qualities of the Tanztheater Wuppertal were only gradually recognised. Many thought that perhaps the ensemble members just couldn't dance very well. There were often direct reactions to this in the pieces; in *Nelken*, for example, Dominique Mercy complains angrily as he delivers a virtuoso taster of his excellent classical technique: a clear indication that this – the technique – is exactly what is no longer important.

For a long time it was also disturbing to some that the company hardly conformed to the normal standards of uniformity or ideals of beauty. To many people the dancers were too fat or too thin, too tall or too short, or not young and pretty enough, thus far too closely resembling the audience – ourselves, in other words. What people failed to appreciate was that dance, reborn in Wuppertal, was far removed from any kind of vanity and had its sights on exactly the kind of everyday life from which the spectators come.

Dance theatre insists on showing people as they really are, not as they should be. Thus it is imperative that the dancers do not perform things their audience cannot do. The dancers have no wish to overwhelm the audience with their breathtaking and highly acclaimed technique but to remind them instead of something which lies within everyone and on which they can rely. With their ability to present what we all are and can do – reduced to its simplest form and concentrated into the essentials – the Wuppertal dancers give their spectators courage. They demonstrate what it means to be at peace with oneself, to acknowledge oneself and be wholly in the world.

Once we have arrived at a place of our own it is possible to meet each other; this is where genuine communication and real intimacy begin. Here too there have always been misunderstandings, such as seeing the working methods as a kind of therapy. But however great a value is placed on individuality and personality; the questions Pina Bausch asks are never private. In a documentary film on rehearsal techniques there is a moment which demonstrates this clearly. It is about crying. The performers try out various ways of crying, then stop. Sceptical questions are raised about whether they should be turning their innermost feelings outwards. No, Bausch says, it is about finding out what crying does to your body. In an interview she once said: "I ask a precise question. When a dancer answers, it is with something we all share. Something we know about – but not intellectually." Individual experience is only a medium used to reveal that which, in fact, "we all share", that which connects the players on stage to the audience. In exposing themselves to experience and getting to the root of emotions, the dancers take the first step and invite their audience to follow them on their journey into uncharted territory. They generate a precisely focused energy in the pieces and let it take effect. They guide the spectator through a switchback ride of emotions, with an intensity rarely found elsewhere. Working with Pina Bausch they have learned that there is knowledge preserved in the body which can be trusted. Its language is precise and always already understood, even before the intellect decodes it. A particular posture, a particular way of walking, standing or indeed dancing: in the Tanztheater Wuppertal all these feed into moments of touching intensity. Its members are experts in fine nuances, the delicate balance of moods, the tragicomic tight-rope walks over the everyday abyss. Courage is coupled with skill, openness with profound knowledge of dance. Curiosity and the delight of discovery are joined by dogged persistence: a bond maintained by some members of the Wuppertal ensemble for over two decades.

What Pina Bausch and her dancers have created over this period is a new type of theatre: a world theatre in which the players, brought together from almost all corners of the world and with diverse mentalities and temperaments, embody various prototypes of human behaviour while possessing their own unmistakeable identities. They dedicate themselves to this work with their whole personality, bringing their diverse shades and tones to it. Dance theatre was and is enriched by its fellow comrades, who have paved the way for a new understanding of dance:

- Malou Airaudo, emanating an earthy melancholy as well as a passionate energy, enhanced by a strength derived from patience and endurance;
- Ruth Amarante, a Bausch dancer par excellence, precise and full of dramatic force;
- Regina Advento, a self-possessed beauty of girlish charm;
- Josephine Ann Endicott, who is able to draw on the whole register of "femininity" from the uninhibited freshness of a child to the aloofness of a *grande dame*;
- Lutz Förster, whose long, lanky dancer's body is able to evoke masculine defencelessness and who shows us how we can be saved by dry, black humour;
- Mechthild Großmann, wide-eyed girl-child or simpering vamp in so many of the productions, but behind the clichéd images she lets the occasional flash of self-assured eroticism be glimpsed;
- Urs Kaufmann, a specialist in well-judged dry humour as well as moments of cautious, exploratory fragility;
- Silvia Kesselheim with her incisive precision, whose sudden silences let us fall into alarming voids and bewilderment;
- Beatrice Libonati, who throws her body into the fight for survival with a disturbing force, memorably – but by no means only – as Judith in *Blaubart*;
- Dominique Mercy, often a tragic clown, underpinning his fidgety Pierrot figure with profound seriousness and great vulnerability;
- Jan Minarek, a brilliant "Simple Simon", a calming force in almost every piece, left unruffled even by escalations of hysteria;

- Vivienne Newport, with her raw, dry charm and the courage to create provocative presences;
- Helena Pikon, tall, thin, quiet and reserved, demonstrating a mute tenacity in solitary arm-entwining dances;
- Nazareth Panadero, a born actress, employing the German language with obvious pleasure and to great effect with a rolling Spanish accent;
- Jean-Laurent Sasportes, a brilliant scatterbrain, an anarchist prepared to unhinge the apparently fixed world of conventions at any moment;
- Julie Shanahan, the perfect embodiment of the diva and the hysteric, lends Pina Bausch's dances a dramatic volatility;
- Janusz Subicz, often overcome with boyish embarrassment which wins us over with its natural honesty;
- Meryl Tankard, a delicate figure, equipped with great comedic talent, able to create masterful parodies of shrill hysteria and just as able to evoke soft, quiet undertones.

Also to be mentioned are the less conspicuous dancers of the Tanztheater Wuppertal who have carried and helped shape the pieces with their enthusiasm and precision: Barbara Hampel, Kyomi Ichida, Jakob Andersen, Bernd Marszan and Francis Viet.

The company has grown younger in the meantime, acquiring some impressive talents, particularly amongst the men: Rainer Behr, Jorge Puerta Armenta, Fabien Prioville and Fernando Suels represent a new generation who have given the beauty of the dances new expression, combining technical precision with great charm.

The list could be continued and would still not do everyone justice. More than 150 dancers, actors and singers have contributed to the Tanztheater Wuppertal's work over the years. Not all of them stayed for the long haul, but they all brought something with them that far exceeded the daily dance routine of a normal ensemble. They were – and many have over and again continued to be – prepared to expose themselves, to commit themselves to the journey of exploration in which questions are more important than smooth, ready-made answers. They are all a testament to the fact that it is possible to make a kind of theatre in which every individual is important, in which everyone counts, where each remains unique, with their own face, their own voice. Showing courage and persistence, Pina Bausch's comrades have enabled a theatre as it ideally should be: a place where human affairs are continually re-negotiated, in which things are tried out and researched, rather than known in advance and dealt with routinely. One in which dance develops models for a possible understanding and a practisable way of living together: a life together which can accommodate differing mentalities and temperaments, showing respect for the individuality of each and every one. This is a theatre in which an exploration of the world – astonishing, painful, disturbing but always moving – begins each time anew.

# Interviews with Pina Bausch

## "Dance is the only true language"

*When I think back to the early days, there was considerable resistance to the work of the Tanztheater Wuppertal – from the audience and sometimes from the press too. How do you cope with working in the face of such resistance?*

The protests were always targeted at particular individuals or particular groups, it was not a general protest. It wasn't that there was nobody who respected this kind of work. Of course sometimes it was difficult, but if you're creating a piece you can't ask: what kind of audience will like this? An audience is made up of a large number of different individuals. So which audience are we talking about? Who is the piece for? You don't know. All I can do is to try to show things, to say things and to find what is important to me. That's the most important thing: what you want to say. That's one of the hardest things – to formulate it properly or give some idea what it's really about; but you can communicate without words, through actions. It's the kind of thing in which you perhaps have an idea of what is behind it. But it's something completely concrete. It is the only gauge you have; to succeed in what you're trying to do, to bring it into some kind of form.

*But sometimes the reactions were very angry.*

It was often a misunderstanding, because people sometimes thought I was trying to challenge somebody or to critisise something in some way. I wasn't trying to hurt anybody. If some people did feel hurt, that was just in the nature of the work.

*Did you never think of giving up?*

Sometimes. I did think about doing something different but never because of the audience. Never. What I do is for an audience after all. If I did sometimes despair that was never the reason.

*Initially, it must have been quite difficult for the dancers to learn new approaches, to develop a way of working in which they have to reveal themselves.*

Of course, it was very difficult at the beginning. The word "dance" was linked to a number of very particular ideas. It was very difficult to understand that dance could exist in a different form. Because dance

229

doesn't consist of a particular technique. That would be highly arrogant, to think that so many other things were not dance. And I believe that it is only a very good dancer who can do very many, very simple things. It's all very delicate. I never ask anything private, I ask a precise question. When a dancer answers, it is with something we all share. Something we know about – but not intellectually.

*But it was a very different process – that of asking questions. Until then choreography meant a choreographer standing there demonstrating steps.*

I demonstrate steps too. They are also something that I create. It's part of the material we work with, just like the many variants that we add: the movements and gestures. Ballet, in earlier days, was made up of gestures too. They weren't just movements, although today many dancers have no idea where they came from.

*Today, the audience is very different. At premieres, applause often breaks out after individual scenes. People come to Wuppertal because the Tanztheater is famous.*

I can't speak for the audience, but the pieces really have nothing to do with that. I am very pleased when I notice people have understood what I'm trying to say. Booing would not be appropriate. Everybody is part of the performance: seeing what you think, what you feel, what connections are created in your head. If someone feels that we have come together in some way, I think that is wonderful. But it's not about making judgements on the choreography. It's about a kind of humanity. There are no special effects, there's nothing on the stage that doesn't belong there. Each object has a purpose. Everything else is left out. It's not that I couldn't do other things. We have deliberately left all that out.

*Don't you ever feel like creating a piece that is totally based on movement?*

I think it develops by itself. I always enjoy movement. It has often been the case that a lot of movement was involved, and for some reason I kept reducing and reducing it and only left it where it felt right. Or the dance happened in such a way that you didn't even notice it. It's always the way it is out of necessity or a whim. I don't want people to think: I'm a choreographer, and now we should dance again. Those aren't the criteria. Dance is much too important. But I see so many other things as dance.

230

*Such as?*

Almost anything can be dance. It has to do with a particular consciousness, a particular inner, physical approach, a very great attention to detail: knowledge, breathing, every tiny detail. How something is done is always important. There are so many things that are dance, even totally contradictory things. Dances have developed from crises, not just from joy, from a whole range of different circumstances. And today we are living in a very particular time in which dance needs to be created in a particular way. But not for egotistical reasons.

*You said once that the pieces seem much funnier today; they weren't seen in that way in the early days.*

People never thought I had a sense of humour. They simply overlooked the fact that it's all much more multilayered. The evenings are like pieces of music: they're not created to be watched once and once only. I see them very often and know how different they can be, what can happen to people, how each tiny nuance can change something.

*Is it not the case that many things were seen as shocking in the early days because they had never been seen in that way before?*

That was the way it was seen at first. But it also has something to do with people's personal idea as to why we have humour at all. I think I am an extremely realistic optimist, not just any kind of optimist. That's the only reality there is: to talk about a possible understanding. Humour has something to do with criticism, but also with love. That's something very fragile, which we can smile about together – the knowledge, perhaps, of how difficult it is. For me that is something real or at least not something utopian. There are many things that I don't see optimistically at all because they aren't actually there. It's only a dream. That can be very pleasant, but it depends on the way you work. I work on things that have to do with our time.

*Today, the Tanztheater Wuppertal has become part of the canon. Is that something of a burden?*

It's just very, very hard work. It always has been and it still is; and looking after these pieces is too. Sometimes it is difficult to summon up the energy, to make sure the enjoyment wins over again.

*What does success mean to you?*

The word "success" is not something I think about. First of all, I think it's such a miracle that we can travel around the entire world with this kind of work – how we can reach out to each other, everywhere, how we can have genuine encounters with each other. It is a really amazing thing that work like this has nothing to do with boundaries, that people can understand each other. At the same time, it is an opportunity for me to be allowed to learn: learn ways of living, music, dances. And to see how, through pieces like this, energy can be directed to where it really makes sense. It changes something. The language spoken is something very exact. We are trying to get our heads round something very precise, something that has always been understood. That is the only real language. The same things always happen at the same moment with the same music. That is something very precise, but it is not something you can see.

*You have been in Wuppertal for seventeen years now. Are you ever afraid that your creative sources might run dry?*

Not really. It's no more difficult than before. It must come from somewhere, we have no idea where. And some part of it is infinite. The only way I can tell this is from my enthusiasm. If I am enthusiastic, everything goes all right. These processes, the low periods, are part of every piece. That has always been the case. As soon as I've created a piece, I want to create a new one immediately. And then circumstances prevent it. Immediately after one piece we are always very tired, sometimes there are shows that have already been planned. But the best thing would be if you could keep going immediately.

*With all that work, do you have any time at all for a private life?*

Everything is so mixed up I really don't know where one ends and the other begins. It's all just my life. It's very difficult, but I have to do it that way.

*You don't feel anything is lacking?*

Now and then I would like to have a little more time. But on the other hand I get such a strong urge to work, so then I have to act on it. And I love being in other countries. I am amazed that I feel at home in so many countries.

232

*You're never homesick?*

I wonder whether homesickness might not in fact be the same thing as the longing to travel. Sometimes I think it's the same thing. I like coming back, and I like going away – these longings we have.

*Can you name them?*

I'll try to avoid naming them. You can see them in all my pieces. I would have to be a poet to recreate any of that feeling in words.

(16 February 1990)

## "You have to be highly alert and very sensitive"

*Pina Bausch, about ten years ago you began to re-construct your entire repertoire.*

No, in fact I've always done that. In 1977 or 1978, we did that during the so-called *Tanzwoche* [dance week]. I've always tried to preserve the repertoire. Of course some pieces were lost because people left – during the first couple of years, for example.

*But after that you only put on one new piece per season and revived one old one.*

Creating just one new piece per season began after my son was born.

*Had it all been too much?*

Maybe at the beginning. But also the repertoire was getting bigger and bigger, the way it had developed, and there was more and more travel where we needed one piece or another for each particular trip. That took up an awful amount of time because pieces had been lost. It's different if I can simply preserve them. I always tried to, but sometimes it didn't work because it was simply too much work. If you wait a year or two, it really becomes a revival, and that creates much more work.

*What is it like to re-encounter the old pieces? Do you ever think: I wouldn't do that the same way now?*

233

I wouldn't put it like that at all. I'd say something more like: unfortunately, I can't do that in that way any more. It's not that I wouldn't do it the same way — I can't think of it like that. It's just that I am no longer in the position to do what I did then. We're in a different place, that's all. We've now gone quite a long way back, back to *Iphigenia* and *Orpheus*, and I was a little scared of confronting those works. I thought I might find it terrible. But it was quite amazing how familiar they felt — with Malou Airaudo and Dominique Mercy. It was as if it was the day before yesterday. When that kind of rehearsal is over, it's amazing that all the feelings that you once had come back again. Each piece has grown over time, and I think it's wonderful that you can preserve them. I can't touch them any more even if I wanted to, I am unable to interfere with them. I can sometimes take something away but I can't add anything, that wouldn't work. I just have to leave them as they are.

*When you say you are in a different place now — what is it that interests you most at the moment?*

The forms that you choose — that develops on its own, it is not something that you construct. Over the last few years what has most interested me has been how you create dances, just as I used to encourage dancers to find certain things by asking them questions. But this has been a new chapter for me: how the dances are constructed. My point of departure is completely different to earlier days, when I was looking for gestures or other things. In that sense, for me, *Tanzabend II*, *Das Stück mit dem Schiff* and *Ein Trauerspiel* all belong together.

*Dance takes on an infinite quality in these pieces.*

Yes. The dances in those pieces are like rosaries, there is something endless about them. Someone new always joins in, but I could also repeat them and start again from the beginning. There is a curve, a circle in them.

*How did you develop the working method in which you ask questions?*

That probably began with *Blaubart*. We had conflicts within the group that upset me very much. I felt a little bit hurt. We had just done the Brecht/Weill evening, and suddenly it was said that what I had done was terrible. That hurt me very deeply.

234

*But the piece was very successful.*

That didn't change the way I felt. I didn't feel that I could do a new piece with those people. I took four dancers and withdrew to a little studio belonging to Jan Minarik, and we started work there – with only a few people. And one by one, at various points, the others came back, but only when they wanted to; I didn't want to have anyone there any more who didn't want to work. During that work, I began to ask questions, to formulate my own questions within this circle; things that were questions for me and also for the others. I only dared do that in a small circle. But it then became an important part of the work in Bochum.

*During the* Macbeth *project.*

There were four dancers, four actors, one singer; the dancers didn't dance, the actors didn't act, and the singer didn't sing. I forced myself to use *Macbeth* as a basis. It was a way of seeing how we could all work together. I couldn't suddenly introduce a series of movements. It was an important piece for finding my way of working.

*How do make the answers to the questions into a composition? How do they fit together?*

Initially, nothing fits together at all. It's an ongoing process of searching and collecting material. In the meantime of course I'm also working on other things. I make a note of everything, and the dancers have to make notes of everything they do as well, so I can ask them again about it. And then I start to sort through it.

*So how do you know how things fit together? Are there particular subjects that begin to crystallise? When one sees the results, everything seems very precisely composed. Is it all instinctive?*

Yes of course – instinct, and a lot of work, it's a mixture of both.

*And what does the work consist of?*

It's very difficult work. It involves trying out every single detail, not just one way, but in all other possible ways. I only accept something if I find it truly beautiful. But sometimes there is not just one possibility but five, and then I wait for a while and turn it around and around, but I don't put it together. It is an enormous amount of work, and you need an unbelievably clear head for it.

*And how do you know when it is right?*

The others have even less idea than me, because they can't see it. But when I enjoy it, then I know it's right. You feel it when it is right, and you feel when it is not right too. But how you get to that point, that's a completely different question. I can't tell you. It suddenly clicks, there is no easy way of getting there, it's a series of jumps. Sometimes, logical thinking will get you there, and sometimes you make large steps towards it, and you don't even know how you could have thought that. They are huge steps; I can't explain how they come. And it can't be forced. All you can do is keep on working, patiently.

*How do you find the right pieces of music for the pieces?*

Matthias Burkert has been working with me for so many years, he knows my taste, which means he knows what I don't like. Just as I am always looking for pieces of music and speaking to people, Matthias is always under instructions to look for pieces of music, and the dancers also bring music with them.

*Does the music have anything to do with remembrance – not with nostalgia but with a repertoire of very different feelings?*

It depends what you want. It can be wonderful to work with music by a single composer. I created *Bandoneon* almost exclusively using music by Carlos Gardel. But there are many, many pieces of music I never knew before which inspire very deep feelings in me. And through variety – it's just like having twenty-six different people in the company – you create a harmony together. That's how the wider world is; it is made up of different things.

*And how do you put the pieces of music together?*

How can I explain it; it's all based on feeling. We look at everything, whether it's terrible or beautiful, we take a look at it all. Sometimes it breaks your heart. Sometimes you know, sometimes you find it; sometimes you have to forget it all and start looking again from the beginning. You have to be extremely alert, extremely sensitive; there is no system. It's a highly intensive period; it is a great skill, being able to abandon so many false turns in such a short period – because you have to.

*How do you find the stage environment for each piece? When they aren't interior spaces, there are often slices of nature: snow, earth, water, a field of poppies, a meadow, fallen leaves, stones. Things that are normally outside moved inside. But you can often see very clearly that you are in the theatre; the stage is left open right to the firewalls. Do you know what the stage will look like right from the beginning of rehearsals?*

No, that comes much later. It's only when you have some idea what is happening that you can think about the space in which it is happening. I can't think: this is a performance space, and I will create a piece there. I can only feel what is there, growing within me; it is only then that I can think: where could that be? It is very important that you do know that at some point. After that, another way of working begins. For me, many different things play a role. What something does to your body: a meadow – you walk on it, and it is totally quiet, and it has a very particular smell. Or water – suddenly your clothes get very long and wet and the water is cold, the sound it makes, or the way the light reflects on it. It's alive in a different way. Or earth – suddenly everything is sticking to your body when you sweat. Those are all essential elements. I like that, partly because of the difference, because it is exhibited so openly on the stage. I was always aware of the fact that I was in an opera house. But you also need to introduce another location, which is like a foreign body.

*And the dancers never wear costumes that would "match" the stage design. In* Arien, *they stand surrounded by water in beautiful evening dresses, like a society that is drowning.*

Well, there is an expression: I'm up to my neck in it.

*Is that the idea?*

It's not trying to be that explicit. It aims for openness. Everything that you already know beforehand is of no interest. Completely different thoughts develop, a whole variety of reasons why that is beautiful – the contrast.

*I have the impression that the colours of the costumes in the pieces are composed too, or does that develop naturally?*

Rolf Borzik's way of working was very different from the way Marion Cito works now. Of course, the pieces at the beginning were very different too. Rolf designed a lot of clothes, but he also sought them out in second-hand shops. He created colour scales for everything. In *Kontakthof*, for example, all the clothes were specially designed. And then the way of working changed. Today, there are a lot of costumes for rehearsals – they are hanging there ready. Anyone who feels like putting something on can do so. Then they rehearse and rehearse, and then things begin to crystallise. Marion is always on the search for clothes, it's an ongoing work which isn't limited to a particular piece. At the same time, it's always open to debate. A lot develops during the work; things suddenly arise. Then you have to find other things or swap them around. Suddenly one thing doesn't fit in, and then something else is produced. Great urgency sometimes produces spontaneous feelings: that's not right. You realise that very quickly. Even if it creates major problems, those are very positive decisions. And the clothes are never abandoned; sometimes I use them in another piece. That always works well.

*Where did the idea come from of putting the dancers in normal clothes? They don't wear ballet dresses or leotards.*

I never create works for leotards.

*Does that have something to do with showing people as they are?*

That was the case right from the beginning. It was also about not wanting to elevate yourself, not wanting to distance yourself, not wanting to disguise yourself. It's something that's very intimate. You have to see the individuals on the stage as people, not as dancers. That would disturb the work. I would like them to be seen as people who are dancing.

*But there are disguises too.*

That is something different; there would be specific reasons for it. In principle it could be anything. For example in *Nelken*, when the men are wearing dresses. Sometimes, at first people think: a man in a dress. But after five minutes it's normal. I find it wonderful that it takes so little time.

*And there is another source of confusion: the animals. For example, the hippopotamus in* Arien, *which is always just there, in the middle of this festive group. It comes up to Josephine Ann Endicott, looks at her with a sad expression, goes away again and takes a bath.*

It's a love story between those two.

*But the animals are always just there. Sometimes I feel as if they don't have the same anger people have.*

But I find the hippopotamus very sad; it is suffering – but from love. The way someone can feel totally alone.

*Do the animals tell similar stories to the people or different ones?*

That really depends. The crocodiles in *Keuschheitslegende* have something very erotic about them. The walrus in *Ahnen* is something completely different.

*How do you know what animals belong in a certain piece?*

It's a decision. For *Arien*, I knew in advance that I wanted a hippopotamus. You have to decide things like that early because it takes so long to create something like that.

*When the most unusual things come together in a wholly natural way (a walrus in a forest of cacti or crocodiles on a painted sea), what does poetry now mean?*

I can't think about that. You can only talk about that afterwards. I'm in the happy situation of not having to analyse my pieces. I only have to create them.

*Is it possible to say what sources these images and movements arise from?*

That is something very delicate. I am afraid of not finding the right words; and it is much too important to me: how you feel, how you express something or what you're looking for. Sometimes I can only find it as it develops. I don't want to interfere with that.

*I always had the sense that your pieces have to do with travel, with being on the move.*

Life is a journey. Isn't it?

(30 September 1995)

## "That we have the will to tackle life again"

*Pina Bausch, you've now been in Wuppertal for more than twenty-five years, longer than most other choreographers stay at one theatre – could you have imagined that back then in 1973, when you started here?*

No, I could never have imagined that.

*Back then you hesitated for a long time before taking on the appointment.*

I was very happy at the Folkwang-Tanzstudio, and I couldn't imagine working in a theatre, with operas and operettas and unions. I didn't really know that much about it, but it was the last thing I could imagine doing.

*When you look back, has much changed in the way you work?*

You don't notice it at all yourself. It's a really slow process, it doesn't happen overnight. For example, I did *Fritz* back then. There was no model for that; even that was a collage. Then I did *Iphigenia* and a piece called *Ich bring dich um die Ecke*, and then *Orpheus*. Those were massive extremes I was moving between. It's not something that developed much later; it was like that right from the start.

*Extremes, because in one case there was a musical template?*

Not just a musical template, but a work which already existed. There was already a certain harmony there – with the music, with the roles. Later, it was more that each individual was important.

*Nonetheless for a while there was a lot of very intense emotion in the pieces, which was provocative to many people, whereas today there is a great deal of joy in the pieces.*

Emotion is always very important. It bores me if I can't feel anything. There is a certain happiness, of course, but happiness is inseparable from the other pole. This understanding with the audience, that you're laughing at yourself or with one another, about ourselves as people. Although that was also there in early pieces like *Renate wandert aus* or *Keuschheitslegende*. But it's completely different every time. Happiness by itself means nothing. Every piece also contains the opposite, as in life itself. That also has something to do with trying to find a harmony.

240

*Do you have the feeling that times are tougher than in the seventies or eighties and that you have to do something different for that reason?*

I do think that these are difficult times, and having to do something... I really can't say that. I always try to follow what I feel at that time.

*There are a lot of new faces in the ensemble at the moment, a fresh and different energy. Is that why there are more dances in the pieces?*

The movements come into being in the same way I once used to find things. It's just a different form. I've been very interested in that. Not the composition itself but the finding of the movement. It's a matter of countless details, which themselves come from responses to a particular subject. It's so easy to forget about that afterwards.

*There are more solos now as well; before there were more large-scale ensemble dances.*

That's a result of this parallel searching: on the one hand it's about things to do with movement, very individual things. That involves me working with every single person, including their movements. That comes from the fact that there are suddenly so many dancers, marvellous dancers. That's also to do with the fact that the dancers put in an unbelievable amount of effort – the responsibility that they have for their stories. That plays a major role in our work. I have done so many big group formations, and this is just what interests me at the moment. I can always come back to that again and again. No one is stopping me from doing it all differently next time. At the moment I'm enjoying how beautifully they dance.

*You once said that something has also changed in the searching for and finding of the dances.*

You're always looking for something new. Sometimes it's just the beginnings of something. We've done so many things, and after I've done something, I'm not interested in it anymore. It's already in one of the pieces. I don't need to keep doing it. Then everyone says, when are you going to do something like *Le Sacre du printemps* again? But we already perform that one. When the time comes, I'll do it, for sure. That's the wonderful part of it, that you're always setting off on a journey again, always opening new doors; doors you *must* open.

*Do you still, with every new piece, experience a fear of beginning such as you did previously?*

I don't know what you would call it, whether it is fear. Nothing has ever changed there. It is something very special when you do a piece. First I embark on a search. The first thing we do is search for material, a very, very great deal of material. From the material we develop, I find – I hope – small things with which I can then carefully start to put something together. It's like a painter who has just one sheet of paper and now has to paint on it: there is this big, big sense of caution. If you do something wrong, it can't be corrected. Suddenly you lose your way. That's why we take a great deal of care and concentration to do the right thing. Nothing is certain. I start something, and I have no idea where it will take us. The only thing that exists is my dancers. That trust which you simply have to have in the moment, that's not easy. That's not just fear, it's also a great hope that you will find something beautiful. You're feeling so many emotions together at that point.

*Do you feel that the pieces change when the cast is different? Or does it turn out the same again?*

It's supposed to turn out the same again. That's the beautiful thing about a live performance: every evening is different. It's a lot of work to maintain a performance so that it really seems as if it were created right in that moment. You can't just drag things around with you and say, okay, let's do that one now. It must be fresh and new, every time.

*The pieces don't change with new dancers?*

Certain things should stay the same. The performance should be such that the piece comes across even on a weak night. Of course it's sometimes very difficult to change the cast of a piece, or it might take longer until it develops, until it's all running properly again. Sometimes it goes very quickly, and sometimes it's much better afterwards. Many things have become much better, even through cast changes. There's no formula at all for it. Some things I haven't even dared to try with a new cast yet, it would really make the piece redundant.

*That's also why many dancers return as guests, because certain roles are linked to certain people?*

242

One reason, yes.

*In another interview you've said that life is like a journey. Everything we see on journeys – the different types of music, the dances, the other cultures – is worked through in the pieces.*

In the pieces I don't know; all I know is I have to work through it myself. It's inside me somehow; certainly, if you mean the co-productions, it is in the pieces as well.

*What is that like, working with people from other cultures?*

I find it wonderful, otherwise I wouldn't do it. It's quite a strain and a lot of work, but it's something which is incredibly important.

*Would I be right in saying that you are a passionate observer of people?*

Yes, definitely. Although I don't know if it's just looking. Feeling, sensing. I look, of course, but it also has something to do with what reaches you, what you see. I'm not someone who just looks or makes notes. That's no use to me at all, whatever I've seen. It's a different way of taking things in, a different kind of awareness.

*When I look at you I see someone who takes everything in very carefully and stores it up inside, before it then emerges in a very different way later on.*

Takes it in, yes. I experience many things; where it all goes, I don't know. I know absolutely nothing. That's quite an amazing thing in itself of course, how little we know.

*Looking back on the twenty-five years, and the work is, of course, still ongoing, is there ever a feeling that the energy might perhaps fade away some day?*

I have no time to be thinking about that, and I don't want to either. The only fear I have is of being swallowed up by other things and having no time to work on pieces. I have no lack of desire to work. On the contrary, I would love to do more. My problem is more the reverse. I would be very happy if some of the load was taken off me in the things which have to do with organisation and I could concentrate more on creative things.

*To be in Wuppertal for so many years – there must be a particular reason for that.*

That's a combination of many things. On the one hand, it was all unplanned; it just happened. For example, I only ever had one-year contracts; but you've got to plan everything in advance, all the guest performances for example, and then before you know it you can't leave because you're planned in. It's a huge amount of planning, also with the travelling; which pieces can you perform where. Suddenly the sets are off to Japan, and then you can't perform the pieces for such-and-such a time beforehand. You need to have a big repertoire to be able to do these things. Or if a dancer leaves and a different one suddenly has to learn twelve pieces. You don't have all that much time. You suddenly find yourself in a certain routine, but some people we have, they do so much work – when someone drops out, you're afraid that the whole thing is going to collapse.

*Where do you find the strength to keep it all moving?*
The dancers who have come here, they haven't come to Wuppertal to sit in their apartments. They all want to have plenty to do. A dancer's working life is limited too, they don't have time to sit around. They are very sad when they don't have anything to do. They want to work, and they all want to be in the next piece if they can. And that's wonderful, too. I can't afford to get tired. There's so much expectation, which is nice as well. I can't just slack off. There's someone there, radiating enthusiasm, saying I want to work now. That lends you strength; it's a reciprocal thing. With the travelling too: what you learn and experience on those journeys, it's so strong. You feel so much, you're so full of these things – it's got to come out somewhere. With a lot of things, we also know how depressing they are, the kind of hardship that so many people are in. But there is also still something which is very beautiful, and we shouldn't forget that.

*You recently put on a piece together with another company for the first time:* Le Sacre du printemps, *with the Paris Opera Ballet.*
I would never have thought it would end up being such a beautiful experience.

*Can you imagine doing that with other pieces as well?*
Well, they all want *Le Sacre du printemps* in particular. Other pieces may also be a bit more difficult for other companies. It depends on the company and on the working conditions you have.

*But it is possible in principle?*

Nothing is impossible. [Laughs.]

*Do you have any wishes for the future as far as the company, the work is concerned?*

That we can create a situation in which we can work a great deal, and that all who take part in that work do it with a great sense of responsibility and happily. Not that people should suffer through it, that people should work and torture themselves, but that there should be a joy there, and that that transfers itself to the audience. How can I say it: that something should expand, should form connections. That a lot of friends are made, not enemies; that friends are made throughout the whole world. And that we have the will to tackle life again and retain some hope. That it has a some kind of positive effect.

(13 September 1998)

**Other interviews**

## "At that point you have to start working miracles"
Marion Cito on creating costumes for the Tanztheater Wuppertal

*Marion Cito, you were initially employed at the Tanztheater as a dancer and assistant. How did you start working with costumes?*

I joined Pina's company in 1976, when Malou Airaudo had just left and they were looking for a replacement. I had seen Pina's shows before and liked her work but was sure she wouldn't be interested in me. I was wrong about that. She was looking for an assistant and asked me to dance with the company as well. So I appeared in *Blaubart, Komm tanz mit mir* and *Renate wandert aus* and a number of other pieces. During that period I built up a good relationship with Rolf Borzik [set and costume designer at the time]. I was interested in costumes and often discussed them with him. When Rolf died, Pina asked me if I would like to try my hand at costume design. At first I thought she was joking. During those first few years, we were not exactly popular in the workshops, and the work was extremely difficult.

*Why was it difficult?*

Back then every premiere led to massive protests. Half the audience would just walk out of the theatre slamming the doors. The atmosphere spread to the workshops. People kept saying the Tanztheater was ruining everything and we had no idea what we were doing. We got anonymous phone calls and threats. If it wasn't for the artistic director Arno Wüstonhöfer, who stood by Pina, the Tanztheater would have been finished after the first year or at the very latest after the second year.

*So you had never considered becoming a costume designer, as a second career, after your dance career?*

Never. But I had always been involved with costumes, even going back to my time as a dancer at the *Deutsche Oper* in Berlin. Any time a costume designer needed a model they always sent me because I enjoyed it. But I never imagined creating them myself.

*How did you cope with taking on such a huge responsibility so suddenly?*

249

For my first production as a costume designer, *1980*, Pina helped out a lot. We looked through lots of books and talked about what we liked in them.

*Were a lot of the costumes bought in?*
Some were, but a lot were prepared in house, even then.

*And did you make sketches of the designs?*
No. I used pictures to show what I wanted to achieve or arranged fabrics around the person's body. Of course I always had to make sure that you could still dance while wearing the clothes; for example, your arms need to be able to move. So you have to find clever alternatives. At the moment, what is most important to me is finding beautiful, unusual fabrics. I search the whole world for them. But even today, every time we start a new show I am convinced that I can't do this. We start out with absolutely nothing: no outline of the piece, no set, nothing. All we have is the cast. So I focus my work on the individual. I have a stock of different fabrics and think about which fabric might suit which individual. The form of the costume comes later. Once I have the basics, I show them to Pina so she can get used to them. Then, while the piece is being developed, I can see which individuals need something more special. The scenes that are only created at the last minute are more difficult to deal with. At that point you have to start working miracles!

*So you start by creating a collection for rehearsals?*
That's something I always have on hand. Then I have my "treasure chests" with the most precious clothes, the ones that you can't use for rehearsing too often because they're too fragile.

*Do you have any other approaches, apart from basing your work on the individual dancers?*
For the Turkish co-production *Nefés* I sought out burnout fabrics because I connect the burned-out designs with Istanbul. Of course that doesn't mean that if we do a co-production with Spain I look for fabrics with big dots all over them! But I do need to feel that the fabrics have something to do with the country, in a broader sense. And of course in all the costumes it has to be possible to dance.

250

*So you have very demanding requirements for the costumes: they must have something to do with the country involved, suit the person involved and, sometimes, be able to withstand a lot of stress.*

And when you put everything together, it has to create a certain image, and everything has to fit together. The work has changed a lot from the earlier years because there is much more actual dance involved. I try to follow this development with my costumes. So far, thank goodness, it has always corresponded to what Pina wants.

*When do the dancers start working with the actual costumes?*

I try to get my ideas straight as early as possible because I have to plan for the production. And because Pina needs to be able to get used to them in her imagination. I don't let the performers use the actual costumes until four weeks before the premiere at the earliest so that they don't get worn out. The problem is that the pieces are only put together at a very late stage, and it's only then that we can see if everything fits together. All the costumes need to be individual but, for example, if all the women in a piece are standing in a row you don't want it to be too colourful. Another problem can be that we realise that a transition between scenes doesn't leave enough time for the dancers to change costume. So sometimes they just have to keep the same one on. Or sometimes we have to create a second version of the same costume in a different material because the individual has to immerse themselves in water.

*So the costumes are really developed in the same manner as the pieces themselves?*

Yes, except that I can't do what Pina does and take everything apart and put it together again differently the day before the premiere! I have to work with what I have.

*How do you manage that?*

I just have to get a sense of what it could become. I do have a fear that one day it might not work. But I am always very open; I won't insist on a particular design if the person can't move in it.

*Rolf Borzik used to create special colour charts for particular pieces.*

Of course, but not by deciding I'll make *her* yellow, *her* green and *her* purple but purely through the fabrics that speak to me. Then

251

there are extras for certain performances. Or sometimes we swap a costume if it looks better on a different dancer, and then we have to alter it.

*Along with your beautiful dresses, you also use grotesque costumes for some figures, for example for Dominique Mercy as an elderly woman.*
In the past, I always used to keep things like that in my cabinet of wonders. The dancer themselves would come to me with an idea, and we would pick something out.

*How can you ever guess in advance that something might be needed?*
Well, I love putting men in dresses, so I always have a selection ready. And sometimes the dancers themselves put something together. One example was Jan Minarik as the Statue of Liberty, in my old stretchy miniskirt with a necklace I'd bought in Palermo. He had an amazing imagination for that kind of thing.

*If the new pieces are only assembled so late, the main problem must be the transitions because nobody knows what they will be beforehand.*
Pina takes a very pragmatic approach to that issue. She often finds solutions that are actually better than our original ideas. But sometimes we have to create something new very quickly.

*Do you have the material for that?*
I have quite a large collection of fabrics that I can use.

*So the workshops have got used to this rhythm?*
Of course. And during the final phase, the production is the absolute priority. Our staff in the workshops knows that it's not that I'm incapable of planning the work properly, but that this is simply how things are. But we do have excellent dressmakers and a fantastic wardrobe mistress, who creates all the patterns. She is a true artist.

*So you hardly buy anything in any more?*
Very little. A while ago I bought an old dress in Paris, totally worn-out, but it had fabulous diamanté, a kind you can't get at all any more. We took the diamanté off and sewed it onto a new dress.

252

*How do you know when a costume is right?*

The most important things are that the dancer looks good in the dress, that the colour suits her and that she can move well in it. Apart from that, of course, a dress for dance should be long; short dresses are a rare exception. You have to learn to work with that. In *Wiesenland*, the stage is at an angle, so the dresses can't be quite so long, otherwise they would touch the floor.

*If a role is re-cast, you have to alter the costume.*

It's not usually a problem. It can get difficult if there are big differences in their size, for example if someone comes on tour with the company as a general understudy. In that case I have to bring costumes from other pieces that might work. Usually, all the fabrics I use for a piece are one-offs, so I can't just have a new dress made. I've even built up a small stock of dressers for dancers who are pregnant.

*I would imagine that revivals of very old pieces could present problems.*

That was the case with *Orpheus and Eurydike*, yes, and with *Keuschheitslegende*. Hardly any of the dancers fitted into the old costumes. It was a lot of work to alter everything, and we had to create new copies of some of the costumes.

*Do you ever have to try to disguise aspects of a dancer's body?*

Not disguise, no. But I do have to take their bodies into account.

*Does it bother you if a costume for a particular piece is abandoned?*

Not at all. Costumes are not independent creations, they are part of a production. If it doesn't work, then we get rid of it. That doesn't bother me in the slightest.

*You've been creating costumes for the Tanztheater Wuppertal for twenty-seven years now. Did you ever imagine that you would be doing this job for so long?*

[Laughs.] I never even imagined that I would be doing it at all.

(1 November 2007)

## "I never stop searching"
Set designer Peter Pabst on his work

*What was it like when you started working with Pina Bausch almost twenty-seven years ago? The company had already developed a particular style, a particular direction. Was that a challenge for you?*

I first encountered the Tanztheater Wuppertal some while before I started working there. At the time I was working at the *Schauspielhaus* in Bochum under Peter Zadek. One day he invited me to attend a rehearsal of Pina Bausch's company in Wuppertal. We spent just half an hour watching a rehearsal for a rerun of *Le Sacre du printemps* and then crept out again quietly. Zadek probably took much more in during that short time than I did, simply because he was sharper. At any rate, he then invited Pina to produce the piece based on Macbeth *Er nimmt sie an der Hand und führt sie in das Schloß, die anderen folgen*. During rehearsals in Bochum, we – Pina Bausch, her stage designer Rolf Borzik and I – often met up, drank a great deal of red wine and talked for hours, not about collaborating, simply because we got on well. After Rolf's untimely death, I got a phone call asking me if I could come to Wuppertal to discuss the stage design for Pina's next piece with her. At the time I thought it would be stupid to say no just because I was afraid of getting burnt. And I didn't realise it would be a life changing, long-term decision.

*Didn't your find it enormously restricting that there was already such a strong precedent determining the stage design?*

I didn't see it as a precedent. There is a lot of misunderstanding about that question. A lot of people seem to think Pina knows exactly what she wants and dictates to us. But that's not the case. The real problem with her way of working is that she flies in the face of everything that a stage designer normally requires for his work. If I'm working on an opera, I have a text and the score. There is an intellectual basis for discussion, and there is a plot. None of that exists with Pina. At the start, there is nothing: no title, no music, no imagery. There is nothing you can rely on. But she also differs in another way from most directors I know: she has absolutely no interest in things that are merely decorative. When something is just standing there, with no other function than to be attractive, that's not enough. A set design cannot merely be beautiful. But the actual subject, how the piece is going to turn out, I find that out very late in the process even though I am the set designer. I have to deal with that. I had the great fortune of working with Peter Zadek as my first director. Each time he was preparing a new production, we would withdraw for several days, look through thousands of images, listen to music and talk. At the end of that process only one thing was clear: things would never turn out the way we had just discussed them. With Zadek I learnt to live with doubt, to put up with not knowing, with having to ask questions at every stage. That made working with Pina easier for me. This isn't about having to cope with the uncertainty towards the person with whom you are working, but the uncertainty towards yourself. I have nothing but a black box that wants something from me.

*The problem in dance is that there is no text. The piece first comes into existence when it is made.*
But many aspects of working with Zadek were very similar. He too develops a lot of material through working with the actors, who contribute a lot, and it was important not to miss out on this adventure.

*Had you ever worked in dance before?*
Never.

*So that was a challenge.*
It would have been if I had had any idea what I was letting myself in for. With time, of course, I began to realise the different conditions dancers demand. But at first I marched in there like Parsifal.

*So how and when do the first ideas emerge for the world in which the dancers will finally be moving?*
Even after twenty-seven years of collaboration it is hard to say. At this stage, it is almost an unspoken process between Pina and myself. We've never had to talk to each other much to develop ideas. One principle of this type of open production is that everyone can contribute. Everyone is very awake to what is being created and to what others say and do. That doesn't reduce my responsibility because I have to choose. But ideas can come from the widest variety of sources. Even so, in the end it's not about

255

the ideas. People always place too much emphasis on the importance of ideas. If I have an idea but it does nothing for Pina, the idea is useless. And exactly the same applies in reverse. The important thing is whether something triggers off something within you. It could be something completely minor, but something that won't go away. Images only begin to develop very, very slowly and don't yet take form. Then, slowly, I begin to create images in my model box.

*And then the discussions start?*

Once we have reached a certain point, we start to talk, but at that point neither Pina nor I can tell whether it is right or wrong.

*There was a phase during which the pieces had very clear themes. Then there were all the co-productions, focusing on individual countries; the music creates a particular atmosphere. Can all these different things serve as possible points of departure?*

Well, the music, for example, is added only at a very late stage. If Pina likes a piece of music she actually avoids using it at first so that it doesn't get "worn out" during the rehearsals. During the course of a production, I create as many as six different set designs, each of which can be a different, strange, world. If I can't be at the rehearsals all the time, Pina will keep me up to date, for example telling me that they are doing a lot of work with water during the rehearsals. Once the first steps have been made in rehearsals, we discuss how it would look in these different worlds and what effects they would have on the dancers or on the scenes.

*Has it ever happened that a set you had designed didn't work for the current production, but you could use it for a later one?*

After twenty-seven years, that's hard to say. Over the years Pina and I have built up such a huge stock of shared experiences and ideas, discussions and memories, that it is very difficult to distinguish them. I can't remember ever having used an entire design in a different production, but that would certainly apply to some of the details. For example, the whales that turned up in the set design for *Ten Chi* we had talked about them before.

*To what extent does the location of a co-production affect the set design? You always go along for the initial research phases abroad.*

Yes, I've always been there, except for the preparations for *Ein Trauerspiel*. Of course the location affects you. But it can also lead to disappointment. The cities that invite the company often have very specific ideas about how we should react to the location. But we don't show either the negative or the beautiful sides of a place in that kind of documentary fashion. It's a world of its own. The only important aspect of the set design is that it should help the dancers to tell their stories, not create an image of a particular city. I try to keep the set designs as open as possible, not to confine them to one particular meaning.

*Yet many details of the set for* Palermo Palermo, *for example, are reminiscent of the south of Italy. There is a collapsed wall, which doesn't refer to the fall of the Berlin wall, but the stones, some of which are shattered, make it difficult to walk around. You often create "physical spaces" like that, ones that change the conditions for the dancers.*

That is partly due to Pina's openness — she will accept a lot of different surfaces, some difficult — and due to the dancers' courage. But the dancers know, ultimately, that neither Pina nor I would ever do anything that would do them any harm: not physically and not in artistic terms. I never let any material be used on the stage without having it chemically analysed. When it rains sand in *Palermo, Palermo*, for example, I had it checked beforehand to make sure that it was not damaging to human health in any way.

*Naturalness and artificiality are important subjects, as is the confusion between the internal and external. This creates a kind of poetry.*

Pina and I are similar in that respect. Rolf Borzik also used water and turf, for example, in his stage designs. But I have always liked working with natural materials too. The reason is simple: it's fun. You see the theatrical space, which is an artificial space, in a different way. There is nothing less artificial than nature. Anything that has already become art, has found its form, is uninteresting as a material. Things that are not yet art are much more interesting. Nature is so varied that it never becomes tired. You can watch the flames in a fireplace for hours without getting bored. You can bend wood again and again; it doesn't suffer fatigue. Natural materials are sensual: earth, water etc. And that makes the images sensual. That sensuality is transmitted to the performers. And that sensuality makes the dancers authentic and makes their performance really good.

257

*When do you finally decide on a particular stage design?*

We try to delay the decision as long as possible, in order to keep the process open. Sometimes, something completely different emerges just before the premiere.

*But then there is very little time left to construct the set.*

That's my problem. Neither Pina nor the dancers should have to worry about that. I have to make that decision, and then I have to manage it. It has always been an impossibility, but somehow, together with the workshops and the technicians, I've always managed to achieve a minor miracle.

*Doesn't the staff in the workshops ever threaten to down tools?*

Amazingly no. It's an interpersonal question. They all work like maniacs because they know I take them seriously. I listen very carefully to their reactions. And of course they all enjoy creating something that should have been impossible in the time available. And they are proud when something impressive emerges.

*But creating a wooden floor like that for* Nefés, *one that can be filled with water from below, is technically complex; you can't construct something like that at the drop of a hat.*

It's extremely difficult, even if it looks simple. If Pina likes an idea she always asks: what else can it do? And then I promise her the sun, moon and stars.

*Like submerging a wooden floor in water.*

I had offered her a set using water, without wood. But I like to make things complicated. Combining wood with dancers is a difficult combination and wood and water is even harder. And then Pina asked, do we have to have the water there the whole time? So I daringly said no. And that's where one of my greatest pleasures begins, namely, to find a way of doing it. For *Wiesenland*, I claimed that it would be possible to lie the moss-covered wall flat so that they could dance on it. But the wall weighs several tonnes, and I was showered with criticism and objections from all sides, some for justifiable reasons of safety. But I take especial pleasure in doing something like that and getting it to work.

258

*Do you solve all the technical problems yourself?*

Yes, I do. I enjoy it. The aesthetic side of things is directed more by your emotions. Putting it into practice challenges your intellect. Making designs work in practice always involves an element of logic. For *Ein Trauerspiel*, I wanted to create a floating island, and I had been dreaming of making a waterfall for a long time. I calculated that I needed 23,000 litres of water and the water needed to be about sixteen centimetres deep. But we were forbidden from putting so much water on the stage. The solution was pumps, provided by the Wuppertal fire service, that allowed us to meet the requirement to remove 23,000 litres of water from the theatre in ten minutes. And that allowed me to create my waterfall, by setting up a closed system. There was no way I would have been able to suspend ten tonnes of water from the ceiling.

*Finding solutions like that at the last minute must take a cool head and a lot of staying power.*

You do need a lot of patience. There is no point trying to hurry Pina up. These things take time. Generally, we make the final decision on the set design four to five weeks before the premiere. But sometimes it has been as little as three weeks. And the dancers, and Pina, also have to have enough time to rehearse everything on the actual set. Everyone reacts admirably. Normally, we would have five or six days for those rehearsals. During that final phase, we add a huge number of small refinements, and the video work is only done at that stage, too.

*You yourself make a lot of recordings during the research phase.*

I always have a small video camera with me, but I don't make recordings in a deliberate way. Except for *Danzón*; for that piece, Pina indicated that she might like a projection with fish to accompany her solo. But otherwise I just record everything that I find curious, interesting or odd. Sometimes we use film that I had recorded at a much earlier date. And then I edit the material, under enormous time pressure, while rehearsals are ongoing, and then Pina changes the piece again. At *Masurca Fogo*, the spectators were already taking their seats while I was up in the projection room editing the last piece of film.

*How do you cope with that level of pressure?*

I'm the kind of person who can cope very well under pressure. I become totally calm.

*Sometimes, during the final dress rehearsals, all the projections are abandoned.*

That happened in *Für die Kinder von gestern, heute und morgen*. Pina kept asking for projections, and I had put together two-and-a-half hours of material. But by the end I had a sense that it didn't fit. You have to be able to waste images, and I can do that. What interests me in video is not the sequence of images itself or the technology but the question of the effect the projection has on the space and on the dancers. Technology doesn't create magic; I need to enchant the audience, and to do that I need strong images. So technical perfection, in the video projections, is unimportant to me.

*Now there are not just the classic Tanztheater spaces full of natural materials; you also work with very bare, black stages.*

I like to call those spaces my Zen pieces. Normally, I create sets consisting of toys for the dancers – like the mountain of flowers in *Der Fensterputzer*. It had to be so soft and comfortable that they felt like playing with it. But with the whales that was the only time that I asked the dancers not to touch something. The other spaces of course have to do with the changing structure of the pieces; in recent years they have involved much more dance as such. Or perhaps it is because I am sometimes trying to catch my breath.

*Yet there is a multitude of details within these black spaces. The rock in* Vollmond *is not pure black; it is a shimmering silver, as if lit by moonlight. And the falling rain keeps changing, from a light drizzle to steady rain.*

I think things have to be made in a sophisticated way so that they retain their vitality. The rock does not just sit there being a rock, although it is that, too. The water in the ditch is not standing still, it is a river that flows, although you can't hear it or see any eddies. For the rain, our first thoughts were of summer. But you can never get artificial light to reproduce the intensity of sunlight. So I wanted different kinds of rain, including a really heavy summer downpour. It reminds me of my childhood; I used to run out into the rain, nobody could hold me back. It was a very sensual experience. I fiddled around with the different types of rain for a long time. There is always a huge amount of technical equipment in the background ensuring that the final effect seems simple and natural.

*That must cost quite a lot.*

It's expensive, of course. Even just the safety precautions, when you are working with water, for example. The wooden floor in *Nefés*, too; we had to be sure it wouldn't splinter, yet it had to be as light as possible and also be water-repellent. In order to make it possible to take the pieces on tour I always have to come up with completely autonomous systems that work independently of the different conditions in different countries. For *Nefés*, though, we have to adapt the floor of the set to each stage so that you can't see that it has been mounted on top of the existing stage. It's always much more complicated with the open sets than with the closed ones. So I try to be present at all our guest performances, as far as my other commitments allow.

*Twenty-seven years is a long time for a collaboration. It's fairly unusual in theatre.*

The whole thing is very unusual; keeping productions alive for such a long time is unusual too. It means a lot of care needs to be taken. At some point the set for *Viktor* became unusable because the walls are spread with glue and have clay thrown at them again and again so that they look fresh and radiate warmth. At some point nobody could even lift the pieces, they were so heavy. So we had to construct new ones, and it was very difficult to reproduce everything.

*Patience and staying power keep recurring as key words for every aspect of this kind of work.*

Patience and art go hand in hand; I learned that from Zadek and Pina. That includes being patient with myself – not expecting myself to do things that are not yet possible. There is no other way of coping with processes that are so open-ended. You are very vulnerable – as if someone had taken your skin off. You try to bring that situation to an end as soon as possible by coming up with an idea. But you have to endure the rawness and question your ideas again and again. You can't ever stop searching.

(15 October 2007)

# Appendix

# Biography

1940    Born 27 July in Solingen (father was a publican)

1955    Begins studying dance at the Folkwangschule in Essen under Kurt Jooss

1959    Final exams in dance practice and dance educational studies. Receives the Folkwang prize for outstanding achievements and a grant from the German Academic Exchange Service to continue her studies in the USA

1960    Becomes "special student" at the Juilliard School of Music in New York. At the same time member of Paul Sanasardo's and Donya Feuer's companies

1961    Dances with the New American Ballet (collaborating largely with Paul Taylor) and with New York's Metropolitan Opera House Ballet

1962–68    Becomes a soloist at the newly founded Folkwang Ballet under Kurt Jooss. Works with the choreographers Kurt Jooss, Antony Tudor, Lucas Hoving, Hans Züllig and in particular Jean Cébron

1968    Choreographs *Fragmente* (music by Béla Bartók) for the Folkwang Ballet

1969    Choreographs *Im Wind der Zeit* (music by Mirko Dorner). Supervises Kurt Jooss' choreography of the dances in Henry Purcell's opera *The Fairy Queen* at the Schwetzingen Festival. Wins first prize in the Cologne choreography competition with *Im Wind der Zeit*. Takes on directorship of the Folkwang-Tanzstudio (till 1973). Teaches at the Folkwang Academy

1970    Premiere of the ballet *Nachnull* (music by Ivo Malec). Guest choreographer at the Rotterdam Dance Centre

1971    Premiere of the ballet *Aktionen für Tänzer* (music by Günter Becker) at the Wuppertal Theatres, danced by members of the Folkwang Tanzstudio. Performances in Germany and the USA

1972    Choreography of the "Bacchanal" for *Tannhäuser* at the Wuppertal theatres, danced by members of the Folkwang-Tanzstudio. Guest teacher of modern dance, guest soloist and choreographer for Paul Sanasardo's company in New York. Premiere of the choreographies *Wiegenlied* and *Philips 836885 D.S.Y.* (Music by Pierre Henry)

1973    Receives the North Rhine Westphalia sponsorship award for young artists. Takes over as director of ballet at the Wuppertal theatres; the company is initially called Wuppertaler Tanztheater, later Tanztheater Wuppertal

1974    Develops the first choreography there: *Fritz*. Plays the title role in the opera *Yvonne, Prinzessin von Burgund* by Boris Blacher. First full-length production, the dance-opera *Iphigenia in Tauris*. Choreography of the revue *Zwei Krawatten*. Beginning of her collaboration with the stage and costume designer Rolf Borzik

1975    Choreographs *Orpheus and Eurydice* and the three-part evening "Frühlingsopfer" (including *Le Sacre du printemps*)

1976    Premiere of the two-part evening "Die sieben Todsünden"

| | |
|---|---|
| 1977 | *Blaubart. Komm tanz mit mir.* First performances abroad. *Renate wandert aus* |
| 1978 | *Er nimmt sie an der Hand und führt sie in das Schloß, die anderen folgen. Café Müller. Kontakthof* |
| 1979 | First overseas tour (to south-east Asia). Invited to the Berlin *Theatertreffen* with the new piece *Arien. Keuschheitslegende* |
| 1980 | On 27 January her partner Rolf Borzik dies following lengthy and severe illness. *1980. Bandoneon* |
| 1981 | Invited to the Berlin *Theatertreffen* with *Bandoneon.* The Tanztheater Wuppertal is given its first extensive showcase at the *Theater der Welt* festival in Cologne. Birth of her son Rolf Salomon (28 September) |
| 1982 | *Walzer.* Appears in Federico Fellini's film *E la nave va. Nelken* |
| 1983 | Takes on artistic directorship of the dance department at the Folkwang Academy (till 1989), thus also becoming director of the Folkwang-Tanzstudio again (until 1999) |
| 1984 | *Auf dem Gebirge hat man ein Geschrei gehört.* Guest performance in Los Angeles as part of the cultural programme for the Olympic Games |
| 1985 | *Two Cigarettes in the Dark* |
| 1986 | *Viktor* |
| 1987 | *Ahnen.* Tour of the German Democratic Republic |
| 1989 | Her film *Die Klage der Kaiserin* is released. *Palermo Palermo* |
| 1991 | *Tanzabend II (Madrid)* |
| 1993 | *Das Stück mit dem Schiff* |
| 1994 | *Ein Trauerspiel* |
| 1995 | *Danzón.* Receives the German Award for Dance |
| 1996 | *Nur Du* |
| 1997 | *Der Fensterputzer.* Production of *Le Sacre du printemps* for the ballet of the Paris Opera. Award of the French order *Pour le Mérite* |
| 1998 | *Masurca Fogo.* Stages Béla Bartók's opera *Herzog Blaubarts Burg* in Aix-en-Provence (with musical director Pierre Boulez). The Tanztheater Wuppertal's 25th birthday is celebrated with a festival |
| 1999 | *O Dido.* Receives the European Theatre Award and the *Praemium Imperiale* in Japan |
| 2000 | *Wiesenland* |
| 2001 | *Água* |
| 2002 | *Für die Kinder von gestern, heute und morgen* |
| 2003 | *Nefés.* Awarded *Chevalier de l'Ordre National de la Légion d'Honneur* in Paris |
| 2004 | *Ten Chi.* Receives the Nijinsky Prize |
| 2005 | *Rough Cut.* Production of *Orpheus and Eurydice* for the ballet of the Paris Opera |
| 2006 | *Vollmond* |
| 2007 | *Bamboo Blues.* Awarded the "Golden Lion" of the Venice Biennale and the Inamori Foundation's Kyoto Prize |
| 2008 | *Sweet Mambo* |

# Works

*Fritz*
Music: Gustav Mahler, Wolfgang Hufschmidt. Scenography: Hermann Markard (costume assistant: Rolf Borzik). Premiere: 5 January 1974, Opera House, Wuppertal
Performers: Hiltrud Blanck (Fritz), Malou Airaudo (mother), Jean Mindo [Jan Minarik] (father), Charlotte Butler (grandmother), Dominique Mercy (man in shirt), Riita Laurikainen (bald woman), Ed Kortlandt (man-woman), Carlos Orta (man), Tjitske Broersma (woman in black furs), Heinz Samm (fat man), Catherine Denisot (girl with long arms), Wolf Werner Wolf (nose), Monika Sagon (aged girl), Monika Wacker (lady with umbrella), John Giffin, João Penalva (two pursuers), Gabriel Sala (overcoat man), Vivienne Newport (girl)

*Iphigenia in Tauris*
Music: Christoph Willibald Gluck. Scenography: Pina Bausch, Jürgen Dreier. Premiere: 21 April 1974, Opera House, Wuppertal
Performers: Malou Airaudo (Iphigenia), Dominique Mercy (Orest), Ed Kortlandt (Pylades), Carlos Orta (Thoas), Colleen Finneran, John Giffin (media), Josephine Ann Endicott (Clytemnestra), Tjitske Broersma (Electra), Hans Pop (Agamemnon), Josephine Ann Endicott, Hiltrud Blanck, Catherine Denisot, Colleen Finneran, Tjitske Broersma, Margaret Huggenberger, Charlotte Butler, Riita Laurikainen, Vivienne Newport, Monika Wacker (priestesses), John Giffin, Ralph Grant, Carlos Orta, Arnaldo Álvarez (Clytemnestras), John Giffin, Ralph Grant, Hans Pop, Arnaldo Álvarez (guards)

*Ich bring dich um die Ecke*
Music: Dance music hits from the past. Stage design: Karl Kneidl. Premiere: 8 December 1974, Opera House, Wuppertal
Performers: Marlis Alt, Malou Airaudo, Pedro Bisch, Hiltrud Blanck, Sue Cooper, Michael Diekamp, Josephine Ann Endicott, László Fenyves, Colleen Finneran, Lajos Horváth, Margaret Huggenberger, Ed Kortlandt, Stephanie Macoun, Yolanda Meier, Dominique Mercy, Jean Mindo [Jan Minarik], Vivienne Newport, Barbara Passow, Hans Pop, Monika Sagon, Heinz Samm, Matthias Schmidt, Monika Wacker, Barry Wilkinson

*Adagio – fünf Lieder von Gustav Mahler*
Assistance: Hans Pop. Music: Gustav Mahler. Stage design: Karl Kneidl. Premiere: 8 December 1974, Opera House, Wuppertal
Performers: Marlis Alt, Malou Airaudo, Pedro Bisch, Hiltrud Blanck, Sue Cooper, Michael Diekamp, Josephine Ann Endicott, László Fenyves, Colleen Finneran, Lajos Horváth, Margaret Huggenberger, Ed Kortlandt, Stephanie Macoun, Yolanda Meier, Dominique Mercy, Jean Mindo [Jan Minarik], Vivienne Newport, Bar-

bara Passow, Hans Pop, Monika Sagon, Heinz Samm, Matthias Schmidt, Monika Wacker, Barry Wilkinson

*Orpheus and Eurydice*
ASSISTANCE: Hans Pop. MUSIC: Christoph Willibald Gluck. SCENOGRAPHY: Rolf Borzik. PREMIERE: 23 May 1975, Opera House, Wuppertal
PERFORMERS: Dominique Mercy (Orpheus), Malou Airaudo (Eurydice), Marlis Alt (Love); "Grief": Marlis Alt, Pedro Bisch, Hiltrud Blanck, Tjitske Broersma, Sue Cooper, Michael Diekamp, László Fenyves, Colleen Finneran, Lajos Horváth, Margaret Huggenberger, Stephanie Macoun, Yolanda Meier, Jean Mindo [Jan Minarik], Vivienne Newport, Barbara Passow, Monika Wacker, Barry Wilkinson; "Power": Heinz Samm, Michael Diekamp, Jean Mindo [Jan Minarik], Marlis Alt, Pedro Bisch, Hiltrud Blanck, Tjitske Broersma, Sue Cooper, László Fenyves, Colleen Finneran, Margaret Huggenberger, Stephanie Macoun, Yolanda Meier, Vivienne Newport, Barbara Passow, Monika Wacker; "Peace": Monika Sagon, Heinz Samm, Marlis Alt, Hiltrud Blanck, Sue Cooper, Vivienne Newport, Barbara Passow, Monika Wacker, Pedro Bisch, Tjitske Broersma, Michael Diekamp, László Fenyves, Colleen Finneran, Lajos Horváth, Margaret Huggenberger, Stephanie Macoun, Yolanda Meier, Jean Mindo [Jan Minarik], Barry Wilkinson; "Dying": Heinz Samm, Michael Diekamp, Jean Mindo [Jan Minarik], Marlis Alt, Pedro Bisch, Hiltrud Blanck, Tjitske Broersma, Sue Cooper, László Fenyves, Colleen Finneran, Lajos Horváth, Margaret Huggenberger, Stephanie Macoun, Yolanda Meier, Vivienne Newport, Barbara Passow, Monika Wacker, Barry Wilkinson

"Frühlingsopfer"
ASSISTANCE: Hans Pop. MUSIC: Igor Strawinsky. SCENOGRAPHY: Rolf Borzik. PREMIERE: 3 December 1975, Opera House, Wuppertal
*Wind von West*
PERFORMERS: Josephine Ann Endicott, Jean Mindo [Jan Minarik], Ed Kortlandt, Tjitske Broersma, Monika Sagon, Marlis Alt, Pedro Bisch, Hiltrud Blanck, Sue Cooper, Fernando Cortizo, Michael Diekamp, Esco Edmondson, László Fenyves, Colleen Finneran, Lajos Horváth, Margaret Huggenberger, Yolanda Meier, Stephanie Macoun, Vivienne Newport, Barbara Passow, Heinz Samm, Monika Wacker, Barry Wilkinson
*Der zweite Frühling*
PERFORMERS: Vivienne Newport, Michael Diekamp (old married couple), Josephine Ann Endicott, Colleen Finneran, Jean Mindo [Jan Minarik], Marlis Alt (the memories)
*Le Sacre du printemps*
PERFORMERS: Marlis Alt, Hiltrud Blanck, Tjitske Broersma, Sue Cooper, Josephine Ann Endicott, Colleen Finneran, Margaret Huggenberger, Stephanie Macoun, Yolanda Meier, Vivienne Newport, Barbara Passow, Marie-Luise Thiele, Monika Wacker, Pedro Bisch, Fernando Cortizo, Guy Detot, Michael Diekamp, Esco

268

Edmondson, László Fenyves, Lutz Förster, Erwin Fritsche, Lajos Horváth, Ed Kortlandt, Jean Mindo [Jan Minarik], Heinz Samm, Barry Wilkinson

"Die sieben Todsünden"
ASSISTANCE: Hans Pop. MUSIC: Kurt Weill. LIBRETTO: Bertolt Brecht. SCENOGRAPHY: Rolf Borzik. PREMIERE: 15 June 1976, Opera House, Wuppertal
*Die sieben Todsünden der Kleinbürger*
PERFORMERS: Ann Höling (Anna I), Josephine Ann Endicott (Anna II), Zsolt Ketszery, Willi Nett, Siegfried Schmidt, Oskar Pürgstaller (the family), Hiltrud Blanck, Tjitske Broersma, Sue Cooper, Colleen Finneran, Margaret Huggenberger, Stephanie Macoun, Yolanda Meier, Vivienne Newport, Barbara Passow, Monika Sagon, Monika Wacker, Pedro Bisch, Fernando Cortizo, Michael Diekamp, Esco Edmondson, László Fenyves, Lajos Horváth, Ed Kortlandt, Jean Mindo [Jan Minarik], Hans Pop, Heinz Samm
*Fürchtet Euch nicht*
PERFORMERS: Mechthild Großmann, Ann Höling, Karin Rasenack, Erich Leukert, Marlis Alt, Hiltrud Blanck, Tjitske Broersma, Sue Cooper, Josephine Ann Endicott, Colleen Finneran, Margaret Huggenberger, Stephanie Macoun, Yolanda Meier, Vivienne Newport, Barbara Passow, Monika Sagon, Monika Wacker, Pedro Bisch, Fernando Cortizo, Michael Diekamp, Esco Edmondson, László Fenyves, Lajos Horváth, Ed Kortlandt, Jean Mindo [Jan Minarik], Heinz Samm, Matthias Schmidt, Barry Wilkinson

*Blaubart. Beim Anhören einer Tonbandaufnahme von Béla Bartóks Oper "Herzog Blaubarts Burg"*
ASSISTANCE: Rolf Borzik, Marion Cito, Hans Pop. MUSIC: Béla Bartók. SCENOGRAPHY: Rolf Borzik. PREMIERE: 8 January 1977, Opera House, Wuppertal
PERFORMERS: Marlis Alt, Jean Mindo [Jan Minarik], Arnaldo Álvarez, Anne Marie Benati, Hiltrud Blanck, Tjitske Broersma, Fernando Cortizo, Marion Cito, Elizabeth Clarke, Guy Detot, Michael Diekamp, Mari DiLena, Esco Edmondson, Josephine Ann Endicott, Colleen Finneran, John Giffin, Ed Kortlandt, Luis P. Layag, Yolanda Meier, Vivienne Newport, Barbara Passow, Hans Pop, Monika Sagon, Heinz Samm, Monika Wacker

*Komm tanz mit mir*
ASSISTANCE: Rolf Borzik, Ralf Milde, Hans Pop. MUSIC: traditional German folk songs. SCENOGRAPHY: Rolf Borzik. PREMIERE: 26 May 1977, Opera House, Wuppertal
PERFORMERS: Josephine Ann Endicott, Gisbert Rüschkamp, Arnaldo Álvarez, Anne Marie Benati, Hiltrud Blanck, Tjitske Broersma, Fernando Cortizo, Marion Cito, Elizabeth Clarke, Guy Detot, Mari DiLena, Esco Edmondson, Colleen Finneran, John Giffin, Ed Kortlandt, Luis P. Layag, Yolanda Meier, Jean Mindo [Jan Minarik], Vivienne Newport, Barbara Passow, Hans Pop, Monika Sagon, Heinz Samm, Monika Wacker

*Renate wandert aus*
ASSISTANCE: Rolf Borzik, Marion Cito, Hans Pop. MUSIC: Pop and golden oldies. SCENOGRAPHY: Rolf Borzik. PREMIERE: 30 December 1977, Opera House, Wuppertal
PERFORMERS: Malou Airaudo, Marlis Alt, Arnaldo Álvarez, Anne Marie Benati, Hiltrud Blanck, Tjitske Broersma, Fernando Cortizo, Marion Cito, Mari DiLena, Josephine Ann Endicott, John Giffin, Ed Kortlandt, Luis P. Layag, Dominique Mercy, Yolanda Meier, Jean Mindo [Jan Minarik], Vivienne Newport, Barbara Passow, Jacques Antoine Petarozzi, Helena Pikon, Monika Sagon, Heinz Samm, Dana Robin Sapiro, Monika Wacker, Erich Leukert

*Er nimmt sie an der Hand und führt sie in das Schloß, die anderen folgen*
ASSISTANCE: Ula Blum-Deuter, Hans Dieter Knebel, Ingeborg von Liebezeit, Klaus Morgenstern, Katharina Schumacher. MUSIC: Peer Raben. SCENOGRAPHY: Rolf Borzik. PREMIERE: 22 April 1978, Playhouse, Bochum
PERFORMERS: Sona Cervena, Josephine Ann Endicott, Mechthild Großmann, Hans Dieter Knebel, Rudolph Lauterburg, Dominique Mercy, Jan Minarik, Vivienne Newport, Volker Spengler, Vitus Zeplichal

*Café Müller*
MUSIC: Henry Purcell. SCENOGRAPHY: Rolf Borzik. PREMIERE: 20 May 1978, Opera House, Wuppertal
PERFORMERS: Malou Airaudo, Pina Bausch, Meryl Tankard, Rolf Borzik, Dominique Mercy, Jan Minarik

*Kontakthof*
ASSISTANCE: Rolf Borzik, Marion Cito, Hans Pop. MUSIC: Charlie Chaplin, Anton Karas, Juan Llossas, Nino Rota and others. SCENOGRAPHY: Rolf Borzik. PREMIERE: 9 December 1978, Opera House, Wuppertal
PERFORMERS: Arnaldo Álvarez, Gary Austin Crocker, Fernando Cortizo, Elizabeth Clarke, Josephine Ann Endicott, Lutz Förster, John Giffin, Silvia Kesselheim, Ed Kortlandt, Luis P. Layag, Mari DiLena, Beatrice Libonati, Anne Martin, Jan Minarik, Vivienne Newport, Arthur Rosenfeld, Monika Sagon, Heinz Samm, Meryl Tankard, Christian Trouillas

*Arien*
ASSISTANCE: Marion Cito, Hans Pop. MUSIC: Ludwig van Beethoven, Wolfgang Amadeus Mozart, Sergey Rakhmaninov, Robert Schumann, songs by the Comedian Harmonists, etc. SCENOGRAPHY: Rolf Borzik. PREMIERE: 12 May 1979, Opera House, Wuppertal
PERFORMERS: Arnaldo Álvarez, Anne Marie Benati, Marion Cito, Gary Austin Crocker, Fernando Cortizo, Elizabeth Clarke, Josephine Ann Endicott, Lutz Förster, John Giffin, Silvia Kesselheim, Ed Kortlandt, Mari DiLena, Beatrice Libonati, Anne Martin, Jan Minarik, Vivienne Newport, Arthur Rosen-

feld, Monika Sagon, Heinz Samm, Meryl Tankard, Christian Trouillas, Monika Wacker

*Keuschheitslegende*
ASSISTANCE: Marion Cito. MUSIC: Nino Rota, George Gershwin, Peter Kreuder and others. TEXT: Ovid, Rudolf Georg Binding, Frank Wedekind and others. SCENOGRAPHY: Rolf Borzik. PREMIERE: 4 December 1979, Opera House, Wuppertal
PERFORMERS: Arnaldo Álvarez, Anne Marie Benati, Gary Austin Crocker, Josephine Ann Endicott, Lutz Förster, Mechthild Großmann, Hans Dieter Knebel, Ed Kortlandt, Beatrice Libonati, Anne Martin, Jan Minarik, Nazareth Panadero, Isabel Ribas Serra, Arthur Rosenfeld, Monika Sagon, Heinz Samm, Jean-Laurent Sasportes, Janusz Subicz, Meryl Tankard, Heide Tegeder

*1980*
ASSISTANCE: Hans Pop, Klaus Morgenstern. MUSIC: John Dowland, John Wilson, Ludwig van Beethoven, Claude Debussy, Johannes Brahms, Edward Elgar, Francis Lai, Benny Goodman, songs by the Comedian Harmonists, etc. STAGE DESIGN: Peter Pabst (using designs by Rolf Borzik). COSTUMES: Marion Cito. DRAMATURGY: Raimund Hoghe. PREMIERE: 18 May 1980, Playhouse, Wuppertal
PERFORMERS: Anne Marie Benati, Lutz Förster, Mechthild Großmann, Hans Dieter Knebel, Ed Kortlandt, Mari DiLena, Beatrice Libonati, Anne Martin, Jan Minarik, Vivienne Newport, Nazareth Panadero, Isabel Ribas Serra, Arthur Rosenfeld, Monika Sagon, Jean-Laurent Sasportes, Janusz Subicz, Meryl Tankard, Heide Tegeder, Ralf John Ernesto (magician), Arthur Sockel (violin), Max Walther (athlete at the bar)

*Bandoneon*
ASSISTANCE: Matthias Burkert, Hans Pop. MUSIC: Latin American tangos. STAGE DESIGN: Gralf-Edzard Habben. COSTUMES: Marion Cito. DRAMATURGY: Raimund Hoghe. PREMIERE: 21 December 1980, Opera House, Wuppertal
PERFORMERS: Malou Airaudo, Anne Marie Benati, Mechthild Großmann, Urs Kaufmann, Hans Dieter Knebel, Beatrice Libonati, Anne Martin, Dominique Mercy, Jan Minarik, Vivienne Newport, Nazareth Panadero, Isabel Ribas Serra, Arthur Rosenfeld, Jean-Laurent Sasportes, Janusz Subicz, Meryl Tankard, Heide Tegeder, Christian Trouillas

*Walzer*
ASSISTANCE: Matthias Burkert, Hans Pop. MUSIC: Franz Schubert, Robert Schumann, national anthems, Latin American dance music, etc. STAGE DESIGN: Ulrich Bergfelder. COSTUMES: Marion Cito. FILM: Frédéric Leboyer. DRAMATURGY: Raimund Hoghe. PREMIERE: 17 June 1982, Carré Theatre, Amsterdam
PERFORMERS: Malou Airaudo, Jakob Andersen, Anne Marie Benati, Bénédicte Billiet, Matthias Burkert, Josephine Ann Endicott, Mechthild Großmann, Urs Kaufmann, Ed Kortlandt, Beatrice Libonati, Jan Minarik, Nazareth Panadero,

271

Helena Pikon, Hans Pop, Arthur Rosenfeld, Monika Sagon, Jean-Laurent Sasportes, Janusz Subicz, Meryl Tankard, Christian Trouillas, Francis Viet, Vitus Zeplichal

*Nelken*
ASSISTANCE: Matthias Burkert, Hans Pop. MUSIC: Franz Schubert, George Gershwin, Franz Lehár and others. STAGE DESIGN: Peter Pabst. COSTUMES: Marion Cito. DRAMATURGY: Raimund Hoghe. PREMIERE: *1st version*: 30 December 1982, Opera House, Wuppertal; *2nd version*: 16 May 1983, marquee in the English Garden, Munich
PERFORMERS (30 December 1982): Jakob Andersen, Anne Marie Benati, Bénédicte Billiet, Matthias Burkert, Lutz Förster, Kyomi Ichida, Urs Kaufmann, Ed Kortlandt, Anne Martin, Dominique Mercy, Jan Minarik, Nazareth Panadero, Helena Pikon, Hans Pop, Jean-Laurent Sasportes, Janusz Subicz, Francis Viet

*Auf dem Gebirge hat man ein Geschrei gehört*
ASSISTANCE: Matthias Burkert, Hans Pop. MUSIC: Henry Purcell, Heinrich Schütz, Felix Mendelssohn Bartholdy, Gerry Mulligan, Johnny Hodges, songs by Fred Astaire and Édith Piaf, Irish bagpipe music, etc. STAGE DESIGN: Peter Pabst. COSTUMES: Marion Cito. DRAMATURGY: Raimund Hoghe. PREMIERE: 13 May 1984, Playhouse, Wuppertal
PERFORMERS: Jakob Andersen, Anne Marie Benati, Bénédicte Billiet, Matthias Burkert, Jean-François Duroure, Dominique Duszynski, Josephine Ann Endicott, Lutz Förster, Kyomi Ichida, Urs Kaufmann, Silvia Kesselheim, Ed Kortlandt, Beatrice Libonati, Melanie Karen Lien, Elena Majnoni, Anne Martin, Dominique Mercy, Jan Minarik, Nazareth Panadero, Helena Pikon, Arthur Rosenfeld, Jean-Laurent Sasportes, Janusz Subicz, Francis Viet, Musikverein Marion (senior citizens' orchestra)

*Two Cigarettes in the Dark*
ASSISTANCE: Matthias Burkert. MUSIC: Claudio Monteverdi, Ludwig van Beethoven, Maurice Ravel, Hugo Wolf, Henry Purcell, Ben Webster, Minnesang, etc. STAGE DESIGN: Peter Pabst. COSTUMES: Marion Cito. DRAMATURGY: Raimund Hoghe. PREMIERE: 31 March 1985, Playhouse, Wuppertal
PERFORMERS: Jakob Andersen, Bénédicte Billiet, Jean-François Duroure, Dominique Duszynski, Josephine Ann Endicott, Mechthild Großmann, Kyomi Ichida, Dominique Mercy, Jan Minarik, Helena Pikon, Francis Viet

*Viktor*
ASSISTANCE: Matthias Burkert, Marion Cito. MUSIC: Pyotr Tchaikovsky, Dietrich Buxtehude, Antonín Dvořák, Aram Khachaturian, medieval dance music, Russian waltzes, New Orleans jazz, 1930s dance music, traditional music from Lombardy, Tuscany, southern Italy, Sardinia and Bolivia. STAGE DESIGN: Peter Pabst. COSTUMES: Marion Cito. DRAMATURGY: Raimund Hoghe. PREMIERE: 14 May 1986, Playhouse, Wuppertal

PERFORMERS: Jakob Andersen, Anne Marie Benati, Bénédicte Billiet, Rolando Brenes Calvo, Antonio Carallo, Finola Cronin, Dominique Duszynski, Jean-François Duroure, Kyomi Ichida, Urs Kaufmann, Silvia Kesselheim, Ed Kortlandt, Beatrice Libonati, Melanie Karen Lien, Anne Martin, Dominique Mercy, Jan Minarik, Helena Pikon, Monika Sagon, Jean-Laurent Sasportes, Mark Sieczkarek, Julie Anne Stanzak, Francis Viet

*Ahnen*
ASSISTANCE: Hans Pop. MUSIC: Claudio Monteverdi, John Dowland, songs and instrumental music from the Middle Ages and the Renaissance, traditional Nubian, Hamar and Senufo music, folk music from Switzerland, Italy, Spain and the Caribbean, early Jewish instrumental music, rock and pop from Japan, dance and popular music from the 1920s and 1930s by Fred Astaire, Ella Fitzgerald and Billie Holiday. MUSICAL ASSISTANCE: Matthias Burkert. STAGE DESIGN: Peter Pabst. COSTUMES: Marion Cito. DRAMATURGY: Raimund Hoghe. PREMIERE: 21 March 1987, Playhouse, Wuppertal
PERFORMERS: Jakob Andersen, Bénédicte Billiet, Rolando Brenes Calvo, Matthias Burkert, Antonio Carallo, Finola Cronin, Dominique Duszynski, Josephine Ann Endicott, Lutz Förster, Kyomi Ichida, Urs Kaufmann, Ed Kortlandt, Beatrice Libonati, Melanie Karen Lien, Anne Martin, Dominique Mercy, Jan Minarik, Helena Pikon, Monika Sagon, Jean-Laurent Sasportes, Mark Sieczkarek, Julie Anne Stanzak, Francis Viet

*Die Klage der Kaiserin* (film, 1989)
ASSISTANCE: Matthias Burkert. COSTUMES: Marion Cito. DRAMATURGY: Raimund Hoghe. CAMERA: Martin Schäfer, Detlef Erler. SOUND: Michael Felber. EDITING: Nina von Kreisler, Michael Felber, Martine Zevort
PERFORMERS: Mariko Aoyama, Anne Marie Benati, Bénédicte Billiet, Rolando Brenes Calvo, Finola Cronin, Dominique Duszynski, Mechthild Großmann, Barbara Hampel, Kyomi Ichida, Urs Kaufmann, Ed Kortlandt, Beatrice Libonati, Anne Martin, Dominique Mercy, Jan Minarik, Helena Pikon, Dana Robin Sapiro, Jean-Laurent Sasportes, Mark Sieczkarek, Julie Anne Stanzak, Mark Alan Wilson, Peter Kowald (double bass), Ilse Schönemann, Rodolfo Seas Araya, Alois Hoch, Josef Ratering

*Palermo Palermo*
MUSIC: Edvard Grieg, Niccolò Paganini, traditional music from Sicily, southern Italy, Africa, Japan and Scotland, Renaissance music, blues and jazz from the USA, etc. MUSICAL ASSISTANCE: Matthias Burkert. STAGE DESIGN: Peter Pabst. COSTUMES: Marion Cito. PREMIERE: 17 December 1989, Opera House, Wuppertal
PERFORMERS: Mariko Aoyama, Anne Marie Benati, Matthias Burkert, Antonio Carallo, Finola Cronin, Thomas Duchatelet, Barbara Hampel, Kyomi Ichida, Urs Kaufmann, Ed Kortlandt, Beatrice Libonati, Bernd Marszan, Dominique Mercy, Jan Minarik, Nazareth Panadero, Jean-Laurent Sasportes, Julie Shanahan, Julie

Anne Stanzak, Janusz Subicz, Quincella Swyningan, Francis Viet, Mark Alan Wilson

*Tanzabend II (Madrid)*
MUSIC: Traditional music from Spain, Italy, Morocco, Egypt, central Africa, Argentina and Brazil, medieval music, 1930s and 1940s jazz, Diamanda Galás, Peter Kowald, laments from Spain and Italy. MUSICAL ASSISTANCE: Matthias Burkert. STAGE DESIGN: Peter Pabst. COSTUMES: Marion Cito. PREMIERE: 27 April 1991, Playhouse, Wuppertal
PERFORMERS: Jakob Andersen, Mariko Aoyama, Anne Marie Benati, Matthias Burkert, Finola Cronin, Thomas Duchatelet, Barbara Hampel, Kyomi Ichida, Urs Kaufmann, Beatrice Libonati, Marigia Maggipinto, Bernd Marszan, Dominique Mercy, Jan Minarik, Nazareth Panadero, Dulce Pessoa, Julie Shanahan, Geraldo Si Loureiro, Julie Anne Stanzak, Janusz Subicz, Quincella Swyningan, Francis Viet, Mark Alan Wilson

*Das Stück mit dem Schiff*
MUSIC: Christoph Willibald Gluck, Georg Friedrich Händel, Walther von der Vogelweide, Matthias Burkert, classical Indian music, dance music and love songs from Ethiopia, Morocco, Namibia, Nigeria and Peru, Bronze Age Scottish horns, Hungarian gypsy songs, Lithuanian prayer, sounds from the Amazon, Cambodia, Nepal and southern Florida, Spanish laments, Renaissance pavanes, popular music from the 1940s and 1950s. MUSICAL ASSISTANCE: Matthias Burkert. STAGE DESIGN: Peter Pabst. COSTUMES: Marion Cito. PREMIERE: 16 January 1993, Opera House, Wuppertal
PERFORMERS: Ruth Amarante, Jakob Andersen, Mariko Aoyama, Hans Beenhakker, Matthias Burkert, Thomas Duchatelet, Barbara Hampel, Urs Kaufmann, Beatrice Libonati, Marigia Maggipinto, Bernd Marszan, Dominique Mercy, Jan Minarik, Nazareth Panadero, Helena Pikon, Felix Ruckert, Jean-Laurent Sasportes, Julie Shanahan, Geraldo Si Loureiro, Julie Anne Stanzak, Janusz Subicz, Quincella Swyningan, Aida Vainieri, Francis Viet

*Ein Trauerspiel*
MUSIC: Franz Schubert, Sephardic songs from Spain, Hungarian gypsy songs, Yiddish songs, dance music from Argentina and Poland, voices from Ethiopia, Gabon, India, Siberia and Turkey, hunting horn music, Renaissance music, Italian tarantellas, jazz by Louis Armstrong, Duke Ellington and Django Reinhardt, Russian and Japanese popular music. MUSICAL ASSISTANCE: Matthias Burkert. STAGE DESIGN: Peter Pabst. COSTUMES: Marion Cito. PREMIERE: 12 February 1994, Playhouse, Wuppertal
PERFORMERS: Regina Advento, Ruth Amarante, Hans Beenhakker, Thomas Duchatelet, Barbara Hampel, Daphnis Kokkinos, Beatrice Libonati, Marigia Maggipinto, Bernd Marszan, Dominique Mercy, Jan Minarik, Cristiana Morganti, Nazareth Panadero, Helena Pikon, Felix Ruckert, Julie Shanahan, Julie Anne Stanzak, Quincella Swyningan, Aida Vainieri

*Danzón*
ASSISTANCE: Marion Cito, Jan Minarik. MUSIC: Francesco Cilea, Umberto Giordano, Gustav Mahler, Henry Purcell, Camille Saint-Saëns, songs from Mexico, Argentina, Greece and Portugal, songs by Ben Webster, Billie Holiday and Johnny Hodges, US and Japanese popular music. STAGE DESIGN: Peter Pabst. COSTUMES: Marion Cito. PREMIERE: 13 May 1995, Wuppertal Opera House
PERFORMERS: Regina Advento, Andrey Berezin, Antonio Carallo, Mechthild Großmann, Barbara Hampel, Daphnis Kokkinos, Marigia Maggipinto, Dominique Mercy, Jan Minarik, Cristiana Morganti, Aida Vainieri

*Nur Du*
ASSISTANCE: Jan Minarik, Marion Cito, Irene Martinez-Rios. MUSIC: Matthias Burkert, Indian flute music, Mexican and Brazilian waltzes, Argentine tangos, songs by Simón Diaz, Alfredo Marceneiro, Elis Regina, Amália Rodrigues, rhythm & blues from the 1950s, percussion music by Chico Hamilton, various popular music, jazz by Harry Cormick junior, Duke Ellington, Sidney Bechet, Dinah Washington, Joe Mooney, Harlan Leonard and his Rockets, Albert Mangelsdorf, etc. MUSICAL ASSISTANCE: Andreas Eisenschneider. STAGE DESIGN: Peter Pabst. COSTUMES: Marion Cito. PREMIERE: 11 May 1996, Playhouse, Wuppertal
PERFORMERS: Elena Adaeva, Regina Advento, Ruth Amarante, Rainer Behr, Andrey Berezin, Stephan Brinkmann, Chrystel Guillebeaud, Barbara Hampel, Kyomi Ichida, Daphnis Kokkinos, Bernd Marszan, Eddie Martinez, Dominique Mercy, Jan Minarik, Nazareth Panadero, Helena Pikon, Julie Shanahan, Julie Ann Stanzak, Fernando Suels, Aida Vainieri, Jean Guillaume Weis, Michael Whaites

*Der Fensterputzer*
MUSIC: Chinese songs and popular music, Chinese, Indian and Mexican drumming, traditional Rumanian gypsy music, fado, Argentine and Cape Verde songs, Iranian guitar music, love songs from the 13th and 16th centuries, jazz by Dizzy Gillespie, Pat Metheny, Nnenna Freelon, Al Cooper, Barney Kessel, Jo Stafford, Frantic Faye Thomas and the Jesse Powell Orchestra, etc. MUSICAL ASSISTANCE: Matthias Burkert, Andreas Eisenschneider, Marion Cito, Irene Martinez-Rios, Jan Minarik. TEXT: Péter Esterházy, Silja Walter, Wisława Szymborska. STAGE DESIGN: Peter Pabst. COSTUMES: Marion Cito. PREMIERE: 12 February 1997, Opera House, Wuppertal
PERFORMERS: Regina Advento, Ruth Amarante, Rainer Behr, Andrey Berezin, Stephan Brinkmann, Raphaëlle Delaunay, Mechthild Großmann, Chrystel Guillebeaud, Na Young Kim, Daphnis Kokkinos, Beatrice Libonati, Marigia Maggipinto, Bernd Marszan, Eddie Martinez, Dominique Mercy, Jan Minarik, Cristiana Morganti, Nazareth Panadero, Helena Pikon, Jorge Puerta Armenta, Anne Rebeschini, Michael Strecker, Fernando Suels, Aida Vainieri, Michael Whaites

*Masurca Fogo*
ASSISTANCE: Marion Cito, Irene Martinez-Rios, Jan Minarik. MUSIC: Balanescu Quartet, tango music by Gidon Kremer, fado, Cape Verde music, Portuguese

drumming by Rui Junior, Brazilian waltzes, various percussion music, jazz by Duke Ellington, etc. MUSICAL ASSISTANCE: Matthias Burkert, Andreas Eisenschneider. STAGE DESIGN: Peter Pabst. COSTUMES: Marion Cito. PREMIERE: 4 April 1998, Playhouse, Wuppertal

PERFORMERS: Regina Advento, Ruth Amarante, Rainer Behr, Stephan Brinkmann, Raphaëlle Delaunay, Chrystel Guillebeaud, Daphnis Kokkinos, Beatrice Libonati, Dominique Mercy, Jan Minarik, Cristiana Morganti, Nazareth Panadero, Jorge Puerta Armenta, Anne Rebeschini, Julie Shanahan, Michael Strecker, Fernando Suels, Aida Vainieri, Michael Whaites

### O Dido

ASSISTANCE: Marion Cito, Irene Martinez-Rios, Jan Minarik. MUSIC: Gustavo Santaolalla, Sephardic songs, Bonga de Sela, Lhasa Kuenza, tango music by Gidon Kremer, instrumental and vocal music by Cyro Baptista, Nnenna Freelon, João Gilberto, Bobby McFerrin, Portishead, Marc Ribot, Virginia Rodrigues and John Zorn, jazz by Chet Baker, Eartha Kitt and Royal Crown Revue, hip hop by Assalti Frontali, etc. MUSICAL ASSISTANCE: Matthias Burkert, Andreas Eisenschneider. STAGE DESIGN: Peter Pabst. COSTUMES: Marion Cito. PREMIERE: 10 April 1999, Opera House, Wuppertal

PERFORMERS: Ruth Amarante, Rainer Behr, Andrey Berezin, Stephan Brinkmann, Raphaëlle Delaunay, Chrystel Guillebeaud, Na Young Kim, Daphnis Kokkinos, Jan Minarik, Cristiana Morganti, Nazareth Panadero, Jorge Puerta Armenta, Julie Shanahan, Shantala Shivalingappa, Fernando Suels, Aida Vainieri

### Wiesenland

ASSISTANCE: Marion Cito, Irene Martinez-Rios, Jan Minarik, Robert Sturm. MUSIC: popular music by Vera Bila, Romano Drom, Ghymes, Taraf de Haidouks, Fanfare Ciocărlia, Peace Orchestra, Elektrotwist, Bohren & the Club of Gore, Bugge Wesseltoft, Sidsel Endresen, Hermenia, Caetano Veloso, José Afonso, René Lacaille, Lil Boniche, Rex Steward, Mel Tormé and Götz Alsmann. MUSICAL ASSISTANCE: Matthias Burkert, Andreas Eisenschneider. STAGE DESIGN: Peter Pabst. COSTUMES: Marion Cito. PREMIERE: 5 May 2000, Playhouse, Wuppertal

PERFORMERS: Ruth Amarante, Rainer Behr, Stephan Brinkmann, Raphaëlle Delaunay, Barbara Hampel, Na Young Kim, Daphnis Kokkinos, Eddie Martinez, Dominique Mercy, Pascal Merighi, Jan Minarik, Helena Pikon, Fabien Prioville, Jorge Puerta Armenta, Julie Shanahan, Julie Anne Stanzak, Michael Strecker, Fernando Suels, Aida Vainieri

### Água

ASSISTANCE: Marion Cito, Irene Martinez-Rios, Robert Sturm. MUSIC: Brazilian popular music by Baden Powell, Caetano Veloso, David Byrne, Gilberto Gil, Bebel Gilberto, Nana Vasconcelos, António Carlos Jobim, Luiz Bonfá, Bob Brookmeyer, Tom Zé, Grupo Batuque, Carlinhos Brown and Rosanna & Zélia, popular music by Susana Barca, Amon Tobin, Bugge Wesseltoft, Sidsel Endresen, Julien

Jacob, Mickey Hart, Tom Waits, Lura, The Tiger Lillies, St Germain, Leftfield, Troublemakers, PJ Harvey, Kenny Burrell and Ike Quebec. MUSICAL ASSISTANCE: Matthias Burkert, Andreas Eisenschneider. STAGE DESIGN: Peter Pabst. COSTUMES: Marion Cito. VIDEO: Peter Pabst. PREMIERE: 12 May 2001, Opera House, Wuppertal

PERFORMERS: Regina Advento, Rainer Behr, Silvia Farias, Ditta Miranda Jasjfi, Na Young Kim, Daphnis Kokkinos, Eddie Martinez, Melanie Maurin, Dominique Mercy, Pascal Merighi, Cristiana Morganti, Helena Pikon, Fabien Prioville, Jorge Puerta Armenta, Azusa Seyama, Julie Shanahan, Michael Strecker, Fernando Suels, Kenji Takagi, Aida Vainieri, Anna Wehsarg

*Für die Kinder von gestern, heute und morgen*
ASSISTANCE: Marion Cito, Daphnis Kokkinos, Robert Sturm. MUSIC: popular music by Félix Lajkó, Nana Vasconcelos, Caetano Veloso, Bugge Wesseltoft, Amon Tobin, Mari Boine, Shirley Horn, Nina Simone, Lisa Ekdahl, Gerry Mulligan, Uhuhboo Project, Cinematic Orchestra, Goldfrapp, Gotan Project, Guem, Hughscore, Koop, Labradford, T.O.M., Prince and Marc Ribot. MUSICAL ASSISTANCE: Matthias Burkert, Andreas Eisenschneider. Text: Péter Esterházy, Michael Caduto, Joseph Bruchac. STAGE DESIGN: Peter Pabst. COSTUMES: Marion Cito. PREMIERE: 25 April 2002, Playhouse, Wuppertal

PERFORMERS: Rainer Behr, Alexandre Castres, Lutz Förster, Ditta Miranda Jasjfi, Melanie Maurin, Dominique Mercy, Pascal Merighi, Nazareth Panadero, Helena Pikon, Fabien Prioville, Azusa Seyama, Julie Anne Stanzak, Fernando Suels, Kenji Takagi

*Nefés*
ASSISTANCE: Marion Cito, Helena Pikon, Robert Sturm. MUSIC: popular music by Mercan Dede, Birol Topaloğlu, Burhan Öçal, Istanbul Oriental Ensemble, Replicas, Bülent Ersoy, Candan Erçetin, Suren Asaduryan, Yansımalar, Amon Tobin, Arild Andersen, Bugge Wesseltoft, Chris McGregor's Brotherhood of Breath, Doctor Rockit, Elektrotwist, Innerzone Orchestra, Koop, Mardi Gras.BB, Astor Piazzolla, Tom Waits and Uhuhboo Project. MUSICAL ASSISTANCE: Matthias Burkert, Andreas Eisenschneider. STAGE DESIGN: Peter Pabst. COSTUMES: Marion Cito. VIDEO: Peter Pabst. PREMIERE: 21 March 2003, Opera House, Wuppertal

PERFORMERS: Ruth Amarante, Rainer Behr, Andrey Berezin, Alexandre Castres, Silvia Farias, Ditta Miranda Jasjfi, Na Young Kim, Daphnis Kokkinos, Melanie Maurin, Pascal Merighi, Cristiana Morganti, Nazareth Panadero, Fabien Prioville, Jorge Puerta Armenta, Azusa Seyama, Shantala Shivalingappa, Michael Strecker, Fernando Suels, Kenji Takagi, Anna Wehsarg

*Ten Chi*
ASSISTANCE: Marion Cito, Daphnis Kokkinos, Robert Sturm. MUSIC: Ryoko Moriyama, Hwang Byungki, Kodo, Yas-Kaz, Balanescu Quartet, Thomas Heberer, René Aubry, Beth Gibbons & Rustin Man, Gustavo Santaolalla, Robert Wyatt,

277

Kreidler, Labradford, Plastikman, Tudósok, Underkarl, Club des Belugas, etc. TEXT: Ruth Berlau, Bertolt Brecht, Georg Büchner, José Saramago, Margarete Steffin, Wisława Szymborska and others. MUSICAL ASSISTANCE: Matthias Burkert, Andreas Eisenschneider. STAGE DESIGN: Peter Pabst. COSTUMES: Marion Cito. PRE-MIERE: 8 May 2004, Playhouse, Wuppertal
PERFORMERS: Regina Advento, Alexandre Castres, Mechthild Großmann, Ditta Miranda Jasjfi, Eddie Martinez, Dominique Mercy, Thusnelda Mercy, Pascal Merighi, Nazareth Panadero, Helena Pikon, Jorge Puerta Armenta, Azusa Seyama, Julie Shanahan, Julie Anne Stanzak, Fernando Suels, Kenji Takagi, Aida Vainieri

*Rough Cut*
ASSISTANCE: Marion Cito, Barbara Hampel, Robert Sturm. MUSIC: Uhuhboo Project, Young-Gyu Jang, Gong Myoung, Eun-Il Kang, Jin-Hi Kim, Nam-Hwa Jung, Sung-Jun Choi, Min-Ki Kim, Sun-Chul Kim, Amon Tobin, Elektrotwist, Jun Miyake, Ryuichi Sakamoto, Yonderboi, DJ Explizit, Balanescu Quartet, Pen-guin Cafe Orchestra, Alex Gunia, Les Reines Prochaines, Mickey Hart, Björk, etc. MUSICAL ASSISTANCE: Matthias Burkert, Andreas Eisenschneider. STAGE DESIGN: Peter Pabst. COSTUMES: Marion Cito. PREMIERE: 15 April 2005, Playhouse, Wup-pertal
PERFORMERS: Regina Advento, Ruth Amarante, Rainer Behr, Andrey Berezin, Silvia Farias, Ditta Miranda Jasjfi, Na Young Kim, Daphnis Kokkinos, Melanie Maurin, Thusnelda Mercy, Pascal Merighi, Cristiana Morganti, Franko Schmidt, Michael Strecker, Fernando Suels, Kenji Takagi, Anna Wehsarg, members of the German Alpine Climbing Association (Elberfeld branch)

*Vollmond*
ASSISTANCE: Marion Cito, Daphnis Kokkinos, Robert Sturm. MUSIC: Amon Tobin, Balanescu Quartet, Cat Power, Carl Craig, Jun Miyake, Leftfield, Magyar Posse, Nenad Jelic, René Aubry, Tom Waits, etc. MUSICAL ASSISTANCE: Matthias Burkert, Andreas Eisenschneider. STAGE DESIGN: Peter Pabst. COSTUMES: Marion Cito. PRE-MIERE: 11 May 2006, Playhouse, Wuppertal
PERFORMERS: Rainer Behr, Silvia Farias, Ditta Miranda Jasjfi, Dominique Mercy, Nazareth Panadero, Helena Pikon, Jorge Puerta Armenta, Azusa Seyama, Julie Anne Stanzak, Michael Strecker, Fernando Suels, Kenji Takagi

*Bamboo Blues*
ASSISTANCE: Marion Cito, Daphnis Kokkinos, Robert Sturm. MUSIC: Trilok Gurtu & Arkè String Quartet, Suphala, Sunil Ganguly, U. Srinivas & Michael Brook, Talvin Singh, James Asher & Sivamani, Mukta, Bombay Dub Orchestra, Anoushka Shankar, Amon Tobin, Bill Laswell, Talk Talk, Michael Gordon, Lisa Bassenge, Emmanuel Santarromana, Lutz Glandien, 4hero, Jun Miyake, Solveig Slettajel, Slowhill, Dschiwan Gasparjan, etc. MUSICAL ASSISTANCE: Matthias Bur-kert, Andreas Eisenschneider. STAGE DESIGN: Peter Pabst. COSTUMES: Marion Cito. PREMIERE: 18 May 2007, Playhouse, Wuppertal

PERFORMERS: Ruth Amarante, Pablo Aran Gimeno, Rainer Behr, Damiano Ottavio Bigi, Clémentine Deluy, Silvia Farias, Na Young Kim, Eddie Martinez, Thusnelda Mercy, Cristiana Morganti, Jorge Puerta Armenta, Franko Schmidt, Shantala Shivalingappa, Fernando Suels, Kenji Takagi, Anna Wehsarg

*Sweet Mambo*
ASSISTANCE: Marion Cito, Thusnelda Mercy, Robert Sturm. MUSIC: Barry Adamson, Mina Agossi, René Aubry, Mari Boine, Lisa Ekdahl, Brian Eno, Mecca Bodega, Jun Miyake, Hazmat Modine, Lucky Pierre, Portishead, Ryuichi Sakamoto, Hope Sandoval, Gustavo Santaolalla, Trygve Seim, Nina Simone, Ian Simmonds, Tom Waits. MUSICAL ASSISTANCE: Matthias Burkert, Andreas Eisenschneider. STAGE DESIGN: Peter Pabst. COSTUMES: Marion Cito. PREMIERE: 30 May 2008, Playhouse, Wuppertal
PERFORMERS: Regina Advento, Andrey Berezin, Daphnis Kokkinos, Nazareth Panadero, Helena Pikon, Julie Shanahan, Julie Anne Stanzak, Michael Strecker, Aida Vainieri